# The Spiritual Life

# The Spiritual Life

Campegius Vitringa

Translated and Edited
by
Charles K. Telfer

**Reformation Heritage Books**
Grand Rapids, Michigan

**Reformation Heritage Books**
2965 Leonard St. NE
Grand Rapids, MI 49525
616-977-0889
orders@heritagebooks.org
www.heritagebooks.org

*Printed in the United States of America*
18 19 20 21 22 23/10 9 8 7 6 5 4 3 2 1

ISBN: 978-1-60178-658-6 (paperback)
ISBN: 978-1-60178-659-3 (e-pub)

*For additional Reformed literature, request a free book list from Reformation Heritage Books at the above regular or e-mail address.*

*Filiis meis carissimis,*
*Victoriae, Joanni, Samueli, et Annae*
*et*
*nepotibus meis dilectissimis,*
*hoc opusculum dedicatur.*

*I have been crucified together with Christ, but I live.*
*Yet it is no longer I, but Christ lives in me.*

—GALATIANS 2:20

# Contents

# Foreword

It bears repeating that the frequent claim of a scholastic dogmatism—devoid of humanistic linguistic skills, lacking the techniques of critical textual exegesis, and set against the spirituality of a rising pietism—fails to grasp the patterns of thought and exposition characteristic of Protestant orthodoxy. A closer examination of the writings of Reformed orthodox theologians, as demonstrated in an increasing number of recent studies, has shown that the early modern exponents of scholastic method and the practitioners of academic disputation were also often engaged in exegetical work and highly skilled in ancient languages. Studies of the era (particularly of the Reformed orthodox) have shown not only significant evidence of piety or spirituality but also direct connections between the production of technical and even polemical expositions of doctrine and the creation of nontechnical but confessionally sound works of spiritual edification.

The writings of Campegius Vitringa the Elder provide an important window into the spirituality, doctrine, and exegesis of the era of orthodoxy and exemplify the interrelationships of these disciplines. Vitringa's work on Christian spirituality, originally published under the title *Essay on Practical Theology, or a Treatise on the Spiritual Life*, is found in the present volume. He also wrote a volume on the proper method of preaching in the church. His numerous biblical and exegetical works included six volumes of observations on various topics and a series of major commentaries on the Old Testament, including a massive two-volume commentary on Isaiah. On the doctrinal front, he wrote a basic work on Christian doctrine in the form of aphorisms or theses that was later expanded into a larger body of doctrine, as well as an elenctical theology dealing with disputed issues. The interrelationship of all three emphases—the spiritual, the exegetical, and the doctrinal—is exhibited in Vitringa's homiletical method, in which the exposition begins in prayer, is rooted in the text, and moves on to both practical and doctrinal applications. This is also evident throughout *The Spiritual Life*.

*The Spiritual Life*, taken by itself, is a finely organized presentation of an older Reformed spirituality that bears the marks of a believer and scholar steeped both in the text of Scripture and a foundational Reformed theology. As with Reformed receptions of other aspects of the older tradition, Vitringa's approach to spirituality evinces an underlying sense of the decline of Christian thought and practice toward the close of the patristic period and an interest in recovering the purity and simplicity of the original Christian message while drawing on the best resources of the Christian tradition.

The treatise begins with four chapters that provide a general definition of the nature, origins, and causes of the spiritual life, concluded by a section of how the spiritual life arises in the individual. A second section presents the spiritual life in three parts—self-denial, cross-bearing, and following Christ. Important here is Vitringa's emphasis on the spiritual life as active, in opposition to the quietistic piety that dominated much Roman Catholic thought of his era and that carried over into Protestantism by way of the highly influential mysticism of Antoinette Bourignon. This emphasis is, arguably, reflected in the phrase in the original title, *Essay on Practical Theology*. Many of the Reformed theologians of the era held theology to be a practical or theoretical-practical discipline, with its practical aspect understood actively as a praxis directing believers toward salvation and godly living. Vitringa's second section also underlines an important and often neglected characteristic of traditional Reformed spirituality and ethics: it emphasizes the spiritual development of dispositions or capacities for virtuous conduct. The spiritual life, in other words, embodies a version of virtue ethics, defined by Vitringa as conforming one's "mores to those of Christ." Vitringa's argument here echoes the Reformed view of the relationship of right reason to biblical revelation: Christian virtues, as identified both in the Gospels and in the Pauline letters, do not set aside the classical philosophical virtues—rather, they include the philosophical virtues even as they provide a deeper truth than can be known purely rationally.

The remaining three portions of *The Spiritual Life*—the challenges facing spirituality, the development of spiritual life in sanctification, and the goals of spiritual life—also contain significant echoes of Vitringa's larger theological project. The connection between spirituality and dogmatics is evident in the definition of theology found in Vitringa's early aphorisms: theology is "the Doctrine [or teaching] that instructs us concerning God and the ways of God toward a certain consolation in this life and salvation in the next."[1] The methods of doctrinal theology and Christian spirituality may be different, but they direct toward the same goals, both penultimate and ultimate.

In presenting the stages of spiritual development, Vitringa employs as a central metaphor the states of human life from infancy to childhood to adulthood that also reflects the concerns of Reformed orthodox theology and the broad outlines of a Reformed understanding of Scripture, both historically and doctrinally. While careful to note the imprecision of metaphors, he makes two significant comparisons: one between the development from infancy to adulthood that is identifiable in a person's life and the development of God's people through the economy of grace to its maturity in the New Testament, and the other between a person's development toward adulthood and the progress of the spiritual life from initial faith and regeneration toward the increase of spiritual capacities in sanctification. There is a probable reflection here of the federal theology of Johannes Cocceius, in which a view of the historical economy of the covenant in its progress from the beginnings of postlapsarian grace toward the New Testament was conjoined with an understanding of the order of salvation in the life of the individual Christian.[2] Vitringa's reading of the spiritual life of Christians offers a deeply biblical account of personal spiritual

1. Campegius Vitringa, *Aphorismi, quibus fundamenta sanctæ theologiæ comprehenduntur: in usum scholarum privatarum* (Franeker, Neth.: Johannes Gyselaar, 1688), i.1 (p. 1).

2. See Willem J. van Asselt, *The Federal Theology of Johannes Cocceius (1603–1669)*, trans. Raymond A. Blacketer (Leiden: Brill, 2001), 278–82. Note that Vitringa did not follow Cocceius in arguing a gradual abrogation of the covenant of works.

development that is closely coordinated with the Reformed understanding of the order of salvation: doctrine provides structure for spirituality, and spirituality breathes life into doctrine.

In sum, Charles Telfer's work on Vitringa marks a major contribution to our knowledge both of this incredibly prolific exegete and theologian and of the era in which he taught and wrote. As Telfer indicates, his project of translating *The Spiritual Life* into English originated during his work on Vitringa's exegesis. The translation therefore complements Telfer's study of Vitringa's commentary on Isaiah, in which Telfer not only analyzes Vitringa's methods in detail but also provides an extended description of Vitringa's many writings and a full bibliography of Vitringa's works, including a listing of the academic disputations over which Vitringa presided. Taken together, the books provide an excellent introduction to Vitringa's thought. The translation of *The Spiritual Life*, taken by itself, offers a major contribution to our understanding of traditional Reformed spirituality.

—Richard A. Muller

# Translator's Preface

The book that you hold in your hand is a remarkable effort by a remarkable man. Vitringa biographer Albert Schultens (1686–1750) called it "a very worthy book that should live and be carried around in our eyes, hands, bosoms and even our very bones and hearts."[1] It began as a course on Christian experience that Vitringa taught at the University of Franeker, one of the three great universities in the Netherlands during the seventeenth and eighteenth centuries. There Vitringa taught biblical and theological courses and influenced students from across Protestant Europe for over forty years.[2] He had a particular concern for international students, as can be seen in the references and affectionate inscriptions he wrote for them. A few of Vitringa's students were so struck with his teaching that they translated and published his class lectures (with his authorization—and sometimes without it) into a variety of languages. *The Spiritual Life* was quickly printed not only in Dutch but in German, French, and even Magyar (Hungarian).[3]

1. From his *Laudatio funebris*; see Charles Telfer, "Campegius Vitringa (1659–1722): A Biblical Theologian at the Beginning of the Eighteenth Century," in *Biblical Theology: Past, Present and Future*, ed. Mark Elliot and Carey Walsh (Eugene, Ore.: Wipf and Stock, 2016), 30.

2. Charles Telfer, "Campegius Vitringa Sr.: 'Praefatio ad lectorem,' in: *Commentarius in librum prophetiarum Jesaiae*, 1716 and 'De interpretatione prophetiarum,' in: *Typus doctrinae propheticae, in quo de prophetis et prophetiis agitur, hujusque scientiae praecepta traduntur*, 1708," in *Handbuch der Bibelhermeneutiken*, ed. Oda Wischmeyer (Berlin: De Gruyter, 2016), 445.

3. For this and other biographical information, see the biography in Charles Telfer, *Wrestling with Isaiah: The Exegetical Methodology of Campegius Vitringa (1659–1722)*,

In Germany, Vitringa's influence was particularly far reaching. In terms of his emphasis on practical godliness, he certainly influenced the Pietists August Hermann Franke (1663–1727), Joachim Lange (1670–1744), and Johann Albrecht Bengel (1687–1752), but some trace his impact even as far as Gotthold Lessing (1729–1781), Johann Gottfried Herder (1744–1803), and German Idealism.[4] And in terms of his emphasis on careful historical and linguistic analysis of the Bible, he was considered a model by many scholars (including Wilhelm Gesenius [1786–1842] and Franz Delitzsch [1813–1890]) far into the nineteenth century. In Britain and North America, Vitringa's commentaries and his writings on Christian experience were significant both in the eighteenth and even into the nineteenth century, particularly at Princeton Seminary.[5]

One of Vitringa's most enthusiastic francophone students was Henri-Philippe de Limiers (d. 1728). He was moved by the beauty of this guide to the spiritual life and translated it for the benefit of his French countrymen in a work entitled *Essai de Théologie Pratique, ou traité de la vie spirituelle et de ses caractères* (An essay on practical theology or a treatise on the spiritual life and its characteristics).[6] Vitringa

---

Reformed Historical Theology Series, ed. Herman Selderhuis (Göttingen, Ger.: Vandenhoeck and Ruprecht, 2016).

4. Klaas Marten Witteveen, "Campegius Vitringa und die prophetische Theologie," *Zwingliana* 19, no. 2 (1993): 359.

5. Brevard S. Childs, "Hermeneutical Reflections on Campegius Vitringa, Eighteenth-Century Interpreter of Isaiah," in *In Search of True Wisdom: Essays in Old Testament Interpretation in Honour of Ronald E. Clements* (Sheffield, U.K.: Sheffield Academic, 1999), 90. "Vitringa's massive apologetic defense of the literal coherence between biblical text and historical reference became widespread by the early eighteenth century, especially in England, Scotland, and North America.... In North America Vitringa's approach was most systematically developed by the old Princeton School, emerging in full form already in one of its founders, A. A. Alexander." Childs, "Hermeneutical Reflections on Campegius Vitringa," 97.

6. The Latin original and the exemplar of this work which I used was published by Saurmann in Bremen in 1717. The French version was published by Strik in Amsterdam in 1721, a year before Vitringa's death. The scholarly reader will note just how much the French version has helped me in translating the Latin original. De Limiers dedicates his translation to Benedict Pictet, "Pastor of the Church at Geneva, Professor of Theology in the Genevan Academy and Member of the Society for the Propagation of the Faith established at London" and expresses his appreciation for Pictet's *Christian Morals* (1692), which overlaps somewhat in content with this present work.

himself approved of his translation. But up until now, this work has not been translated into English.

Translating Vitringa is as stimulating as it is challenging. Stylistically speaking, Vitringa's principal translator into German, Anton Friedrich Büsching, remarked, "[Vitringa's] style is manly, serious, clear and rich in expression. And when the topic requires, his Latin is magnificent and noble."[7] Although Vitringa's page-length sentences may have seemed noble and Ciceronian in the eighteenth century, I have reduced many of his long expressions to a more manageable size while still attempting to cleave to the thought of the original. I have produced a version that is somewhat more literal than the French while enabling Vitringa to speak in contemporary English. I have left out references to unfamiliar books and certain sections of little interest to moderns (the original Latin and the other versions are easily available to the curious through the Post-Reformation Digital Library). Regarding the mistakes that surely remain, I can only say with de Limiers, "If there are certain defects in this work, one must hold the translator alone responsible. But even as we ask grace for the faults that escaped us, we ask those familiar with the original that they acknowledge the difficulty of the enterprise we have undertaken."[8]

The project of bringing this book into English was conceived while I was a doctoral student. As I was slogging through a translation of Vitringa's rather technical Isaiah commentary, I read *The Spiritual Life* and was enraptured by its lofty vision. Some sections of this book were so uplifting, even breathtaking, that I resolved to try to bring something of its beauty into English. De Limiers spoke well of "the piety and the unction that one can feel so well in the original."[9] If you happen to find the detail in some of the early chapters less than scintillating, please do not put this book down without reading the later material. Chapter 12 on the means of grace, chapter 15 on God's chastening us,

---

7. A. F. Büsching, "Fortsetzung des Lebenslaufs des selige Herrn Vitringa: von seinem natürlichen und sitlichen Character," in *Auslegung der Weissagung Jesaiae* (Halle, Ger.: Johann Gottlob Bierwirth, 1751), 2:8–9.

8. Campegius Vitringa, *Essai de Theologie Pratique, ou traité de la vie spirituelle et de ses caractères*, trans. Henri-Philippe de Limiers (Amsterdam: H. Strik, 1721), Avant-Propos du Traducteur, n.p.

9. Vitringa, *Essai de Theologie Pratique*.

and, of course, chapter 18 about our life with Christ in eternity are particularly helpful and have some glorious insights. Profiting from the perspective of our forebears is excellent for our spiritual health, and though parts of old books may seem prosaic, those who press on surely will be inspired by many arresting and delightful passages.

The university course that Vitringa taught, which led to *The Spiritual Life*, was undertaken partly to "avert the criticism often made in our day that theological professors only deal with abstract theology and neglect practical theology."[10] I hope you will see that Vitringa's whole life, in preaching and in practice, was an extended refutation of the idea that truth can be separated from practical godliness, or faith from charity. "Practical theology" in Vitringa's course meant in part the classic discussion of virtues and vices, but he wanted to "trace the streams to their source." Vitringa wanted to "see where the bubbling springs come from. Life comes from life, and I wanted to explain how all the lively acts of the true virtues come from the fountain and principle that produced them, which is regeneration."[11] Thus a class in ethics evolved into a discussion about the states, the progress, and the affections of the spiritual life.

It is beyond the scope of this preface to set *The Spiritual Life* in its fuller historical context (either tracing the influences on Vitringa or the specific impact that the book had on other people).[12] Though it should prove interesting to those interested in early modern spirituality, theological anthropology, and ethics, I have intended this work for a popular rather than a scholarly audience. But I do hope Vitringa's book will provide one more piece of evidence of how vibrant Christian life and thought was at this period of Reformed high orthodoxy, contrary to its stereotype as a hidebound and dead period of Protestantism.[13]

---

10. Campegius Vitringa, *Typus theologiae praticae, sive de vita spirituali, ejusque affectionibus commentatio* (Bremen, Ger.: Saurmann, 1717), Praefatio.

11. Vitringa, *Typus theologiae praticae*. Praefatio, 16.

12. For some introduction to the background, see Luca Baschera, "Ethics in Reformed Orthodoxy," in *A Companion to Reformed Orthodoxy*, ed. Herman Selderhuis (Leiden: Brill, 2013), 519–52.

13. For periodization, see Richard Muller, *Post-Reformation Reformed Dogmatics: The Rise and Development of Reformed Orthodoxy, ca. 1520–1725*, vol. 1, *Prolegomena to Theology*, 2nd ed. (Grand Rapids: Baker Academic, 2003), 31.

This book breathes the refreshing air of *Nadere Reformatie* spirituality, the heartfelt, orthodox devotion of Dutch Further Reformation piety. To a certain extent, this quality is evident from Vitringa's own preface to the reader.

I have include an excellent biography of Vitringa to introduce the author of *The Spiritual Life*. It is my edited translation of the German *Lebenslauf* (lit. life-course) done by Anton Friedrich Büsching (1724–1793), who published it alongside his own translation of Vitringa's famous Isaiah commentary.[14] Büsching had a high view of Vitringa both as a scholar and as a devoted Christian, but he did not produce a hagiography. The *Lebenslauf* is typically eighteenth-century German in its accuracy and thoroughness. Readers who love scholarly details and are looking for an unedited version may find it in my doctoral dissertation.[15] I trust you will find this life sketch to be a stirring and edifying portrait of a notable but often overlooked servant of Christ.

*Tolle, lege*—take up and read this work, and you will find Vitringa to be not just a profound theologian and insightful exegete of Scripture but an honest and helpful counselor for your own pilgrimage and spiritual life as a Christian. With so little of Vitringa having been translated, I am delighted that this much-appreciated book now makes its appearance in English.

—CKT

---

14. Campegius Vitringa, *Auslegung Der Weissagung Jesaiae, übersetzt und mit Anmerkungen Begleitet von M. Anton Friederich Büsching. Mit einer Vorrede von Herrn J. L. von Mosheim Mit Lebenslauf von Vitringa*, trans. M. Anton Friederich Büsching, 2 vols. (Halle, Ger.: Johann Gottlob Bierwirth, 1749). Parts 1 and 2 of this *Lebenslauf* are taken from this 1749 publication of the German edition of Vitringa's commentary on Isaiah. Part 3 was added at the beginning of volume 2 in the 1751 edition: Anton Friederich Büsching, "Fortsetzung des Lebenslaufs des selige Herrn Vitringa: von seinem natürlichen und sitlichen Character," in *Auslegung der Weissagung Jesaiae*, vol. 2 (Halle, Ger.: Johann Gottlob Bierwirth, 1751). Let me again thank W. Kendrick Doolan, a former teaching assistant, for his valuable German translation assistance *auld lang syne*.

15. Charles Telfer, "The Exegetical Methodology of Campegius Vitringa (1659–1722), Especially as Expressed in His *Commentarius in Librum Prophetiarum Jesaiae*" (PhD diss., Trinity Evangelical Divinity School, 2015).

# Acknowledgments

I have incurred many debts in the course of translating and editing this work. None is so great as what I owe to Mrs. Louise Wright, who has worked with me through the Latin and French originals. *Merci beaucoup!* I thank my colleagues at Westminster Seminary California, particularly Dr. John Fesko, dean of the faculty, whose suggestions were quite helpful. Thanks to Jay Collier of RHB and Andrew Buss of CES for their excellent work. Thanks also to Allen Rae, to teaching assistant Jason Vanderhorst, and *magnas gratias* to Tori Telfer, editor extraordinaire and my favorite best-selling author in history.

I thank Dr. Richard Muller for his support of my early interest in Vitringa and for writing the foreword. I thank Dr. Ferenc Postma, doyen of Vitringa scholars, for his encouragement. And I would like to recognize the famously beautiful and well-furnished library of the Reformed Collegium Illustre in Sárospatak, Hungary, which (despite the mistaken footnote in *Wrestling with Isaiah* that they had thrown away Vitringa's personal papers) has maintained a rich collection of Vitringa materials and manuscripts for over three hundred years.

CAMPEGIUS VITRINGA P.S.S.Th. Doctor ejusdemque & Historiæ S. Prof. Ordin. Franequeræ Natus d. XVI Maj. a.C. MDCLIX. Denatus d. XXXI Mart. a.C. MDCCXXII.

B. Akkama Pinx.                                                                 P. Tanjé Sculp.

Vitringam Frisii decus Lycaei          Et magnum columen vides. videbis
Expressam variae eruditionis,          Et sacrae effigiem libros per omnes,
Quos plenos pietate fabricavit,        Doctos, quis neget? et laboriosos.
                                                            P. W.

# The Life and Work of
# Campegius Vitringa Sr. (1659–1722)

## Part I: Biography

Campegius Vitringa is indisputably considered one of the greats. He gained respect and a lasting name not only for his sincere godliness but also for his broad and deep scholarship and his great service to the church. I hope that distant posterity learns about his life and background, his excellent writings, and his commendable character qualities. This is the order I shall follow in the following sketch.[1]

In Leeuwarden, the capital city of Friesland in the north of the Netherlands, Campegius Vitringa first saw the light of this world on the sixteenth day of May in the year 1659. His father, Horatius, was chief secretary of the provincial high court and eventually became judge of the city of Leeuwarden. For the love of the Protestant faith, some of his ancestors suffered persecution from the Spaniards under the Duke of Alba. Forced to forsake their considerable fortune, they fled north from Belgium to Friesland. Vitringa's mother, Albertina von Haen, was well known for her many virtues but died when Campegius

---

1. Campegius Vitringa, *Auslegung Der Weissagung Jesaiae, übersetzt Und Mit Anmerkungen Begleitet von M. Anton Friederich Büsching. Mit Einer Vorrede von Hern J. L. von Mosheim. Mit Lebenslauf von Vitringa*, trans. M. Anton Friederich Büsching, 2 vols. (Halle, Ger.: Johann Gottlob Bierwirth, 1749). Parts 1 and 2 of this *Lebenslauf* are taken from this 1749 publication of the German edition of Vitringa's commentary on Isaiah. Part 3 was added at the beginning of volume 2 in the 1751 edition: Anton Friederich Büsching, "Fortsetzung des Lebenslaufs des selige Herrn Vitringa: von seinem natürlichen und sitlichen Character," in *Auslegung der Weissagung Jesaiae*, vol. 2 (Halle, Ger.: Johann Gottlob Bierwirth, 1751). The main sources for Büsching's *Lebenslauf* are Schultens, von Hase, Nicéron, and personal correspondence with J. G. Michaelis (one of Vitringa's students).

was young. His father remarried, but again little Campegius lost his stepmother to death after a short time.

Campegius was the second son of the family. His father had an affectionate love for his children, and he attended to their upbringing with the greatest possible diligence. He trained them in the fear of God and tutored them as carefully in the arts and sciences as time allowed. This careful nurture from his father was not without effect. From childhood Campegius demonstrated a reverence for God and called on His gracious presence as he bent his knee. When a God-fearing heart is connected to a sharp head and to earnest industriousness, a happy outcome is inevitable. Casparus Rhomberg, the rector of the school at Leeuwarden, regarded him highly and sought to cultivate his excellent mind, sharp discrimination, remarkable teachableness, and unflagging thirst for knowledge. He also publicly praised his modesty and piety as an example to others. He even produced a couplet in Latin for him, "Blossom, O choicest portion of our school, that you may be the flower and honor of your lonely father."

Rhomberg was impressed not just because of Vitringa's mastery of Latin but because he learned Greek well and had read through the New Testament at least four times. So he added Hebrew to Vitringa's curriculum. The young scholar was so industrious that, except where obscure words and difficult passages tripped him up, he became able to translate any part of the Old Testament from beginning to end without the help of a version—a rare and admirable expertise for one so young!

Vitringa transferred to the university at the age of sixteen in 1675. His farewell address at grammar school commencement was an oration in Latin entitled, "On Christian Endurance." He delivered it with such skill, such agreeable speech and gestures, and with so much brilliance that the hearers were left astonished. The famous Herman Witsius [1636–1708], at that time still a preacher in Leeuwarden, was on hand for this presentation. He was so moved by the quality and vivacity with which the young man spoke that he could not restrain himself from weeping. Soon thereafter when the learned Witsius was called to the university of Franeker as professor of theology, he became not only Vitringa's teacher but also his special patron, as we shall see from later developments.

Campegius moved to the illustrious university at Franeker together with his oldest brother, Wigerus, who, truth be told, had never proven himself to be much of a scholar. But "Kempe" (as he was known to his Dutch-speaking friends) studiously sought to better himself. He tackled a wide variety of subjects, including all the disciplines preparatory to the study of theology. Vitringa studied history and chronology carefully. He patiently worked through all the *Chronicles* of [Johan] Carion [1499–1537]. He read the best Greek and Latin authors carefully and collected important quotations into a series of notebooks, which served him for a lifetime. When the professor of history, [Michael] Buschius [d. 1681], became ill, Vitringa took over his lectures for a time. He studied mathematics and astronomy with Ravius, and logic, natural sciences, and the other branches of "philosophy" with Johan Wubbena [d. 1681], who testified that he was "born for philosophy." He even produced a disputation, "On Fire," and defended it successfully against many skilled opponents.

Vitringa wanted to become solidly familiar with the biblical languages and availed himself of the finest teachers there. He listened to Nicolaus Blancard [1624–1703], who gave instruction in Greek literature. And he had Witsius as a private tutor in Greek. They read together the beautiful *Zyropaedia* of Xenophon, and checked the Latin translation themselves. He studied biblical Hebrew with Johannes Terentius [1628?–1677]. And after Terentius died, Vitringa went on to the study of rabbinical Hebrew and Aramaic through private study with a local Jewish teacher. Spending much time learning Rashi [1040–1105], Vitringa gained for himself access to an unhindered reading of the rabbis.

Vitringa spent two years at Franeker studying and writing on theology. The good catechetical education he had received as a youth gave him a solid foundation for his work with theologians Nicholas Arnold [1618–1680] and particularly with Herman Witsius, who was well-disposed toward him and for whom he had a high esteem. In his third academic year he produced three disputations on the origin of monasticism and defended them to great acclaim.

But Vitringa was not content with this state of his knowledge and burned with desire to see and to hear still other great scholars, especially the theologians of the university at Leiden who were famous at that time. He knew some of them by reputation and others through their writings. His previous teachers sent along excellent references for him. The famous Witsius wrote among other things that he considered him worthy to someday be successor to his position, which later took place.

He arrived happily at Leiden. Here he admired the excellent eloquence of Friedrich Spanheim Jr. [1632–1701], the uncommon acuity of Christoph Wittichius [1625–1687], and the prodigious erudition of Stephanus Le Moine [1624–1689]. He followed these men who were so great in his eyes, but not blindly since the desire for truth above all else had mastered him. He managed to navigate the controversies of the day in full boil at Leiden over the philosophy of [René] Descartes [1596–1650] and the theology of [Johannes] Cocceius [1603–1669], and won the esteem of all parties for his impartiality and freedom from bias.

Shortly after his arrival, the famous Professor Spanheim held a public disputation in which Vitringa took the opposition. He conducted himself so admirably that he not only earned the respect of Spanheim but amazed the whole assembly. Everyone praised the scholarship and oratorical abilities that Vitringa demonstrated even as a youth. After a year in Leiden, having conducted extensive research, he gave three disputations on the second psalm. During the first, Le Moine held the chair, Spanheim during the second, and [Antonius] Hulsius [1615–1685] during the third. The last, held on the ninth of July 1679, enabled him to graduate with highest honors in theology. He was twenty years old at the time.

At that time Vitringa very much wanted to go to England, especially to visit Oxford, but his father refused, partly from the hope that he would be given a position as professor of Eastern languages in the academy of his homeland (i.e., Friesland). Though he did not get the academic post just then, it came to him a few months later through an alternate route. Meanwhile, our young doctor was able to employ his gifts for the building up of the church. In Leeuwarden he was received as a candidate for the holy ministry on the third of June 1680. His natural congeniality and honest eloquence won his preaching thorough approval. The administrators of the university saw how useful he would be for his homeland and sought his advancement. They favored him with the position of professor of Hebrew language and holy antiquities by a unanimous vote. He took up this call on the nineteenth of August 1680. This position opened when Witsius departed for Utrecht and his successor, Johan van der Waeyen [1639–1701], stepped in as professor of theology, leaving the position as professor of Hebrew language to Vitringa, who then was twenty-one years old. On the eleventh of January 1681 he presented his inaugural address, "On the Duty of an Honest Interpreter of Holy Scripture." This magisterial presentation became even more notable due to the personal presence of Heinrich Casimir [1657–1696], Prince of Nassau-Dietz and hereditary Stadholder in Friesland.

Vitringa handled the duties of his position so well that, upon the departure of [Johan] Markius [1655–1731] to Erdningen, Vitringa was called to be professor of theology. On May 10, 1683, he gave a fine inaugural address, "On the Love of Truth." Ten years later, when [Jacobus] Perizonius [1651–1715] had been called to Leiden, Vitringa was also made professor of sacred history.

As Vitringa's fame as a scholar spread, it won him a call to the University of Utrecht, which unfortunately brought him all kinds of trouble. When Witsius was called from Utrecht to Leiden in 1698, the directors of Utrecht had earmarked Vitringa as his successor, promising an annual salary of 2,000 Dutch guilders. Though Vitringa had accepted this call, its consummation was unexpectedly blocked. It seems that [Willem IV, Prince of Orange, 1711–1751] the Stadholder of Holland and Utrecht (who had with his wife, Mary, just become king and queen of England) had been unjustly prejudiced against Vitringa, thinking that he was a proponent of Cocceius's dangerous doctrines. It is likely that Melchior Leydeker [1642–1721], a theologian at Utrecht, had a large part to do with this. The termination of the call to Utrecht arrived on the very day before Vitringa was to undertake his journey to Leeuwarden to receive a dismissal from the directors of the Friesian university. The directors were pleased at this turn of events, thanked him for his service, and assured him that they wanted him to continue in his present position.

Vitringa responded to this faithfulness in kind when the directors of the University of Utrecht called him again in 1702 on the same generous terms. Though they sent particularly respectable men to urge him to accept, Vitringa rejected the call. This magnanimous response so impressed and moved the directors of the University of Franeker that they matched this lordly salary offer, which no professor but the famous jurist Ulrich Huber [1636–1694] had ever enjoyed.

The Utrechters still did not give up hope to steal him for their university. The next year directors of the city of Utrecht renewed for the third time an offer to teach for them. But they now added two further enticements: not only a theological professorate but a position as city preacher that would bring the yearly salary to 2,800 guilders, along with a special gift of 8,000 guilders (in compensation for the four years of salary he had not received because of their failure to fulfill the first call they made to him). You might expect that this superabundant windfall would have altered Vitringa's previous resolution. But Vitringa showed his devotion to his fatherland, and no amount of money or honors could tear him away. It was love, not stubbornness or pride, that led him to remain at the University of Franeker.

As he began, Vitringa continued to serve faithfully as professor. The considerable influx his school experienced for the entire forty-one years he was there demonstrates in part how much he was esteemed. He was sought out by such a quantity of Hungarian, Polish, French, Scottish, German, and Dutch young people that his lecture hall often was not able to accommodate the multitude. Many learned and distinguished men resulted from his excellent instruction. All his students cherished a great love and esteem for him and considered themselves truly fortunate to have had him as a teacher.

Though he was growing old, in 1716 Vitringa had the joy to see his twenty-three-year-old son Campegius Jr. installed as an assistant professor of theology at Franeker. Vitringa Sr. continued to weaken, largely due to overwork and his habit of studying at night. His hearing declined after an infection, and during the last year of his life he suffered a series of strokes. But as the signs of his dissolution came nearer, he was able to speak about his imminent death to his friends with joy. Even on the very day that he himself died, he was able to comfort his daughter-in-law at the death of her grandmother. He testified that he had joy at the thought of his own death and that he did not feel particularly burdened about it. At 4:50 in the afternoon of March 21,

1722, he suffered a stroke and lost speech, movement, and all feeling. Someone quickly fetched a doctor, who used powerful means for his strengthening and recovery. But the nerves were so debilitated and the sickness taken hold to such an extent that at approximately ten thirty that night, under the tears and prayers of his own dear ones, he gave over his well-prepared spirit into the hands of his Creator and Redeemer. He was one month and sixteen days short of being sixty-three years old. His son had traveled to Holland and was not present at the time of his father's death.

Considering Vitringa briefly as a family man, he married Wilhelmina van Hell [1660–1728], a pastor's daughter from Haarlem, in the fall of 1681. They had a peaceful and happy life together. She supported and encouraged him in his frequent ill health and was always a great comfort to him. They had five children together. The oldest son, Simon, made a very hopeful beginning but later fell into the way of vice and caused great pain to his parents. At the end of his life, however, he reformed himself and died in the presence and under the prayers of his excellent father. The second, Horatius, died young at age two. The Vitringas had a daughter, Johanna Margaretha. The records contain little about her except that she married Wilhelm Ruitz, a well-to-do merchant and elder of the church at Haarlem, who died a few weeks before Vitringa.

Vitringa's third son, also named Horatius, became a young scholar of note and left behind touching proofs of his academic industriousness. But he died in 1704 at eighteen years of age to the indescribable pain of his tender father. Vitringa wrote,

> Indeed, in these recent years (in which the sun's appearances have been less bright to me) I have been hard pressed by the divine hand and struggled with troubles. Among which you, my clever and precious son Horatius, have left me indeed plenty of reason for bitter grief. You were carried off by death before your time, in the very flower of your age. You were my delight and showed such uncommonly promising erudition. Although I cause these things to be inserted here to honor your memory, I do desire for you a fully peaceable rest. And I will neither envy your happiness nor rebel against the rule of the divine will.

The fourth son, Campegius Jr., was born on the twenty-third of March in 1693; studied in Franeker, Leiden, and Utrecht; and in 1715 became a much-appreciated professor of theology in Franeker. In the following year a call came to him from Zerbst, which he turned down since he wanted to aid his father. But he did not long survive him, and on the eleventh of January 1723 he went the way of all flesh. His widow later became the wife of the famous Old Testament professor Herman Venema [1697–1787].

## Part II: A Bibliography of the Author

I will now go on to produce an account of the excellent publications of the blessed Vitringa, which have been received by the learned world with almost universal approbation.[2] They are filled with very broad and deep scholarship and contain countless traces of his God-fearing heart. His books have been useful both to the church and to the scholarly world. And I trust that these books with their many beneficial insights will be treasured for years to come.

In 1683, shortly after he became a professor, he produced his first book, *A Survey of Sacred Things*, at twenty-two years of age. Throughout his life Vitringa added to this collection of essays, most of which were written as summaries of the public disputations in which the author participated. They amounted to six volumes dealing mostly with the exegesis of Scripture, though some raise theological questions or explore New Testament church history. [Theodor Christoph] Lilienthal [1717–1781] said that "not only does one find there a treasure of exegetical knowledge, but also they will be of use as an example wherever the clarity of Scripture is assailed." [Johann Franz] Buddeus [1667–1729] called them "books bursting with remarkable learning." They were reprinted numerous times in the Netherlands and Germany.

Vitringa's second work is his *Ruler of the Synagogue*, which arose out of his research in the talmudic and rabbinical writings and was published in 1685. It enters into the debate about the nomenclature

---

2. Unfortunately, apart from this work and short selections from his Isaiah commentary, Vitringa's only writings to be translated into English are an abbreviated form of *On the Old Synagogue* and *Outline of Prophetic Teaching*.

used in the early synagogue (e.g., titles such as bishop, elder, deacon) and how the order and constitution of the early church related to that of the synagogue. The book defends Presbyterianism with its parity of church leaders and critiques [John] Lightfoot [1602–1675], who was a champion of Episcopalianism. Unfortunately, it became the spark for an extensive debate with Vitringa's colleague Jacob Rhenferd [1654–1712] (who had been passed over in favor of Vitringa for the chair of theology and was not well disposed to him). Both men produced polemical works in a series of exchanges. Vitringa acknowledges the strength of Rhenferd's arguments at points, and one happy outcome of the conflict was the production of a greatly strengthened work, *On the Old Synagogue*, ten years later. [Albert] Schultens [1686–1750] appreciated *Ruler of the Synagogue* for its erudition and Vitringa's personal example throughout the debate for "remembering virtue and upholding the name of a Christian when assailed by a bitter adversary."

In 1687 Vitringa published a two-volume *Introduction to a Proper Understanding of the Temple as Seen by Ezekiel*, in which he argues (a) that Ezekiel's famous temple was modeled after the plan of Solomon's temple, (b) that the prophecy of it was literally fulfilled in the building of the temples of Zerubabel and Herod, and (c) that at the same time this was a particular foreshadowing of the glory and excellence of the New Testament church of the end times. He wrote this work in Dutch for the benefit of his unlearned countrymen. But since Vitringa departed from the views of the famous Cocceius at points, the latter's son, Johannes Heinrich Cocceius [1653–1719], wrote a refutation to which Vitringa produced a rejoinder. It is worth noting (a) that Vitringa appreciated both the "literal sense" as well as a "mystical or spiritual sense" in the biblical text and (b) that he recognizes Cocceius's many contributions but was willing to disagree with him where truth required.

In 1689 Vitringa became involved in a heated dispute with another colleague, the famous philosopher and theologian Herman Alexander Röell [1653–1718]. Among others at Franeker, Vitringa was concerned that Röell gave human reason too high a place. He was especially concerned about Röell's teaching (a) that the second person of the Godhead was indeed true God but not actually and truly engendered of the Father (which seemed to introduce a type of tritheism or more exactly Sabellianism) and (b) that the death of believers was a punishment. Pieces both in Latin and in Dutch were produced in the course of the back-and-forth that ensued. Though Röell disturbed the peace of the local churches with his teachings, Vitringa distinguished himself for not losing proper restraint despite the use of many heated expressions on the part of his antagonist.

Next, our author produced a useful little work, *Summary of the Teaching of the Christian Religion*, which went through many editions beginning in 1690 and was translated into Dutch.

I have mentioned it already, but Vitringa published his *On the Old Synagogue* in 1696. It is a precise and in-depth study of the offices, ministries, and worship of the synagogue in relation to those of the early church. [Johann Georg] Pritius [1662–1732] called it "an outstanding work," and [Hieronymus] Grundling [1671–1729] said it was indispensable for understanding church history.

In 1705 he produced his *Examination of the Apocalypse of John the Apostle*. Schultens called this "a work of solid judgment…a lighthouse amidst the most dense clouds." Grundling, [Joachim] Lange [1670–1744], and [Johann Gustav] Reinbeck [1683–1741] went on record to praise it. In the second edition, which was published thirteen years later, Vitringa himself said it had become "a book valued by learned Europe…even men with fair judgment of the Roman sect." In the preface he lays out his hypotheses: what he sees as the foundational principles on which the entire system of the book's teachings rests and on which the teachers of the Christian church must come to agreement if they wish to achieve harmony in the interpretation of apocalyptic prophecies. He seeks to establish these principles through comparing different parts of the book itself that are parallel to one another, through comparing related prophecies from the Old Testament, and through ascertaining the purpose of the author.

The year 1706 saw the publication of his little book *Discourse on the Usefulness, Necessity and Authority of Church Synods*. Such a work is typical of Vitringa's concern for the practical life and health of the churches. In 1708 he came out with a revised edition of his *Outline of Sacred History and Chronology from the Foundation of the World to the End of the First Century AD*. He presents a chronology of biblical history in connection with Mesopotamian sources, and he gives students a helpful set of rules as they approach the study of history and chronology. [Johann Benedict] Carpzov [1675–1739] called it a "nice abridgement of nearly everything which has been written more at length." Vitringa went on to attach another work to this edition entitled *An Outline of Prophetic Teaching*. This was written for theological students to help them understand the function of prophets in biblical times, the nature of biblical prophecy, and sound rules for correctly understanding and interpreting the prophecies. Though not slavishly, he generally follows the hypothesis of Cocceius concerning the seven periods through which the New Testament church will have to pass. He interacts with [Benedict] Spinoza's [1632–1677] godless *Tractatus theologico-politicus* on prophecy somewhat as well. [Johann Jakob] Rambach [1693–1735] said that among the smaller compendia this was one of the best and most useful historical helps on the art of interpretation. Schultens calls these two outlines one of Vitringa's "gifts to the public."

Vitringa's best work, a monument to his great learning and incomparable skill in expounding the Holy Scriptures, is his *Commentary on the Prophecies of Isaiah*. The first volume appeared in 1714 and the second in 1720. The value of the preface for laying out a solid approach to interpretation and of the thorough commentary itself for its careful handling of words and of historical matters is well known. Despite its great length, the work went through many editions in the Netherlands and Germany and has been received throughout Europe with great applause. Buddeus said it was "the model of a perfect commentary in every respect." [Theodore] von Hase [1682–1731] called it "a distinguished treasury of vast and rare learning." Rambach said Vitringa should be considered "among the ornaments of our age." Lange said that "in terms of exegetical method, exposition and laying the foundations for a proper understanding of…Isaiah, the best and most excellent commentary of the famous Dutch theologian Campegius Vitringa stands out." Schultens said, "The public acclaims you, Campegius Vitringa, as one of the greatest examples of interpreters." Another proof of the value of this work is that it has been appallingly plagiarized!

Though Vitringa did not prepare the text with an eye to publication, his colleague Johannes d'Outrein translated from Latin and expanded Vitringa's reflections into *Exposition of the Gospel Parables*. This came out in 1715 and was translated into German as well. It examines the literal and spiritual meanings of the parables and can be of great assistance in preaching because suggestions for practical applications accompany each section.

In 1716 Vitringa published *The Spiritual Life*. This work came out of his lectures on Christian practice at the university. Its usefulness is shown by the fact that it went through many editions and was translated into German, Dutch, French, and Hungarian.

The last of Vitringa's writings published while he was alive is his *Observations on the Proper Form of Preaching*. This was first published in 1721 as an effort to improve preaching in the Dutch churches. It also gives suggestions on public prayer. Schultens said of it,

> This was the swan song of a most faithful minister of Jesus Christ, whose permanent concern was not for the academy only, but indeed he expended himself for the protection of (and in watchful care for) the church universal. And he made the attempt as his final will, even as he had continually instilled such wise counsels and precepts and such practical discipline into his students, to press the concern on all their minds (even with his voice dying and his hand weak) that by dividing and dispensing the true, solid, vital, living, spiritual, and fully rational word of God in preaching, they were to feed the Lord's flock and to lead them to the springs of living water.

Numerous books were published after Vitringa's death that stem from his notes and from his lectures, which were recorded by others. Theodore von Hase published a useful *Sacred Geography* in Vitringa's name in 1723. This would have become a major work on biblical geography if Vitringa had not been hindered by death.

The next year a book entitled *Observations on the Miracles of Jesus Christ* was published in Dutch and soon translated into German. It was prepared for publication by Campegius Jr. before he too died, and was completed by his successor Venema. Though it would have been better if Vitringa Sr. himself had finished it, it helps the reader understand the spiritual meaning of the miracles, how they throw light on the transformations of the believer's spiritual life and in part point to the future transformations and destinies of the church.

Another book collected from his lectures on the Bible is his *Epistle of the Apostle Paul to the Congregations of the Galatians and Also to Titus*. The lectures were in Latin, but this work is a Dutch version published in 1728, which contains some excellent insights. It was often cited and praised by Johann Christoph Wolf [1683–1739] in his *Curis philologicis et criticis*.

Similar to this is his *Exposition of the Apostle Paul's Epistle to the Romans*, which treats the first eight chapters of that letter and was translated into Dutch. Lilienthal said about the work, "It contains many beautiful things, especially the word studies. He is able to analyze things and unwind the many difficult connections involved in this epistle. This *theologus pacificus* has done as much as possible to avoid *controversiae*, but has diligently carried out the *exegesis*."

After finishing his commentary on Isaiah, Vitringa pushed himself despite his bodily weaknesses to complete a commentary on the prophecies of Zechariah. He reached 4:6 before succumbing to death. The prolegomena alone is an adequate introduction to this prophet. Venema, who followed Campegius Vitringa Jr. both in his professorate and in his marriage, received all of Vitringa Sr.'s manuscripts. He published this unfinished work in 1734 under the title *Commentaries on the Book of the Prophecies of Zechariah*. That same year Venema published Vitringa's *Commentary on the Song of Moses (Deut. 32)* and noted that it "is able to throw light on many very difficult and contested passages."

This is a catalog of all the books and writings by Vitringa that I know.

### Part III: The Sequel of the Biography of the Late Vitringa— Regarding His Natural and True Character

Though I may lack the skill to describe vividly the beautiful character of this blessed man, the truth should make up for my lack of elegance.

Vitringa was rather tall, thin, and had a noble and pleasant appearance. His face had something honest, modest, solid, and serious about

xxxvi        THE LIFE AND WORK OF

it. His eyes were clear, cheerful, and pointed to a calmness of spirit. His body had been weak since he was a child, but his habits of intensive studying debilitated him even more. Over time he developed a stoop, not because of age but because he was constantly reading and writing. He pressed himself continually [literally, he tried to keep himself in sweat day and night] even though he became exhausted because of it. He was often seriously ill and more than once was very close to death. But God, who apparently wanted the best for His church through him, marvelously strengthened him and sustained his dilapidated dwelling for longer than one might have expected. In 1702, he was plagued by a violent kidney stone pain that threatened him with imminent death; only through God's help and the skill of Dr. Latanäus was he eventually freed from this troublesome affliction. In the same year he was also beset by another infection, which was very strong and settled into his ears, causing deafness, an affliction that troubled him the rest of his life. It taught him much patience, but he was able to maintain his daily work schedule.

He was still able to govern his voice well for his public lectures at the university. And in private conversation he used a hearing horn. But if the person's voice was still not sufficiently audible and Vitringa could not understand, he would graciously ask the person to have patience with his weakness, which was ordained by God. This hardness of hearing made it difficult for him to participate in the public debates and disputations, and he sometimes required the other participants to put their arguments into writing, to which he would respond in public. When he was asked his thoughts on vexed and difficult questions, he requested people to present the issues in written form, to which he would give thorough answers.

God often manifests his riches in vessels of clay. Vitringa's body was weak and frail, but God furnished him with many gifts. His mind was keen, fruitful, and wide-ranging. His intellect was deep and sharp, and his style of writing was not only thorough in detail but pleasant and even witty. His outstanding commentary on the prophet Isaiah is read with as much pleasure as profit. He seemed continually able to turn mountains of difficulties into comfortable plains for the gratification of his readers. Vitringa was not infallible (for only God can claim that!).

But throughout his life he had a careful system of note taking and an accurate memory, which combined to make him a dependable scholar. Vitringa climbed to an advanced level of scholarship. He had a sound, accurate, and well-ordered knowledge of philosophy and other disciplines ancillary to the study of theology, the queen of the sciences, which was his focus. He was a great connoisseur and lover of history. This is abundantly clear from his writings, especially his *Outline of Sacred History and Chronology from the Foundation of the World to the End of the First Century AD*. He particularly recommends the study of history to theological students, along with the study of chronology, geography, and antiquities. All should learn to see in historical events not only the actions of men but the hand of the most-wise Ruler of the world as well.

In terms of languages, Vitringa attained a thorough knowledge of the old Latin and Greek writers and went on to attain a wide grasp of Hebrew, Aramaic, and rabbinic literatures. He would never have become such a great interpreter of Holy Scripture if he had not become a master and skillful critic of all these languages. In terms of his own writing, he sometimes invented new Latin words in order to bring out a proper sense of the stress of the biblical languages. But his style is manly, serious, clear, and rich in expression. And when the topic requires, his Latin is magnificent and noble.

Vitringa preached as well as practiced the principle that ministers should have a broad liberal arts education in preparation for their theological studies. Those who argued for a shorter, streamlined course of training were seriously mistaken. Ministers must become people of broad scholarship. Knowing great thinkers of earlier times produces humility and modesty and teaches us to be patient with those who hold opinions other than our own in secondary matters. Haughty pride typifies the semischolarly, and superficial scholarship tends to stir up unnecessary disputes.

Vitringa believed that piety goes hand in hand with learning. The theologian should be able to give an accurate opinion on any subject that pertains to his area of science [*Wissenschaft*]. But he will only attain to this (unless it be given him by an extraordinary grace of the Holy Spirit) through labor and strenuous effort. Walking with God

xxxviii THE LIFE AND WORK OF

by faith in Christ does not dull but sharpens the mind. Meditation on spiritual things and the practice of true piety provokes rather than stifles academic achievement and true scholarship. The true Christian must seek the honor of God and not his own in all his studies. Because he truly reverences God, he dedicates to God and the benefit of His church all his intellect, all his diligence, and all his labors, which are God's gifts anyway. Christianity can boast above other religions that true piety and true scholarship and rationality shine most brightly when they are combined.

We have seen how highly Vitringa praised the combination of learning and godliness. Let us now examine his own attainments in each, starting with his scholarship. Of course, the sound theologian needs to be a skilled interpreter of the Holy Scriptures since they comprise the foundation of our faith and conduct. Who is unacquainted with the fruits of Vitringa's exceptional exegetical skill? He will surely take a permanent place among the greatest and most respected interpreters of the priceless Word of the Lord. He read, studied, and interacted daily with the books of the Holy Scriptures throughout his life. It was his particular concern to clarify for others the more difficult and obscure parts of the Bible, particularly in the prophetic books. In his day Dutch theologians were divided into the Cocceians and the Voetians. But Vitringa managed to steer clear of any party spirit. Cocceius was his friend as was [Gisbertus] Voetius [1589–1676], but his dearest friend was truth. As you can see from the famous preface to the Isaiah commentary, he was able to make use of as well as disagree with Cocceius. Through his love of truth, Vitringa was able to keep a good conscience and to please God and those quiet minds who love the peace of Zion.

His presentation of Christian doctrine was balanced and biblically supported. His teaching and writing lacked the polemical strife that typified some others. Even in conflicts he did not allow himself to be drawn in by vehement and immoderate opponents or to be stirred to similar behavior. He handled the controversies with Rhenferd, Cocceius Jr., and Röell in a calm and praiseworthy manner. His sound arguments and humility earned him the respect of all reasonable, truth-loving, and honest people. As a Lutheran myself, I do not appreciate his defense of the Reformed church concerning predestination and particular redemption (I appreciate Vitringa very much but not blindly). But it serves as a singular honor to Vitringa that Lutheran and even Roman Catholic writers settled on him the well-deserved title of "irenic theologian" and have rushed to shower him with fine and solid compliments.

Another demonstration of Vitringa's ability is his beautiful book *The Spiritual Life*. He was able to motivate people for the Christian life and to stir them up to pursue a Christian lifestyle very affectively and with proper biblical support. For this reason, he was also a pleasant and edifying preacher. From the pulpit as well as from the lectern he addressed audiences of many eager listeners.

Rambach calls Vitringa a *miraculum viri docti et pii*, a marvel of a learned and pious man. Having dealt with his learning, let us now consider its principal ornament: his unfeigned godliness. Vitringa did not teach godliness and live godlessness. The high opinion of many Reformed and Lutheran men about his writings is confirmed unanimously by those who knew him in person. He was a godly man and a regenerated as well as an enlightened and illuminated theologian.

Vitringa not only gained the respect of men through his great scholarship but of God through his true Christianity. He belongs to that rare group of scholars who become not only learned but wise. Vitringa's example undermines the harmful prejudice that thorough scholarship and a genuine fear of God cannot be brought together properly or usefully. He served his generation while his eye was on the next world.

Vitringa understood the vast difference between virtues exercised by a person in a state of grace (which one enters through true faith) and the outwardly good deeds of a person still in the state of nature that are performed out of fear of divine punishment or for purely earthly motivations. Many people are satisfied with an outward profession of Christianity but do not consider the inner state and motivations of their hearts. Vitringa felt that the power of Christianity consists in the inner communion of the soul with God in Christ and the constant sense of this communion in all the activities of life. His exposition of Isaiah 28:10 is particularly beautiful, and I hope it makes an impression on many others besides myself. There he affirms that merely theoretical erudition means nothing in the kingdom of God, which consists not in words but in power. Though founded on knowledge, living faith alone makes the mind capable of grasping spiritual and heavenly things. He who without the Holy Spirit studies the truths of our faith simply from books but without a taste and feeling for these truths may easily go astray. He may quote others well, but he has no felt or experiential knowledge consistent with these truths, which contributes more to understanding these things than merely intellectual and bookish efforts that do not involve a person's soul and spirit.

Unfeigned piety expressed itself in the various areas of Vitringa's life. In his preaching and lecturing, people often sensed the divine anointing in a special way. Vitringa became a bright light in the church and the academy and was esteemed by his colleagues, his students, his congregation (of which he was an elder), and the entire community. Though due to his deafness he could not hear the preaching, he continued to attend public worship so that at least he might edify others by his example. And he always had open the text of the preacher on which he engaged in private devotions. He was a vigilant servant who attended day and night on the coming of his Lord and kept himself in readiness for it. He was very careful in the use of his time and redeemed it. The health and safety of the kingdom of God on earth was very dear to him. Does he not write very movingly about the deterioration of the inner condition of the Protestant churches in his preface to the commentary on Revelation? Vitringa's humility was apparent. He refused all flattery and praise, which in fact made him more honorable in others' sight.

In all things Vitringa acted wisely, respectably, and conscientiously. Throughout his life he showed himself to be a fair, upright, and friendly person. He was affectionate, pleasant, and agreeable in his relations with others. His friendliness was readily apparent and yet he was also circumspect. Intimate with his friends, he dealt gently with his opponents. He did not enjoy visitors who merely came to pay compliments. But he made himself fully accessible to his students, whom he loved like a father, and often conversed with them about the truths of Christian doctrine. He showed a special love for international students, whether Reformed or Lutheran, who in return had a special respect for him. No one at the Franeker University ever had his auditorium so full of listeners as did Vitringa over the years. He was concerned to be useful and always sought the welfare of the university. He was elected to serve as academic rector twice. In the university council he expressed his views forthrightly but modestly. He advocated strenuously for what was just and good. He gladly promoted the honor of others and was neither jealous nor envious of their good fortune but looked on it with joy. He praised the virtues of even his opponents and strove to commend every person's honest efforts in keeping with their merits but without flattery.

This has been an incomplete description of the praiseworthy qualities of the blessed man. One category in a useful biography seems to be missing—an account of his accompanying faults. I honestly testify that I have not been silent when some of them were known to me, but rather I know none. That the remarkable and accomplished man should err a little in his views, feelings, or outward behavior is easy for anyone to believe. He was just a man. And as with all of us, the greatest prudence and wisdom does not always keep us from missteps. Even great souls err and may be oblivious to their own faults. That Vitringa had such faults I do not doubt. By the grace of God, however, his integrity and accomplishments so predominated when you consider his whole life that the failings are entirely lost from view.[3]

---

3. End of this *Lebenslauf* [Biography]. Following this, with typical German thoroughness, Büsching included "Certain Additions and Corrections to the First Two Sections of the Lebenslauf." It consists of many details irrelevant to our purposes here, but I will include a letter to Vitringa from his relative, Professor Lambertus Bos [1670–1717], who comments on the death of Vitringa's son Horatius in 1704: "You see here, honored cousin, attached to my own [just published] little work, an example of the diligent labors of your most learned young son, now blessed, whose death you received as a most grave blow, whom you properly still grieve so, and we also.... For if God had supplied him with longer life, he would have been your most outstanding crown, the honor of the family, of us and of everyone who saw his gifts, his joy and fruitfulness, his talent in literature, the ornament of his homeland. For in him were indeed excellent character qualities which held promise that he would be a great man, and showed forth a faithful likeness of yourself."

# The Spiritual Life

# Vitringa's Preface

The spiritual life is something pure, holy, and precious. The subject is worthy of serious attention by all who would promote their sanctification and are desirous of eternal life. For the spiritual life leads to eternal life. We cannot have one without the other. The first is the beginning of the second; the latter is the consummation of the former.

At first the topic seems simple and easy to understand. What is the spiritual life but the exercise of true and living faith through love? The practice of truth, godliness, and every virtue in accordance with the teaching of Jesus Christ? Full obedience to the precepts of the gospel? Or as the apostle Paul puts it, "love from a pure heart and a good conscience and a sincere faith" (1 Tim. 1:5)? Nothing could be clearer!

It might seem unbelievable if it were not confirmed by experience, but by the fourth century the form and features of the Christian religion (most beautiful when properly displayed) began to degenerate from its early and attractive purity and simplicity. As gangrene winds its way through the body little by little, nothing has been more exposed to the instability of the human mind and the mockeries of ignorant men than the exercise of piety. The strength of superstition and the twisted thinking of man corrupted the simplicity of early Christian practice. By that time all kinds of absurd and harmful practices had become established as ways attaining a more perfect spiritual life.[1]

---

1. Here Vitringa goes into a lengthy survey of the strengths and weaknesses of movements in favor of the solitary or the monastic life in the late classical and medieval periods. He gives particular attention to the Quietism of Miguel de Molinos (1628–1696), which he rejects in favor of a fundamentally active view of the spiritual life. For further discussion

You can see, dear reader, how the simple discipline left for us by the authors of our faith has been exposed to so many errors sprouting from the human mind. It seems it is difficult to walk the straight road. Man loves detours, forks in his spiritual path. He would rather be unique and outstanding than walk the old paths with other Christians.

May heaven grant that this little book might be free from such defects and communicate a more accurate and pure depiction of the spiritual life. I have certainly labored to conform it to the teachings of the authors of Scripture and to rational experience, the two most dependable principles to follow on such a question. For true godliness has been the same in every age of the world since its beginning. There is only one way: the ancient way, the straight way, the way of faith, hope, holiness, love, righteousness, and justice in which the patriarchs, prophets, and saints of old walked. By precept and example, they commended this way to their posterity as the true way of life. Jesus Christ Himself as well as His apostles set out this way of life most clearly; they showed what strengthened it and what its limits were. And Christ gave to all His people the most perfect example of every virtue.[2]

In this work I want to go deeper than a survey of vices and their corresponding Christian virtues. I want to examine the work of the grace of God in the hearts of men: its beginning, progress, and perfections, along with the vicissitudes, affections, and distinguishing characteristics of the state of grace. Hopefully we will learn the difference between true virtues (exercised by faith in a state of grace) and counterfeit virtues (exercised in a state of nature out of a fear of divine judgment and from carnal affections). Many people are ignorantly content with an outward profession of Christianity but pay little attention to the condition and internal movements of their soul. The

---

of this material, see my "Campegius Vitringa (1659–1722), Exemplary Exegete and Theologian of the Spiritual Life," *Hapshin Theological Review* 6 (2018): 69–90.

2. At this point in his preface Vitringa expresses his appreciation for the writings of the church fathers on this topic (particularly Clement of Alexandria, Cyprian, John of Damascus, and especially Augustine's *On Morals*) and how he wanted to go deeper than just a survey of vices and virtues. He notes, "Among the ancient Latin writers, I am acquainted with no one who has better explained the nature of the spiritual life than Augustine: the way it is generated, its affections, and the tender feelings with which a soul in the state of grace clings to God and never loses Him from view."

strength of Christianity consists in an interior commerce of the soul with God in Christ and a continual consideration for him in all the actions of life. But many are ignorant of these things since the pastors of souls have not always taken the necessary care to explain them.

I will not drag this out except to say that most of what is in this little book I wrote for my students. I expanded it in various places and now timidly send it to the press. Even if I have rightly understood these things and been able to write without serious errors, I know that the real test is not to write about what makes a good man but to put it into practice. As Augustine says, it is easy to affect an appearance of virtue but difficult to be virtuous. The important thing is not to call yourself or to seem a Christian, but to be one. How difficult a thing it is to submit to Christ Jesus all the affections of your soul! To wish for nothing other than what God wishes and to reject all that is displeasing to God! You who are a new Christian, if you are unaware of this, how many things experience will teach you! When it pleases the heavenly Father to lead you through the valley of shadows, the way of temptation, of affliction, and of the cross, then you will experience what kind of a man you are: how shaky your steps are, how little progress you have made in the school of Christ, how painful it is for a beginner like you to follow after your Lord and to carry His cross. In a word, you will learn how difficult it is to keep in good spiritual condition through the ups and downs of life and amid today's corrupt customs and not to do anything unworthy or shameful. The way of life is a narrow way. It demands a life of strict and exacting discipline and does not allow you freedom to wander to the right or to the left. The spirit is free in the Lord, but the flesh has no liberty. Watch yourself then, Christian, and be careful not to come off as more holy than you are.

As I write, my own imperfections rise up before me, and I feel them deeply and penetratingly. Who can effectively hide from his own faults and weaknesses without willingly blinding and deceiving himself? There is no other remedy than to resort quickly and confidently to the grace of God. With all humility and diligence, we forget what lies behind and strain forward to what lies ahead (Phil. 3:13). Though we may stumble repeatedly, the just Judge will receive us, since He is touched with sympathy for our weaknesses. And we will be able to find mercy with the Lord on that great and brilliant day. Amen—so be it!

Farewell, reader. Look on the fruit of my labor with favor. May God use this work for your benefit and for the benefit of His church. And may you grow more and more in the knowledge and grace of the Lord Jesus in the hope of eternal life.

Written at Franeker in Frisia [Northern Netherlands]
July 13, 1716

# PART 1

## The Nature of the Spiritual Life

CHAPTER 1

◇

# The Spiritual Life and Its Characteristics

The Scriptures portray the spiritual life as the state [*status*] of a man in Christ who has been liberated from slavery to ignorance, corruption, lust, and the vanity of the age, and brought into communion with God. This takes place through the principle of true faith and love for God that the grace of the Holy Spirit has put in him through regeneration and sanctification. He now finds himself having a good conscience and putting into practice all kinds of virtues and good works in accordance with the precepts of the divine law, to the glory of God in Christ our Redeemer. And this in turn results in his neighbor's edification and his own consolation and everlasting welfare. Both the Old and New Testaments refer to this state as a state of "life"[1]: "Make me understand the righteousness of Your eternal testimonies that I may live" (Ps. 119:144); "Abandon foolishness and you will live" (Prov. 9:6); "Truly I say to you that the time is coming and is already here when the dead will hear the voice of the Son of God and those who hear will live" (John 5:25); "We are buried together with Him in death so that, as Christ was raised from the dead to the glory of the Father, thus we too might walk in newness of life" (Rom. 6:4); "For through the law I have died to the law so that I might live to God; I have been crucified together with Christ, but I live. Yet it is no longer I, but Christ lives in me; and the life which I now live in the flesh I live by faith in the Son of God who loved me and gave Himself for me" (Gal. 2:19–20).

---

1. Vitringa's Scripture quotations in Latin are largely his own translations, which have been followed in this version.

The spiritual life is a state of action, a state of continual and conscious activity. To live is to exist by the force of an internal principle
and to be in action with consciousness. All life is like this. Living is
a series of acts that emerge from a principle. There is an immaterial
force, a cause or principle that produces life. The activity that characterizes the spiritual life of a man in Christ can be clearly distinguished
from other forms of life.

There are, of course, other distinct types of life: natural life, social
life, life under the carnal economy (i.e., in Old Testament times), and
the perverse life of sin and wrongdoing. Natural life is the state in
which a person acts—for his own preservation—out of the principle
imbued into all living beings. The natural functions of eating, drinking, protecting oneself against the weather, and all kinds of bodily
activities belong to this type of life. Social life consists in the activities
one carries out as a member of civil society. A third type of activity was
lived out by the people who were part of the external Old Testament
church of God. This was a "carnal economy" involving certain religious ceremonies instituted by Moses. Paul calls this "living Jewishly"
in Galatians 2:14. He has this type of life in mind in Colossians 2:20:
"Therefore if you have died with Christ, you are free from the elemen-
tal principles of the world. Why then do you follow its ordinances as if
you were living in the world?"

Sin, of course, affects the three types of life I have mentioned (natural, civil, and Mosaic), but it can be viewed as a fourth type of human
activity. This life is typified by vice-riddled lusts. In his corrupt nature,
man has become a slave of sin, separated from communion with God
and deprived of His love. The sinner is either ignorant or negligent of
God and gives himself over to the vilest actions (forbidden by God and
reason) to satiate his lusts. It may be that he abandons himself to self-
indulgence, carnal longings, or injustice; to greed, hatred, strife; or to
a long list of offenses against God and man. Because of his deplorable
ignorance and blindness, he may even imagine his own vices please God
and are truly religious acts.

Such is the life of sin and lust, the fleshly life of which the apostle
speaks in Ephesians 2:1–2: "And you He has made alive when you were
dead in offenses and sins in which you previously walked in keeping

with the course of this age" and also 1 Peter 4:2–3: "So that for the rest of our time in the flesh we should live no longer in accordance with human lusts." He then explains this carnal life more clearly: "For it is enough that we have lived in past time doing what the Gentiles delight in: living in sensuality, lusts, drunkenness, gluttony, wild reveling and the shameful worship of idols." And so it follows that every other kind of activity (whether belonging to natural life, civil life, or the carnal economy of the Jews), if it does not spring from the principle of faith and of love for God but comes from the principle of lust, must be considered as a part of the life of sin.

Only this fourth category of life, the life of sin, is opposed to the spiritual life. The spiritual life is compatible with but nobler than the first three categories of life, however. Both natural and civil activity stem from natural motivations and the principle of self-preservation. The principle behind the spiritual life is the love of God in Christ—that is, the desire to be in communion with God. This is a sublime and spiritual affection. The goal of spiritual activities is not the preservation of our natural life or social status but our spiritual state (i.e., our communion with God), and it involves the pursuit of heavenly glory and the happiness that the gospel promises. The person who lives this holistically spiritual life is properly called a "spiritual man" (1 Cor. 2:13; Gal. 6:1).

The spiritual life is fundamentally different from (though not incompatible with) the activities of a Jew under the old economy. It was possible for a person to fulfill all the exterior duties and ceremonies of the law of Moses so that he was considered a good citizen in the Jewish church and republic but still not live in God and from God. It was possible for a person to "live Jewishly" but have no share in communion with Him and miss out on His love. Old Testament "Jewish life" involved merely external activities. And, of course, a person can indeed live spiritually without keeping the rites God imposed on the Jews under the old economy. These regulations were a matter of externals and "the law of a carnal commandment" (Heb. 7:16). Such exercises, when separated from faith and hope in the promises, are called activities of the flesh in 2 Corinthians 5:16: "We regard no one according to the flesh." That is, greatness is not a matter of whether or not one practices the external religion of Moses. Even though we once regarded Christ

"according to the flesh"—that is, according to the life that He lived as
a Jew before His resurrection from the dead—"we regard Him thus no
longer." In this way the apostle makes a distinction between the Jew
under the old economy, whom he calls the one "born according to the
flesh" (Gal. 4:29), and the spiritual man under the new economy.

It is important for us to note again that though the spiritual life is of
a different quality than natural, civil, or Mosaic activity, it accords well
with these types of life. When "animal," "social," or "carnal economy"
activities are subordinated to the spiritual life, they are perfected and
sanctified by it. The principle of faith and of love for God rectifies and
emends all their actions, directing them to a more noble end than they
would naturally tend. The type of life that is entirely opposed to the spiritual life is living "according to the flesh" (Rom. 8:5), acting according
to the will and lusts of the sinful nature (Eph. 2:3). This type of activity
stems from an ignorance of God (especially in the case of idolatry and
superstition) or from the desire of the corrupt nature to obtain that
supposed highest good (apart from God and communion with Him)
that a man makes the object of his lust. He may abandon himself to
greed, ambition, sumptuous living, or sensual pleasures. He may follow
after the pomp of the world and the vainglory of the age. He may give
himself over to injustice, hatred, envy, and similar vices that produce the
most twisted and criminal disorders. All these vile affections belong to
the "fleshly lusts" (1 Peter 2:11). The life of sin is not natural, but fleshly;
it is not civil, but bestial. In such a state man degrades the excellence
of his nature and often makes himself inferior to the beasts. Such a life
cannot be reconciled with the spiritual life in any way.

The following are the defining characteristics that constitute the
spiritual life: (a) It is the life of a "man in Christ" (as the apostle puts it
in 2 Cor. 12:2). Being regenerated by the grace of God and endowed
with the Holy Spirit, such a person is united in the closest connection
to God by faith and hope. "Christ lives in me" (Gal. 2:20). "If anyone
is in Christ Jesus…" (2 Cor. 5:17). (b) It is the life of a man in Christ
liberated from slavery to sin, lust, and the vanity of the age. The apostles
speak this way in Romans 6:11: "You also must consider yourselves to
be dead with regard to sin but alive to God through Christ Jesus our
Lord" (cf. Eph. 2:3; 1 Peter 4:2–4). (c) The spiritual life flows from the

ceaseless principle of true life and love that comes from God, as Jesus says: "The water which I will give him will become in him a fountain of water springing up to eternal life" (John 4:14). This principle is infused by the regenerating grace of the Holy Spirit (see Ezek. 36:26; John 3:5).

(d) The rule of this life is not natural instinct, civil law, or bare rationality but the light of the Holy Spirit Himself. It is the holy and spiritual law of God connected in both Old Testament and New Testament times to the word of grace. It is particularly the spiritual law of the kingdom of heaven announced by Christ our Lord. Therefore, to live spiritually means, as the saints often express it, to practice the law of God and His precepts. The sacred poet speaks elegantly in Psalm 119:17, "Do good things for your servant that I may live and keep Your Word," as does the apostle in John 15:10: "If you keep My precepts, you will abide in My love." To be sure, the type, rule, norm, and model of this state of activity is the very life of God Himself (of which I will soon speak); it is the life of Christ Jesus raised from the dead; it is life under the new economy; it is the life of the good angels in their state [*status*] of holiness, serving God with freedom and joy; it is the life of all the saints inasmuch as they are imitators of God and of Christ (Eph. 5:1). The spiritual life manifests itself in an eager pursuit of all the virtues and every possible good work that we know to be the will of God (Phil. 4:8).

(e) The spiritual life is connected to the joy of a good conscience. "You have put more joy in my heart than when their grain and wine increased" (Ps. 4:7) and "Your joy no one will take from you" (John 16:22). Paul calls this the "joy of faith" (Phil. 1:25). I regard this joy and peace of conscience to be an essential characteristic of this life. It comes from a greater or lesser sense of God's favor in accordance with the varying conditions that believers go through. (f) The goal and focus of a person living spiritually is the glory of God in Christ and the edification of one's neighbor: "Let your light shine before men in such a way that they may see your good works, and your Father in heaven might be glorified" (Matt. 5:16); "Whatever you do in word or deed, do it in the name of the Lord Jesus [a Hebraic expression meaning "to His glory"], giving thanks to our God and Father through Him" (Col. 3:17); "Therefore encourage and build up one another" (1 Thess. 5:11).

(g) Finally, the spiritual life is a condition of everlasting activity. This life will never end but will lead into a future state of glory. The spiritual life that we live on earth will be absorbed into the heavenly life that awaits us: "He who believes in the Son has eternal life" (John 3:36); "He who keeps My word will never see death unto eternity" (John 8:51)—that is, he will be preserved from eternal ruin.

The life whose characteristics we have been describing is beautifully typified by the apostle as the "life of God" (Eph. 4:18), an admirable title distinguishing it as the most noble type of life. It deserves to be called such (a) because it is a particular gift of the grace of God that produces this life in a person; (b) because it perfectly unites a person with God, and especially since a person cannot live this life except in communion with God; (c) because in this life God, by the operations of His Holy Spirit, directly influences a person and joins him intimately to Himself; and (d) because it is a spiritual life, formed after the type and example of the spiritual life of God Himself. In such a life one sees to a certain extent an image, an imitation, and certain marks of that most perfect life that God lives, which is why those who live this life are considered "partakers of the divine nature" (2 Peter 1:4).

We can consider the spiritual life either as *common* to all ages of the church or with a *special* focus on our present economy of the new covenant. The patriarchs were in communion with God, lived by faith (a gift of divine grace), and exercised themselves in the practice of every virtue for the glory of God (see Hebrews 11; Gen. 5:24; 17:1; Mic. 6:8). This is the common experience of all the saints. But under our present New Testament arrangement, there is a higher degree of spirituality than was the case under the old economy, as the church is sanctified by the more abundant and more efficacious grace of the Holy Spirit in virtue of the obedience of Christ Jesus, and the church has the joy of liberation from all the burdensome carnal exercises practiced under the old economy (cf. Deut. 30:6; Ezek. 36:26; John 3:5). The life of Christ Jesus raised from the dead is the model for New Testament spiritual life (Rom. 6:4). Since Christ has been raised from the dead, He has been liberated from the yoke of the Mosaic law and is said to "live unto God" (Rom. 6:10). He is in a state of the perfect, joyful freedom in communion with the divine glory that also characterizes the life of believers, as we will examine in detail.

CHAPTER 2

∽

# The Origins of the Spiritual Life

So far we have been describing the characteristics of the spiritual life. To live means to be full of activity, and that activity stems from a foundational principle [*principium*]. Our next task is to consider the beginning and origin of this life so that we might even better understand its nature. The spiritual life is the fruit stemming from certain good capacities and dispositions [*habitus*] infused into a man in Christ by the grace of the Holy Spirit and diffused throughout all his faculties, among which faith in Christ Jesus is the foremost and the one that directs all the others.[1]

These capacities and dispositions [*habitus*] that are the sources of spiritual life I would list as follows: illumination of the soul (i.e., the ability of a mind to grasp and digest spiritual things), rectitude of judgment (i.e., integrity and wisdom), faith in Christ Jesus, hope and full confidence in divine grace, love and reverence for God, goodwill toward one's neighbor, and finally, purity and moderation of the affections (i.e., temperance). These pure and reasonable capacities and dispositions are the source of the spiritual life. All the particular actions of the spiritual life bubble over from this fountain and foundational principle [*principium*]. The following texts support such an understanding: Ephesians 1:17–18; 1 Corinthians 2:14–15; Colossians 1:9; and the words of Peter

---

1. Vitringa generally uses the term *habitus* to refer to a spiritual capacity or a spiritual disposition of soul (whether of the mind or of the will). Since the term is occasionally misunderstood today, I have noted his use of it at certain junctures below. See Richard A. Muller, *Dictionary of Latin and Greek Theological Terms, Drawn Principally from Protestant Scholastic Theology* (Grand Rapids: Baker, 1985), 134.

set it forth particularly well: "You yourselves, brothers, make every effort to add to your faith virtue, etc." (2 Peter 1:5–7).

Life is something unified and indivisible, and it is reasonable to see a single source behind the various activities of life. Similarly, the divine Word teaches that among the principles which motivate the spiritual life, there is one original source, one outstanding fountain to which the others can be traced back. It sums up the entire life of a believer and is referred to in various ways: "the knowledge of God," "the fear of the LORD," "having the eyes of the understanding illumined," "faith," or in other places "the love of God." Though all these notions seem disjointed, they actually cohere and cannot be separated from each other. These all point toward the same thing and form a single complex object—"the root of the matter," to use the phraseology of Job 19:28.

The source of spiritual life is a sincere love for God that is graciously produced in a person's soul by the Holy Spirit by granting them faith in the word of grace—that is, the message of the gospel with its promises. But this one principle of faith presupposes other graces, such as an illumination of the mind, a love for God, a respect for Him as Father, and obedience to Him as Lord. None of these things appears in a person except by divine grace. So although this single source of the spiritual life is simple and indivisible, it can be discussed under different names, which we will now endeavor to do.

For example, the love of God is spoken of as a source of the spiritual life: "You shall love the LORD your God with all your heart" (Deut. 6:5); "And the LORD will circumcise your heart and the heart of your descendants that you may love Him with your entire heart" (Deut. 30:6); "He who loves Me will keep My word" (John 14:23); "Love for God has been poured out in our hearts by the Holy Spirit" (Rom. 5:5); "The goal of the commandment is love from a pure heart, a good conscience, and a sincere faith" (1 Tim. 1:5). Though the concept is sprinkled in texts throughout the Word of God, the apostle John in his first epistle presses home splendidly the idea that love for God is at the heart of the spiritual life.

Reason and experience affirm the same thing. Whenever a person reflects on his inner motivations, he feels that all his actions and even his affections are motivated by a particular desire that directs and dominates all other feelings. Is this desire and motivating influence anything other than love, the desire that each one has for whatever he considers to be good? So it is with love for God in the case of a Christian. If all our activities and affections must be regulated by the law of God, we must have within us a source principle in keeping with such affections and activities. This must be love for God. If every action of the spiritual life has glorifying God as its highest goal, how can this goal be reached except in a mind where there is a sincere affection for God and an ardent desire to glorify Him? It is precisely this desire that we call love for God.

Love for God is an affection of the soul in which a person, despite being in an estate of misery and sin, feels that his summum bonum, his highest good, is to be in communion with God and that this communion is offered to him by Christ Jesus. This delight in God causes him to seek communion with Him with all his might and his deepest longings. Furthermore, he seeks Him in the way prescribed by the word of grace. And consequently, as long as he is in this world, he directs all his efforts to the glory of God in Christ. And it becomes obvious to all that what he esteems as his highest good is communion with God in Christ, preferring it above all other temporal, carnal, and perishable good things.

The source of the spiritual life is precisely this love for God. Where it reigns in a human heart, it absorbs and subordinates to itself all feelings and desires. It becomes that most noble, most excellent affection that Moses describes as loving with all the understanding of the heart. It is the firm conviction and wholehearted choice that prefers God and communion with Him by grace to be infinitely superior to all other goods. Joshua calls this loving God with all the soul (Josh. 22:5). Our soul is oriented around a single integrating affection, and we submit to God all our desires for earthly things, even the things that contribute to the preservation of our bodies. This is to love God "with all our utmost"—that is, with the entire devoted intentions of all our faculties.

Additionally, this love that I have described as the true source of the spiritual life is not born in sinful man except from true faith (faith, of course, has as its object the word and promise of grace). This is why faith is commended everywhere in the Word of God as the source of the spiritual life. Faith itself may be designated as "the love of God." The apostle joins these two together in 1 Timothy 1:5, where the basic principle of the spiritual life is said to be the pure love of God from an unfeigned faith. The apostle implies the same thing: "Whatever is not of faith is sin" (Rom. 14:23); "It is impossible without faith that anyone should please God" (Heb. 11:6); "The life which I now live in the flesh, I live by faith in the Son of God" (Gal. 2:20). Compare these with Old Testament texts such as "The just will live by his faith" (Hab. 2:3–4); "If you will not believe, you will not be established" (Isa. 7:9); and "The one who believes will not make haste" (Isa. 28:16). In these texts, faith is that thing by which a person acknowledges with a humble and grateful mind that he owes his entire salvation to divine grace.

When we speak of faith as the source of the spiritual life, we do not have in mind a naked faith or a mere historical assent to the doctrine of the gospel, something that takes place strictly in the mind and never becomes an affection. Such "faith" James calls dead (James 2:20) since it never produces the fruit of good works. What we understand as faith is that living act of a man who, persuaded of the greatness of his misery, bondage, and the liberating grace that is offered to him in Christ, seeks that liberation most earnestly. He receives Christ Jesus, having a most pure affection of love for God in Christ and a burning desire to be in communion with Him. He claims Christ for himself as a gift from God. When a person by grace responds in this way, he is joined tightly to Christ Jesus, and by this union he becomes a participant in the spiritual, heavenly, and divine life of which we are speaking. When this faith is in a person's heart, it does not allow him to be lazy, unemployed, or stagnant; such faith is always "working through love" (Gal. 5:6). It is a flowing spring from which every kind of good thought, word, and action bubble forth. This faith is the very life of the mind and soul. It distinguishes the living person from the dead, the carnal person from the spiritual. Where there is such faith, there is life. The love of God is birthed from this faith, is founded on this faith, or rather, this faith is itself par excellence the love of God and of the truth.

The love of God has two aspects, both of which spring from faith. First is that desiring love by which a person comes into communion with God in Christ. Second is that dutiful love by which a believer, having become a recipient of the grace of God, devotes himself entirely to His service in order to testify to his gratitude. The first kind of love is nothing other than faith itself, and the second is the consequence of the first. Until a sinner is convinced of divine grace, he flees from God as a terrible and fearful being. But once he perceives the good news of consolation, the word of grace promised in Christ Jesus, then he begins to feel the movement of life in himself. He is enfolded in the love of God by the Holy Spirit. He ardently desires communion with Him. And when he has obtained this communion, then, totally absorbed by the flames of divine love, he clothes his soul in a holy and spiritual affection so that he might gladly give himself, all he has, and all his faculties over to God his liberator, to whose glory he gladly consecrates all the moments and actions of his life. It is this affection, which is a desire born from faith, that we call the love of God.

It is not difficult to understand why the love of God, this source principle of spiritual life, is sometimes called by Paul an illumination of the eyes of the mind (Eph. 1:18). Since faith is an act of the mind, it presupposes a corresponding condition in the intellect that precedes the reasonable exercise of such an act. In other words, no one can truly believe in Christ Jesus unless his intellect has been prepared and illumined by the Spirit of God so that he can clearly understand the truth set forth in the gospel and perceive the case for the covenant of grace in its essential details. The Scriptures call this work of the Spirit "revelation" (cf. 1 Cor. 2:10; Matt. 11:25) or "illumination" (cf. 2 Cor. 4:4).

Revelation is that clear and efficacious illumination of the understanding of the mind that banishes the prejudices and carnal affections that are obstacles to true faith. It convinces the mind of the truth of the gospel and leads it to embrace this truth with all its strength by faith. And such is the order and connectedness of these affections produced by grace that the illumination of the mind precedes faith, and faith in turn engenders love for God. But these affections are at root a single, unified, and multifaceted capacity [*complexus habitus*], which is the source of the spiritual life.

This illumination of the understanding (as with the faith that springs up after it) and all the resulting affections and actions of the soul are utterly dependent on divine grace. Christ by His Spirit makes a man's soul alive, stirs it into action, and establishes it as His residence. This is why the grace of God, Christ Jesus, and His Spirit are often recognized as the source and foundational principles [*principia*] of the spiritual life: "By the grace of God I am what I am" (1 Cor. 15:10); Jesus speaks of "The water which I will give him," i.e., His grace (John 4:14); "Walk in accordance with the Spirit" (Gal. 5:16), that is, according to the faith administered by the Holy Spirit; "Christ lives in me" (Gal. 2:20).

Lastly, reverence, or "the fear of God," is another scriptural expression for the source of spiritual life. "The fear of the LORD is the beginning of wisdom" (Ps. 111:10). Wisdom and prudence give birth to the activities and operations typical of the spiritual life. The fear of God is composed of three things: loving God in Christ as Father, revering Him as Lord, and fearing Him as Judge (1 Peter 1:17). This reverence for Jehovah is a tender and filial affection of the soul and keeps a person from doing anything to offend Him. It too is born from faith, as is love toward God. In fact, it is another name for love because one cannot have love for God without reverence for Him (Deut. 6:5; 10:12).

CHAPTER 3

⚜

# The Causes of the Spiritual Life

Having considered the nature and source of the spiritual life, we must now seek to understand its causes since one cannot arrive at a full knowledge of something without examining what produced it. We need to learn by what means the spiritual life is produced in the soul that receives it. There are three types of causes involved in the production of the spiritual life: the *meritorious* cause, the *efficient* cause, and the *material* cause. These matters are set forth clearly in the Word of God.

According to Scripture, the *meritorious* cause of the spiritual life is the obedience of the Son of God in accordance with the laws of the eternal covenant contracted between Himself and His Father. He offered this obedience to the point of death, and even the death of the cross. The Lord Jesus Himself sets forth two causes of the spiritual life. One He calls water; the other He calls Spirit. These should not be confused but viewed as truly distinct according to the Savior's intention. He says, "Unless a person is born from water and the Spirit, he cannot enter into the kingdom of God" (John 3:5).

In this text, water is understood to be the purest and perfect obedience of Christ Jesus, which was offered to God in keeping with the demands of divine justice through His most painful sufferings, without which there could be no forgiveness of sins. Nor except by this obedience could the gift of the Spirit of regeneration and of sanctification be obtained for the elect. In the Word of God, the obedience of the Son is set forth as the cause of all the spiritual benefits that we receive. When He Himself spoke about water and the Spirit, Jesus conformed the meaning of His words to those of Ezekiel. "I will sprinkle you with clean water, and you will be made clean; I will put a new heart in you, and my Spirit I will put in your midst" (Ezek. 36:25–26). We see a similar teaching in Zechariah 13:1: "In that day a fountain will be opened for the sake of sin and impurity." This too we should understand as setting forth the obedience of Christ, the true cause of the remission of sins and of the purification of hearts from all spiritual uncleanness—that is, from every carnal and vice-ridden affection. This is just what the apostle says when he speaks about pure water in Hebrews 10:22, surely a reference to the obedience of Christ the Son of God. When Paul notes in Titus 3:5 that "according to his mercy he saved us, by the washing of regeneration, and the renewal of the Holy Spirit," this washing refers to the grace given in Christ—that is, His obedience or righteousness, the true cause of the spiritual life. One can see this easily from the parallel passage in 2 Timothy 1:9, that God saved us not because of our works but because of His own grace which He gave us in Christ. Furthermore, John said that Christ came not only by water but by blood (1 John 5:6). Here again, the obedience or righteousness of the Son of God is set forth as blood because of the custom established under the old economy of using expiatory sacrifices by which an effusion of the blood of a substitute was accepted. And this same obedience of Christ Jesus is called water since it is the cause of both our justification and our sanctification.

All these scriptural phrases lead us to this conviction, which presupposes and illustrates the entire doctrine of grace: that it did not fit with the ways of divine justice for God to dispense His grace to fallen humanity without the intervention of one who would sanctify His name and satisfy His offended justice. So God the Father, out of pure grace toward the elect, ordained His Son as Sponsor and Mediator, who, having clothed Himself with human nature, could offer to Him a pure, entire, and perfect obedience through sustaining the heaviest suffering and a violent and shameful death. In this death Christ shed all His blood and offered it to His Father as a substitutionary victim in order to merit righteousness [*justitiam*], life by the Spirit, and eternal salvation for the elect. God's intention was that through Christ's obedience and by the effusion of His blood, those who believe in Him and truly repent might obtain perfect redemption and the remission of their sins along with the grace of adoption, of renewal, of vivification, of sanctification by the Holy Spirit, and finally the glory that is the fullness of grace in its consummation (Isa. 53:10; Rom. 8:3; Heb. 2:13). This is the foundational and principal teaching of the Christian religion, which explains for us the first and meritorious cause of the spiritual life. From this teaching it is clear that the blood of the Son of God, since it is that of an expiatory, substitute victim, is the water and the fountain of life: in short, the cause of the justification and sanctification of the elect.

This wonderful mystery of our faith is publicly represented for us in baptism, the first sacrament of grace. Baptism is like a bath of regeneration and shows us the fountain and cause of the spiritual life. It was instituted to teach us that we owe both our purification from spiritual stains and our resurrection to a spiritual and eternal life to the blood of Christ as the meritorious cause. Without a communion in His blood, no one can hope to participate in these benefits.

All the washings, sprinklings, and purifications that were practiced under the old economy by means of blood and water, in accordance with the precepts of the law of Moses, were figures established by God to represent this great mystery of our faith. We will only draw out one example here since it illustrates so directly the cause of the spiritual life: the washing basin set in the temple near the altar of sacrifice and used for the purification of lepers and those who were unclean by contact with a dead body. This washing basin at the entrance to the temple and opposite the altar taught Old Testament believers that there existed a mystical, figurative, and antitypical washing basin by which an impure person could be washed from his sins and gain the benefit of sanctification. But even as the washing basin received its effectiveness from the altar (i.e., from the sacrificial victims that were offered on the altar; and of course no one could be purified unless he had part in the sacrifice), so we learn that there is no purification from our sins nor any true sanctification of our souls except through communion in the blood of Jesus Christ who had to offer Himself to God the Father as a substitutionary victim.

There are other, even clearer examples of such types in the rites instituted for the purification of lepers and those who were unclean through contact with a dead body. The first is found in Leviticus 14 and the second in Numbers 19. Every leper was considered a dead person since his flesh was dead and motionless; the leper was looked on as a kind of cadaver walking among the living. Therefore, the purification of a leper was his vivification, the renewal of his life. The case was similar for the person who had touched a dead body. According to the law of the old economy, he was considered dead since he had come into communion with death through contact with a dead body. Therefore, the cleansing of a person who was unclean through contact with the dead is another example of renewal to life [*vivificationis*].

Both the leper and the person unclean by contact with a dead body are a picture of man in his natural condition outside communion with God and deprived of any sensitivity to true life. Or rather, the leper prefigures man under the sorrowful judgment of God subjected to the power of spiritual death in a condition of unbelief and hardheartedness, deprived of any movement of the true life of the soul and groaning under the condemnation of eternal death. Now a rite was observed in the purification of lepers and the unclean through contact with the dead, where they took the blood of a bird that had been killed or the ashes of a red heifer mixed with spring water—that is, as Scripture puts it, living water—and they would sprinkle with that water those whose impurities caused them to be regarded as dead people. This showed what Christ would do for His people: the obedience that Christ demonstrated through the sufferings of His passion would become the meritorious cause of the spiritual life of believers.

Second, the *efficient* cause of the spiritual life is God Himself, or as some texts in the Word of God express it, the Spirit of God (e.g., James 1:18; Titus 3:5). Producing such a transformation requires an omnipotent power, and this operation must have God as its agent. The spiritual life cannot be produced in a person unless he is delivered from the power of error and corruption, the dominion of sin, and the power of the devil. This liberation requires a power no less than divine. It is surely the work of God to regenerate and bring a person from the state of spiritual death into a new state of spiritual life. "To regenerate" means to transform the foundational principles and character of the soul itself. Is it within the power and strength of any created being to renew and bring into submission the mind and all the faculties of a person? Can any deny that it is God alone who creates a clean heart and new spirit (Ps. 51:10, 12)? Regeneration fashions a man into the image of God, and who but the Lord Himself can remold and form the human soul? Regeneration has no efficient cause but God Himself. The apostle expresses this elegantly in Ephesians 2:10: "You are God's own workmanship, created in Christ Jesus for good works." Psalm 100:3 says, "He Himself made us and not we ourselves." John 1:13 speaks of those "who were born not by blood [those born naturally], nor by the will of the flesh [as Ishmael became the son of Abraham], nor by the will of a man [as Jacob adopted the sons of Joseph], but who were born by God." What a glorious and amazing gift of grace it is to be a child of God not just by adoption but by the birth of regeneration!

Third, we can speak of the Holy Spirit as the *material* cause of the spiritual life. In accordance with the outworkings of the council of peace between the Father and the Son and based on the achievements of the Son, this work of grace is administered by the Holy Spirit to the redeemed elect.[1] In the economy of God, the Spirit makes the new life a reality for the redeemed. Jesus speaks about being "born of water and of the Spirit" (John 3:5), and then He talks about "everyone who is born of the Spirit" (John 3:8). Since the Spirit of God is not only the *efficient* but also the *material* cause of the new life, we may say that He communicates His spirituality to natural and earthly human beings in such a way that it is begotten in them. This is why regeneration is called in Titus 3:5 the "renewing of the Holy Ghost" and why the apostle in 2 Corinthians 3:3 calls the Corinthians (alluding to Jer. 31:33 and Ezek. 36:26) "an epistle of Christ Jesus not written with ink but by the Spirit of the living God onto the tablets of hearts of flesh."

Who is better suited to such work than the Spirit of God? "It is the Spirit who gives life" (John 6:63). And what is regeneration other

---

1. The "council of peace" (generally termed the *pactum salutis*, "covenant of salvation") refers to the agreement between the members of the Trinity made in eternity regarding the work of salvation. The term *consilium pacis* itself is drawn from Zech. 6:13. See Richard Muller, *Dictionary of Latin and Greek Theological Terms: Drawn Principally from Protestant Scholastic Theology* (Grand Rapids: Baker, 1985), 80.

than making a person come to life? It is the Spirit who imbued movement into every created thing (Gen. 1:2). It is He who arranged and beautified the entire natural order so elegantly, as it says in Job 26:13: "By His Spirit He made the beautiful heavens." What work is more fitting and more holy for the Spirit of God than to imbue the movement of true spiritual and heavenly life into the souls of men, displaying in them the divine beauty and splendor? The regeneration of a man is his sanctification [*santificatio*]; to whom would you attribute this divine work other than the Holy [*Sancto*] Spirit?

Every operation of grace that leads to the reformation of our spirit must come from the Spirit of God (for it is the Spirit who acts on the human spirit). Consequently, in the style of Scripture, every work of grace that disposes and leads a person to salvation is attributed to the Holy Spirit: for example, when he is imbued with intelligence, wisdom, or faith; when his understanding is made ready and attuned to grasp spiritual things; when his intellect is illumined and his judgment purified, his affections put right, and his entire mind, spirit, and body are sanctified (cf. 1 Thess. 5:23). That is, when a person is cleansed from every spiritual stain and put in a suitable state to seek the glory of God in Christ, all these effects are particularly attributed to the Spirit in the Word of God, as is obvious from 1 Corinthians 6:11; 2 Corinthians 4:13; Ephesians 1:17; and especially Romans 8:2, where He is expressly called the Spirit of Life.

In sum, all true spirituality in man (notably the spiritual principles and affections as well as the acts that testify to true life in the soul) depends on the Spirit of God, the author and source of all spirituality. This Spirit, who produces such a wonderful effect in man, is the Spirit of Christ (Rom. 8:9) as well as the Spirit of the Son (Gal. 4:6) since the entire operation of grace is dispensed according to the will of the Son and of the Father. This benefit, of course, does not apply to any except those who belong to the people redeemed by Christ and is limited to the boundaries of His kingdom. But surely the voice that raises the dead from their sins and failings is the voice of the Son of God (John 5:25) whose will the Holy Spirit executes in the divine economy. Let us discuss in greater detail how this happens in our next chapter.

# CHAPTER 4

~

# The Way Spiritual Life Is
# Produced in Man

Everybody understands that the spiritual life cannot be produced in a person except by the operation of the Holy Spirit. But how does the Spirit produce spiritual life in the human spirit? What are the characteristics of this spiritual operation? Thankfully, Scripture has given us metaphors to help us formulate an idea about the nature of this process. First I will set out what the work of producing spiritual life in a person is like (its *nature*), and then I will address questions about exactly how God communicates the principle of new life to man (the *means*).

The most appropriate notion we can employ here is that of generation and regeneration (see John 1:13; 1 John 3:9; 1 Peter 1:3, 23; Titus 3:5). All people receive their natural (or "animal") life through natural regeneration. And Scripture often uses the ideas of generation and regeneration to picture the efficacious, supernatural, and indeed marvelous operation of the Holy Spirit in the souls of men bringing into them the principle of spiritual life by means of the word of grace. And in turn this principle produces in people a chain of living actions (not dead works) that redound to the glory of God and the edification of one's neighbor. Put briefly, regeneration is an operation of grace by which a person goes from being natural or carnal to being spiritual. To understand properly the full force of this idea, let us first explore why this operation of divine grace is called *generation*, then why it is called *regeneration*. Explaining each of these properly will show us the inner nature of this great benefit.

The work of divine grace is called *generation* because the characteristics of natural generation can be seen in it. And we will consider its three principal attributes in this order: (a) Generation is an act of God by which He communicates true life to a person, life par excellence, the spiritual life; (b) this life bears within it a resemblance to the life of the God who generated (i.e., produced) it; (c) this life is produced by God in a person by means of something that has the form of a spiritual seed, the word of grace.

First, as natural generation is an action in which one living being produces another, so it is with the generation of God. Life is communicated from one subject to another. God is a Spirit whose life is the exemplar of all true spiritual life. By His power, God engenders in a person those foundational principles and abilities that give rise to the spiritual life. He illumines the intellect, graciously revealing Himself inside the mind of a person; He purifies the judgment, giving it an aptitude for discerning spiritual things; He stirs up in a person a thirst for communion with Christ Jesus and a living faith in Him, pure affections, and the sincere desire to acquire every virtue. We have seen above that these make up the groundwork and foundations for a person's spiritual life.

Second, the life that God produces in a person by generation is an ectype or reproduction of the most perfect life of God; it has been copied in accordance with His image and resemblance. In the phrase of the apostle, it is the "life of God" (Eph. 4:18). Paul is not referring to a life of any sort whatsoever, but the production of a life like that of its author. The "life of God" refers to the life that comes from spiritual generation. Of course, God is the first cause of the life of all creatures, but that does not mean that everything He enlivens should be called a "child of God" or that we see His image in every living thing. There are types of life very different from the life of God; animal life is one such kind. But of all living beings, the only ones that can glory in having a part in the very life of God are those who have been formed to have activity along the lines of the activity of God. The life of God is that perfect and blessed state of activity in which God perfectly contemplates and loves Himself. And, in keeping with the principles of justice, goodness, and honesty that are proper to the divine nature, He works ceaselessly to uphold and display His own glory in that state of perfect happiness, sufficiency, acquiescence, and rest.

It is appropriate for us to speak of different types of life in human beings in a way that we cannot speak of God's life since it is unified life (we can only make logical, not substantial, distinctions about it). The following is a description of what may be called the life of God in man. When a person has been delivered from the state of ignorance, error, and vanity and has been made a participant of the divine light and glory, he endeavors to do the following: to contemplate and understand God in all the glory and perfection of His nature, to judge God and His ways rightly, to love God and the truth, to long for communion with God, to seek the glory of God with all his mind, to give himself over affectionately to the practice of every virtue, to separate himself from carnal and perishable things, to join himself to God as closely as possible, and to receive with joy and consolation the influence of His light and grace. Angels and men in the primal state of their nature were capable of participating in this active life of God and deserved to be called "sons of God" (Job 38:7; Luke 3:38). And, indeed, those persons in whom by divine grace this life has been restored are called "partakers of the divine nature" (2 Peter 1:4). No title more august or magnificent can possibly be given to a human being. Therefore, this spiritual and reasonable life is the true image, ectype, and copy of the very life and vitality of God; and from the life of the copy one may glimpse the original, the very nature of the divine life. There would be no spiritual life in the world if there did not exist the most perfect Rationality, the archetype and original of that life.

Third and finally, there is another resemblance between natural generation and divine generation: the working of divine grace only takes place by means of something that has the form of a spiritual seed. I do not mean to offend the delicacies of any reader, but scriptural writers speak in terms of the word of grace as spiritual sperm. In nature, sperm is that part of a living being designed for the generation of other living beings. It can be called its most excellent part since it contains life in itself, and is the source of life. Similarly, Scripture uses this conception to set forth the gospel. When joined with the power of the Holy Spirit, the word of promise produces life: "Of His own will He engendered us by the word of truth" (James 1:18); "Being born again, not of corruptible seed, but of incorruptible, by the word of

God, which lives and abides forever" (1 Peter 1:23). Peter alludes to Isaiah 40:8 when he adds in verse 25, "'The word of the LORD endures forever,' and this is the word which was preached as gospel to you." The metaphor of seed underlines a beautiful spiritual reality. The gospel is the only means of illuminating, rectifying, and exhilarating the mind of man that can restore him to his right senses. Only this seed can produce in a person the movements, affections, and exercises of the true spiritual life. For the word of grace is a word of life, not death. Narrowly considered, the word of the law is a word of death and execution. "For the letter [that is the law] kills but the Spirit makes alive," as the apostle says (2 Cor. 3:6). The word of the law condemns sinful man; it terrifies him; it threatens him with the divine wrath and curse; it strikes him down and lays him out; it afflicts him with pain and sadness. The law does not lead a man to God; rather, it leads him away from God. This is why the word of the law cannot by its nature be a means of regeneration.

But the word of the gospel explains to a man the riches of divine love and grace. This word of grace offers the remission of sins and eternal life to the one who believes in Christ Jesus the true Mediator. It gently invites a man to communion of God. This good word, a word of consolation, a living word, can restore the life of a soul and, as it were, bring it back from the dead. This word is like a light accompanied by warmth, as is the case with the sun that illumines, warms, and—penetrating into the depths of the earth—produces the movement of life in everything that receives the influence of its rays. So it is when one reads this word of the gospel attentively or hears it preached and expounded faithfully by ministers. When animated by the Holy Spirit, the gospel lifts the conscience, illumines the mind, purifies the judgment, instructs a person in the true faith, sanctifies him, purifies and consoles him. It leads him to contemplate the glory of God as it shines forth in Christ Jesus. It produces the stirrings of true life in the heart of a dead man, a motion of sincere spiritual love and of a holy longing for communion with God, by which the believing soul, separating itself from all other things, is intimately united to its Creator.

And so it happens that a man who had never until that moment been conscious of any other movement within himself (other than those that spring from the fountain of natural or corrupt desires) begins to experience within himself a principle of new life, a principle that is the effect of a heavenly work, the kindling of an eternal and inextinguishable fire that excites his soul to noble acts in keeping with his new nature. He feels in his heart a fountain of living water that springs up continually and never runs dry. The man affected in such a way by this principle of new vivacity considers having this life to be infinitely more to his advantage than all the things worldly people esteem so greatly. He considers himself happy with this one possession; this one pearl is all his riches, and he derives from it a continual source of consolation. For he is certain that in having the initial enjoyment, he possesses eternal life in its entirety. In being blessed with the firstfruits, he is confident of the entire harvest of future glory (see Ps. 19:8–11; 119:103–17).

Thus far we have been explaining the metaphor of generation. But let me add a few more comments about the nature of the work of divine grace. Just as natural generation produces a whole man with all his parts and faculties, so it is with divine and heavenly generation: it results in a new man with all his parts and spiritual faculties. Such language is used in places such as Ephesians 2:15; 4:22, 24; and Colossians 3:9. We should understand this "new man" according to the language of Scripture as an integrated system of faculties and spiritual qualities with which a man is newly equipped. The work of generation affects all aspects and faculties of the natural man—his intellect, his judgment, and his will. He is transformed into a new form, clothed with new vestments, and a new man, as it were, is produced within the man (Rom. 12:2; 2 Cor. 5:17). Figuratively speaking, this new form is called a "new man" because the newly produced form gradually abolishes and destroys the old form of the man. Additionally, as in nature, the formation of the unborn child precedes its emergence from the mother's womb. Spiritual birth, just as natural birth, requires its own proper interval of time. Often the child does not emerge from the womb without great effort and sharp pains for the one giving birth. Experiences similar to these take place in those whom God grants divine generation. The apostle James uses conception and birthing metaphors to help us think about these things in James 1:15, 18. An infinite number of adults to whom God communicated His grace have experienced being under the hand of God while His Spirit engaged in various preparatory operations, molding the unborn child of the new man before he was fully formed and finally burst forth to appear in public. Also, it often happens in such cases that with the approach of grace, a person is seized by great struggles of soul and deepest anxieties that spread thick darkness over his laboring mind. Even as he struggles greatly against this, he constantly seems to be succumbing to temptation. Then, suddenly, God floods him with the unexpected light of grace and leads him to the fountains of divine consolation. He becomes enchanted with God and ravished in all the affections of his soul. So he bids goodbye to the world, renounces carnal desires, and clings to God with a firm purpose never to be separated from Him. That is the crisis moment, the hour of favor when the work of God's grace comes to completion.

We have been considering this benefit of grace as an act of *generation*. We will go on to consider this divine work under the rubric of *regeneration* (see 1 Peter 1:3; Titus 3:5). Christ the Lord says in John 3:3: "Except a man be born again, he cannot see the kingdom of God." This expression can be taken in two senses: that one must be engendered from above or that one must be engendered again or anew. Both of these senses are appropriate, but I think John had the second in mind as he reported the Lord's speech, both because Nicodemus interpreted it as "to be born a second time" and because this interpretation goes well with the ideas conveyed by the Greek words for regeneration used by Scripture writers. This generation refers to another prior to it, and so it is called regeneration—that is, a second or a repeated generation. There are various opinions as to what this prior generation may refer to: to the first producing of human beings, or to natural human generation or even to the typical "generation" of the Jewish people when they were brought out of Egypt, formed into a people, and endowed with various benefits by a paternal care (Deut. 14:1; 32:6).

I do not deny that the first may be correct, and many accept it because in the beginning when human beings were first produced by God, since they were in His image, they could be called the "sons of God" (as was Adam in Luke 3:38 and as was the case with angels [Job

38:7]). In this sense they were not only created but engendered by God. For when they came forth from the hands of God their Creator, they had in them a principle of activity that tended toward what was good, praiseworthy, and for the glory of God. So, then, one cannot deny that they possessed true life. But when they lost this through a voluntary defection from God, and though all their posterity was subjected to the power of spiritual death, it pleased God out of His mercy to renew in certain of them, by the operation of His Holy Spirit, the spiritual life that they had lost. And so this divine action with respect to the previous generation can be called a re-generation. But frankly, I do not think that scriptural authors had this in mind. Even if one can say that the first humans were generated by God, the idea does not convey what we normally mean by engendering.

Additionally, nothing in the discourse of the Lord with Nicodemus suggests that He had in mind the figurative generation of the Jewish people. He is speaking in this passage about the regeneration of individuals, and the implication is that various races are in mind. I agree that a Jewish person, in order to be transformed in a spiritual way in keeping with the new economy, needed liberation from the fleshly ordinances of the old economy, but this does not support the idea that Jesus was speaking of generation in a metaphorical or typological way to refer to the Jewish nation. It seems clear to me that the term *regeneration* refers back to birth and to the natural manner of engendering people. In other words, just as one receives natural life from his parents, so in this act of grace that we call regeneration God communicates a spiritual and much more excellent life to a person (cf. John 1:13; 3:3–21).

So far we have been discussing the *nature* of this work of grace and its characteristics. But we must go further and say something about the special *means* by which God dispenses this grace. These are deep matters since God administers His grace in a very free way. And I cannot claim to have plumbed the depths of these mysteries. But I will assert what any minister of the gospel should set forth if he wants to avoid the censure of Jesus on the culpably ignorant, "Are you indeed a teacher of Israel and do not know these things?" (John 3:10).

The dispensation of this grace varies in accordance with the economy of divine providence. In other words, His distribution of grace is accommodated and different in Old and in New Testament times. The Lord dispenses His grace to His chosen people in a variety of ways. Of course, the Lord redeems all His elect by the blood of Christ Jesus, claims them for Himself, and transfers them into a state of fellowship with Himself. But among these He generally communicates His grace to children in a different way than He does to adults.

With regard to minors of a tender age, we are persuaded (and it is confirmed by the experience of many examples) that God often graciously communicates with young children at an early age in which their faculties of intellect and judgment are just beginning to develop. A few of the outstanding examples in Scripture are Jacob, Joseph, Samuel, Solomon, Jeremiah, and John the Baptist. Throughout the economies of all times there are many well-known examples, but I will mention only two more: Timothy, who, by the care of his grandmother Lois and mother Eunice (women most highly to be praised), had received the seeds of piety through the knowledge of the Word of God, "from a tender age" (2 Tim. 3:15; see also 2 Tim. 1:5), and from early church history we have another example in the person of Origen.

Clearly the Holy Spirit is pleased to inhabit young souls. He enables them to grasp, each according to his ability, His sacred lessons; He inspires in them a reverence for religion and the divine name; He excites in them the sparks of the love of God and an affection for Himself; He teaches them to observe the duties they owe to God and to their parents, and as they grow in age, to separate themselves from their bad influences, to approach God through prayer and thanksgiving, to bend their knees before Him and to reverently implore His help in cases of doubt and difficulty; He leads them to trust in Him as father with a true inner sense of love, affection, and filial obedience, and to join themselves more and more to Him through Christ. This is so that as they grow in age they might grow too in the knowledge and love of God, more and more increasing in grace as they mature. In all of these gracious operations, the Spirit of God so accommodates Himself to their tender faculties that often one sees in them a knowledge of divine things beyond their age (in many well-known examples from history this has particularly been noted in those near to death). They speak of the grace of God with such conviction and freedom, and they explain the precious foundations of their hope with such heartfelt outpouring that those who witness it are stunned.

Regarding adults to whom the Lord in grace reveals Himself, we can distinguish between those outside the communion of the church and those inside. Some whom God calls and effectively regenerates are outside of communion with His people. They have lived up to that time in a natural state of ignorance and lust, apart from any public profession of the true religion. Such is the condition of pagan Gentiles until illumined by the light of the gospel of Christ Jesus. God also impresses His grace on other unconverted persons who may have lived a long time in the external communion of the church. Some people make an outward profession of being Christians but without having any sensible movement of true life. They put themselves to no trouble to seek God or communion with Him. They content themselves with being civil and concern themselves about a merely outward discharge of the duties required by society or even religious duties expected in the church. But none of this means they have been freed from the lusts of deep vices. Such is the life of a man in the state of nature and of lust while deprived completely of the life of God.

In adults of the first type who are ignorant of the true way of salvation, such as the Gentiles to whom the apostles ministered the gospel, the operation of grace proceeds in this way: the Holy Spirit makes them attentive to the winsome word of grace, illumines their intellect, and enables them to discern both the miserable and condemned state in which they find themselves and the dignity, rationality, and divinity of the Word. The gospel arouses in them faith in the Lord Jesus and, flowing from faith, love for God in Christ, joy, consolation, and gratitude that lead them to glorify Him who lavished them with such great benefits. Acts is filled with such examples (cf. Acts 13:48; 16:14, 32; Gal. 4:15). In such cases, the work of grace is not preceded by convictions over a long period of time, nor were there strong external expressions of grief, shame, or regret for past sins and the errors of earlier times. All these sentiments may be quickly absorbed by a sense of the greatness of God's mercy and by the joy and solid consolation

with which their souls were affected by the Spirit. Such was the case
with the Thessalonians who received the word of the gospel, "with the
joy of the Holy Spirit" (1 Thess. 1:6). The Spirit confirmed this grace
in them with rejoicing and enduring consolation.

But in the case of those who have been in the communion of the
church for some time but have despised or neglected the grace that
has been offered to them, God does not always draw them to Himself in such an easy way. Such people are often under the convicting
hand of God, and perhaps for a long time the Spirit is forming the
infant before he is born as the new man. They may experience sharp
convictions and deep struggles of the soul. The Spirit by means of the
Word knocks at the door of the person's heart (Rev. 3:20), but the man
may refuse to open and admit the Lord because he is charmed by the
lusts of sin. As the Scripture expresses it, this is convicting (or elenctic)
grace. Such was the case in Amos's day, where, "They hate the one who
rebukes in the gate" (Amos 5:10). That is, people push back against
the instruction of their consciences, which convict them of crimes and
warn them of their duties (Job 33:16; 2 Tim. 3:16; John 16:8). But
such correction is part of the Lord's work, as He said to the Laodicean
church, "I rebuke and chasten those I love" (Rev. 3:19).

Wherever the Word of God is heard, taught, and expounded there
will be *elenchus*: rebuke and conviction, medicine for corrupt minds.
Such grace always accompanies the preaching of the Word of God in
every economy and at all times and places. This is "convicting grace"
by which the Holy Spirit presses a man when he is hearing or meditating on the Word of God to think seriously about the end of his life or
about the hope of a better life. The Spirit powerfully convinces him of
his state of condemnation before God and the severity and penalty of
the offenses he has committed in his previous life. And as He does this
He sets before the man's eyes the ugliness of sin and the inappropri-
ateness of the present course of his life. He shows him the inevitable
severity of divine wrath if God were to close the door of grace and put
an end to the patience He has long extended to the man. The apostle
calls this the terror of the Lord (2 Cor. 5:11), the fear of the justice of
His judgment, and the alarm and horror of the infernal state.

Even though they may not yet produce the saving effect of regeneration, these convictions often bear some fruit in a person's life. Convicting grace is distinct from regenerating grace. The typical effect of these pangs of guilt is to put such a person (not entirely deprived of spiritual feeling but not yet ready to renounce the world and its lusts) into a state of struggle and distress. There is combat as the Spirit struggles with the flesh, and often there are times of deep anguish. Such convictions also produce imperfect wishes for conversion, half-hearted willingness, and unsettled desires for change. A person might like to be converted, but the flesh is nevertheless victorious. The habit of sin and the pleasure, sweetness, and benefits that seem to come from it have become through custom the man's second nature. And these things and many others press him to shut the door against the Spirit who is knocking.

A person in this conflicted situation may try to choose a middle way. In order to calm the sting of his conscience he brings the actions of his life under review. He determines to have done with his more serious sins. He will now moderate the course of his life in a wiser direction. He will indeed address God and seek a relationship with Him in the public exercises of religion. He will now humble himself before God in order to make himself worthy of God's favor (such people are vividly portrayed in Isa. 58:2). Often during calamities, whether public or private, convictions produce this kind of effect. Of course, it is easy enough to repress one's conscience when life seems to be going well and a person is getting along, enjoying what he believes to be the signs of God's providential favor. But in calamities God presses home His chastisements on a person's soul, warning him of divine wrath and of his need for repentance, stirring his conscience and pulling him out of his lethargy.

In this middle-of-the-road response, a person agrees to open up one of the rooms of his soul to God but not allow Him to occupy the entire house of his soul. He still reserves for himself a part where he can have commerce with the sin in which he takes the greatest delights. He divides his affection between himself and God, and from one heart he produces a divided heart (Ps. 12:2). This is a form of hypocrisy since God demands a united heart, a heart in which love for God is so dominant that all other affections are subordinated to it (Isa. 38:3). Tragically, many in this divided state live for years in the external communion of the church without going forward to another stage. After the initial impulse toward conversion and repentance, they return to the old apathy and lukewarmness. Forsaking God and His grace, they return to their old ways (James 1:24–25; 2 Peter 1:9). The prophet Hosea (Hos. 13:13) speaks of those in the pangs of birth who will not continue; they do not allow the birthing pains to have their proper fruit. They lack the courage and will not go through the effort and pain to bring forth the new man. They are like those giving birth where the infant dies. Hosea likens this spiritual "middle condition" of the people to a cake of bread baked on a single side and only partly usable. A man in this spiritual condition may make some progress and be a person "not far from the kingdom of God" (Mark 12:34; cf. Acts 27:28, which uses a similar expression meaning "only slightly distant"). Such a one may be quite close to being a Christian and yet never reach a true state of grace.

But grace never fails in those whom God has destined for salvation. At the point of time when this great work is decreed by order of divine providence to take place, it comes to its completion and perfection. Convicting grace is converted into regenerating grace. At that time God makes a striking impression on the mind, illuminating, overpowering, and influencing the affections in such a powerful way that the shadows are pushed back and the scales fall from the eyes (Acts 9:18). Carnal lust is restrained and conquered, and the entire man is kindled and set ablaze by the love of God (Deut. 30:6). The person devotes himself wholly to God in Christ Jesus with all his affections (Acts 15:26), and out of perfect love joined to sincere gratitude he wills that everything that he is and has might be sacred to God and Christ (Luke 7:47), offering himself with all his faculties as a sacrifice to God (Rom. 12:1).

The following subjects now present themselves to his mind with great distinctness: the ugliness and deformity of sin; the shame of his present state; the vanity, uncertainty, and inconstancy of worldly things; the bitter fruit of the sins for which he repents; the attractiveness of communion with God; the beauty of the ways of God in saving a miserable sinner through Christ Jesus His Son; the excellence of His person; and finally the delightful and ravishing effects of communion with God in Christ. Now the man clearly sees. Now he is so affected with the sight of these things that he immediately breaks every bond with which had been bound, renounces all dealings with sin, and prostrating himself with the deepest humility before the throne of God, he commits himself to His grace. In this way the Lord Jesus takes possession of the entire house of the soul with all its rooms, living there, reigning there, and sharing a life with the man (John 14:23), dwelling and feasting with him (Rev. 3:20). So it is that God comes to a soul; so it is that He reveals Himself and joins Himself to a person by grace. Such is the pattern that Augustine left us in his book *Confessions* regarding his own conversion and regeneration.

Two beneficial characteristics always accompany and complement this great work of regeneration when it takes place in adults. First, the operation of divine grace and the emergence of the new man never take place except through vigor and great exertion. There is no place for inaction or slackness. The man convinced of the ugliness of sin rejects it with horror and casts it away like clothing stained with menstrual blood. "Get away from me!" he says (Isa. 30:22). Effectively called to Christ and persuaded about the necessity of having communion with God through Him, he does not merely go, he runs (see Song 1:4; Ps. 119:32; Isa. 40:31). Blazing and ardent, "fervent in spirit" (Rom. 12:11), he does nothing with sloth or indifference.

Second, the operation of divine grace always brings corresponding changes to a person's affections and actions. One man weeps in repentance, shame, and mourning over his unworthiness and the irregularities of his previous life (Jer. 31:19). Another man embraces Christ Jesus with both arms by faith. Another rejoices in the firm confidence that he has the right to stand squarely on God's grace. These affections are particularly dominant in a person who experiences a second renewal, a person who already had come into communion with God but fell back into some serious sin. In the present new economy, it often happens that when a person is regenerated, all his grief is absorbed by a sense of the love of God, and the pangs of guilt are graciously swallowed up by the consolation and joy of the Holy Spirit. This delight, I say, is connected with the most tender love and the deep and active stirrings of gratitude in the soul as in the sinful woman of Luke 7:47.

These are the ways of God as I see them, though of course they vary from case to case. God leads some to Himself through the anguish of deep sadness similar to desperation. Such people finally succumb to God after being under His hand for a long time (Ps. 32:3–4). God draws others to Himself through the cords of love (Hos. 11:4), where He reveals Himself to them in grace. He makes His goodness stand out to them, shows Himself to them in the abundance of His beauty and the riches of His immense love, and affects their minds with such strong consolation that they become, as it were, drunk (Jer. 31:25). Who can explain everything relevant to this discussion? The variety of God's ways is beyond conceiving, let alone explaining. The ways of God working with the souls of men are astonishing, marvelous, and thus often impenetrable.

Because God dispenses this grace to His elect people in various ways as He pleases, sometimes early and sometimes later in life, and since this work of mercy depends utterly on His will alone, we cannot seek a reason or rule for it, except to say that all the ways He displays His grace are ordered by His own good providence. The conversion of Paul is a beautiful example of this.

There are many other portrayals and metaphors used by the Holy Scriptures to picture this work of divine grace, such as new creation, calling, resurrection, vivification (bringing to life), circumcision of the heart, writing the law on the heart, drawing the soul to God, the gift of faith, conversion, and many other depictions. They are analogous to those I have mentioned and illustrate the principles I have laid out here. But further detail here is not in keeping with my original plan for this work.

PART 2

The Parts of the
Spiritual Life

# CHAPTER 5

~~

# Self-Denial

We have considered the characteristics of the spiritual life, its sources, and how it is produced in a person. Next we must consider how it manifests itself outwardly. What are its fruits? The root principle of the spiritual life is faith, and all the activities of a spiritual person (i.e., one who is in Christ) can be referred back to faith as the fountain from which they perpetually flow. But this unified life expresses itself in different areas, different kinds of activities. It is extraordinarily useful to meditate on the different parts and distinct duties of the spiritual life. According to our great Teacher, the spiritual life has at heart three principal duties and parts: self-denial, cross-bearing (endurance/patience), and following Christ. We will deal with the first of these in this chapter and the other two in following chapters.

Let me note in passing, however, that patience involves a humble and thoughtful submission to God amid adversities, and following Christ refers to that devotion to Him that involves the intense desire to acquire every virtue and to perfect holiness of life in imitation of Christ Jesus, the most perfect exemplar of every virtue. As He said, "If anyone wants to come after Me [that is, to hear Me and be My disciple], let him deny himself, take up his cross, and follow Me" (Matt. 16:24). These marvelous words sketch out the entire discipline of the Christian life, and a person's progress should be measured in accordance with this canon and rule. The person who stirs himself up to observe these duties lives "according to the Spirit" and deserves to be called a true Christian, a disciple and follower of Christ Jesus. He has a share in His grace, His unction, and His light. The person who has no experience of these exercises is a Christian in name alone. He should be reckoned as still in the state of death rather than life. He has no share in the kingdom or economy of the Son of God. Let us now consider self-denial, the first and foremost of these things, in detail.

Self-denial is when a Christian willingly renounces all his sins and vices, everything that flows from the fountain of his old corrupt nature, through a serious and sincere repentance. But not only this, self-denial is the virtue by which the believer is willing to lay aside even the helps and comforts of this life, any good thing whatsoever, if it is in the interests of the glory of God of Christ Jesus. He esteems every-thing as lesser in value than communion with God. And he is willing if necessary to part with his riches, honors, prerogatives, connections, and even temporal life itself. He subordinates all things to the value of fellowship with God and pleasing Him. And so he uses all external goods, whose use is permitted by the divine law, with such moderation of soul and affection that it is obvious his highest happiness does not consist in things that have to do with this temporary life.

From the definition of self-denial that I have given, this virtue involves three distinct but interrelated things. The first part of self-denial consists in renouncing all the vices of the corrupt nature of every sort, a duty absolutely demanded of every disciple of Christ Jesus. The second part of self-denial is to renounce anything delightful to the flesh—including all innocent and permissible pleasures and even life itself, which is so dear to each of us—if the glory of Christ Jesus, the advancement of the gospel, or the interests of the kingdom of God demand it of us. The third and final part of self-denial is to make use of the temporal goods whose enjoyment is permitted by the law of Christ with such moderation of our affections that it is manifest that they do not constitute our highest happiness. The use and enjoyment of good things is always to be subordinated to the control of sanctified reason. These are the three aspects of self-denial.

In my definition, self-denial has a broader meaning than repentance and involves a number of other matters. The virtue of repentance is described in Scripture by a variety of terms, including turning, return-ing to one's self, or having a change of mind (cf. Jer. 31:17; Mark 1:15). In repentance, a believer in communion with God (or the person who, encouraged by the word of the gospel, aspires to that communion) renounces all vices whatsoever. He abstains from his sins connected to the corrupt nature since he is convicted of their ugliness, indecency, and noxious consequences. He detests, hates, and distances himself from his sins with a sincere and constant desire to be changed. He embraces a better form of life, completely opposed to the first. Out of love for God he seeks diligently all the opposite virtues and is led by the Holy Spirit to seek to glorify Christ and to edify his neighbor. Such repentance from vices and pursuit of virtue is to "depart from evil, and do good" (Ps. 34:14; cf. Isa. 1:16–17). The two activities can never be separated from each other, but the idea of repentance most directly refers to the first part: that is, abstaining from vices. Since we cannot properly understand this virtue unless we are acquainted with the vices, let us spend a few pages discussing these faults from which we must repent.

It is difficult even to enumerate the vices that are the object of repentance, since the weeds flourish in so many fields and arise in so many fecund varieties, and each seems to have its own numerous subspecies of sins and crimes. Among them are impiety, atheism, profaneness, hypocrisy, superstition, injustice, malice, selfish ambition, pride, greed, intemperance, hatred, envy, false speech, disobedience to parents and superiors, cruelty, inhumanity, vanity, immodesty, self-love, rash judgments, excessive chattering, and the inordinate desire for the honors, comforts, and advantages of this world. These are almost random examples to which innumerable others could be added.

Everyone who has studied ethics recognizes that the numerous types of vices can be traced to chief or root vices. The ancients held four cardinal virtues: prudence, fortitude, justice, and temperance. And they understood the opposing cardinal vices to be imprudence, laziness (faintheartedness), injustice, and self-indulgence. Their approach and method for understanding virtues and vices is parallel. But not everyone organized the species or the number in the same way. John Cassian [ca. 360–435] listed eight capital vices, and John Wycliffe [ca. 1325–1384] (an outstanding man of his time whose memory I wish to honor here) lists seven capital vices and the same number of virtues. They are (each with its opposite) pride/humility, envy/charity, wrath/patience and meekness, sloth/piety and godliness, avarice/a regulated attachment to temporal goods, gluttony/abstinence, and luxury (self-indulgence)/chastity.

Here are my thoughts on the matter: the apostle Paul refers all kinds of vices to two classes—impiety and worldly lust. He says that "because the grace of the gospel has appeared to all men, they must deny ungodliness and worldly lusts and live temperately, justly, and piously in this present age" (Titus 2:11–12). He wisely traces all vices back to these two categories. Injustice, malice, idolatry, superstition, profaneness, and irreverence for holy things are species of impiety. And all other faults can be traced back to lust—that is, an immoderate and overweening affection and desire toward some carnal thing: a person's unregulated longing for something either within himself or outside himself. This is a very nicely made division of the material. But to get a little wider view of the cardinal vices and to understand them more distinctly (without disturbing the apostolic order!), I will discuss five: impiety, malice, injustice, lust (an inordinate love for oneself and for carnal things), and finally, laziness. Now a few words on each.

Impiety or ungodliness is the vice of irreverence toward God and disrespect toward sacred things. Among a wide variety of faults, impiety includes all idolatry and crass superstition, which are offenses against conscience. The direct offenses of impiety include atheism (the denial of a God whose free providence governs the universe), profane thoughts about God, profanity in words, denial of God's providential care toward humankind, lying under oath, and any other false calling on the divine name in the profession or exercise of religion. The indirect offenses of ungodliness include self-will in the worship of God and a casual and irreligious approach to holy things. It is also an offense to be religious only when it goes well with our own temporal interests (Lev. 26:21, 23–24). Idolatry and superstition are often described as the greatest of all vices (e.g., Deut. 29:18; cf. Psalm 10; Isa. 5:18; Mal. 3:14). Impiety is summarized in the words of the godless: "The LORD will not do good, neither will he do evil" (Zeph. 1:12). Atheism is the worst and most serious of all vices. It is an offense against the clear light of reason and in effect changes light into darkness and darkness into light, and, as the prophet says, "Woe to those who call evil good and good evil, who put darkness for light and light for darkness" (Isa. 5:20).

Connected to impiety, malice is that vice by which a person is inclined to harm those he should help. It proceeds from the fountain of his corrupt nature and inborn depravity. It leads a person to rejoice when things go bad for others and to take pleasure when they have trouble, even if it results in no personal benefit (see 1 Peter 2:1; Rom. 1:29; Col. 3:8). The effect of this fault is "to do harm" (Mark 3:4). The nature of this vice is perfectly described in Jeremiah 11:15: "When you do evil [i.e., when you harm another], you exult with joy." This vice surely comes from a corrupted nature by which a man wills his neighbor evil, and if he has the ability and opportunity will work for his detriment and do him evil, even if he gains nothing by it. This vice also involves the tendency to judge one's neighbor in the worst possible light, to interpret his words and deeds perversely, to flay him with slanders, to peck away with jokes at his expense, and if possible, to oppress and destroy him. This is what the prophet calls slaying or killing with the tongue (Jer. 18:18). This vice proceeds from the deep depravity and inborn corruption in fallen human beings. Malice so infects the hearts of some that they want good to happen to no one other than themselves. This stems from envy, which is the most common form of malice (described by the Lord in John 8:44). This vice is so nasty, base, deformed, shameful, and so contrary to the upright nature created in human beings that indeed it points to the image of Satan. For this reason, he is called "the evil/malicious one." Malice deforms man as the image of God and turns his affections in a direction completely opposite the nature of God. God is not only just, upright, pure, and holy, but also good, generous, and patient to all His creatures. Without having any obligation to do so and without regard to His own utility, He treats them liberally with largesse and does them good out of His great kindness. We see in malice all the contrary qualities.

Injustice applies to similarly broad areas of life. Some divide the discussion of injustice and its corresponding virtue, justice, into questions of exchange, commerce, and the business of human society; questions of how social leaders should dispense honors and privileges impartially in accordance with the merits of each one; and questions about each person exercising proper liberality toward others. But justice and injustice always boil down to the same foundational question.

Injustice is the vice of denying others their due, while justice is the virtue of rendering to others what is proper to them. By "what is due to a person," I mean that which is owed to him in accordance with reason; equity; the laws of human society; the covenants, conventions, and particular considerations that have a place among men; and the merits of each person in particular. In society, each member has something that he regards as particularly his own and that does not belong to another: something he loves as his own and that he disposes of at his pleasure alone. Each person has his honor, his dignity, and his reputation. He has the exclusive right to something—for example, his goods or his pay. What is his and what is another's is prescribed and defined by law, reason, and the mutual respect that men owe to each other, founded on justice, law, and the contracts established among them.

Whoever therefore denies to another what rightfully belongs to him commits the sin that we call injustice (1 Cor. 6:9). No matter what motive leads a person to commit injustice (whether malice, hatred, envy, lust, the longing to steal others' goods, or some other inner depravity), it is a most repulsive fault. Though it comes in an infinite number of forms (beyond the limits of this short work to even sketch out), the worst and most shameful injustice is when judges pervert the law and defraud the innocent of their rights. This happens when those in power ingeniously devise exceptions to the most certain and clear principles of law, or when they focus on terminology and neglect the substance of a matter. In such a way they oppress others and condemn them unjustly. Injustice is a vice so serious and so detested by God (but so dominant at times in ancient Israel) that the prophets Isaiah, Jeremiah, Amos, and Micah strongly cried out against it in their day (see Isa. 10:1; Amos 2:7–8; Mic. 3:9–11).

Lust I place fourth in the list of capital vices. Lust, according to the Holy Scriptures, refers either to a forbidden love for something that is falsely considered good or to the excessive love for truly good things. This root vice is a large tree with many branches. Following the division of the apostle in 1 John 2:16, we will consider "the lust of the eyes" (i.e., greed, the excessive and immoderate desire to acquire and possess the wealth and riches of this world), "the lust of the flesh" (i.e., overindulgence in the pleasures of the palate and of the body:

sexual impurity and wantonness, homosexuality, and carnal vices that I do not intend to review), and finally "the pride of life" (i.e., selfish ambition). Sinful ambition is the excessive desire for the honors that distinguish the conditions of men in this life as well as the pride, arrogance, and external display with which people occupy the higher positions in society. This vice is extremely common in the human race and indeed ruins it, as Peter suggests: destruction and mischief are in the world by lust (2 Peter 1:4).

All the other vices we have reviewed come from the corrupt and twisted nature that all men have in common from birth, but they manifest themselves in various degrees. We would not say that all men are equally unjust, malicious, or ungodly, although the seeds of all these corruptions exist in them all. It is the different kinds of lust active in people that makes the difference. All humans are born in slavery to lust and the carnal affections that drag our wills toward the love of false goods. We are all "flesh" in this servitude to desires for fleshly, external, and visible goods. We are all pushed about by carnal affections for things that please the senses: pleasures of the belly and of the body, worldly delights, comforts, beauty, health, strength, honors, and a high reputation. But it is false to put perishable good in the place of true goods that are eternal. Communion with God in Christ is where we find our true riches. This is the summum bonum that constitutes our true security. To love as our summum bonum anything inferior to the true highest good of fellowship with God is to lust after something false. Whatever a man loves, esteems, and prefers (whether in himself or in the world) above and before communion with God is a counterfeit and adulterated good.

Now the love of oneself is instinctual to all. God put in us the instinct for self-preservation, and it is a virtue rather than a vice to love oneself in a proper manner. What is forbidden is "self-love," which is the excessive desire and affection toward those things that have to do with our visible and external condition. The vice is to love one's person and one's possessions (things that have to do with the external state of man) excessively, to pursue them with too great a love and to make these inferior goods one's summum bonum. No other sin is more common or more fertile in giving birth to others than this vice of lust. Lust is the "sin which doth so easily beset us" (Heb. 12:1), as is recognized by everyone except the one who is ignorant of his own heart.

Among the root vices, I give the fifth and final place to sloth or laziness. At first glance it seems to be a type of lust—that is, the excessive desire for the comforts and pleasures of this life. But sloth is a very common vice with a much wider meaning. First, sloth leads a person to neglect looking into what is true and what is his duty (and from this comes a culpable ignorance). Second, sloth leads a person to neglect putting his duty into practice or to carry out his duty in a cold or careless fashion. The ancients called this *accidia* (negligence) (Prov. 6:6; 26:13). The Lord mentions this in Matthew 25:26 as does the apostle Paul in his epistles to the Thessalonians and to Titus. Laziness is the opposite of proper diligence and zeal. It is a damaging fault, shameful in a person gifted with excellent faculties for activity and fit for work. It may come from a native indolence or a natural weakness or slowness. It may be instilled by habit, or it may be that other desires have enticed a person and drawn him away from his labor. It spreads itself throughout the entire man—that is, over every duty and exercise to which he is obligated by the law. This is why I have ranked this as one of the chief and root vices.

There are two main varieties of sloth to which the others can be easily referred. The first is neglecting to search for the truth and to understand one's duty in the matter of religion. The fruit of this carelessness is a culpable ignorance, condemned by the writers of the old and new covenants as the fountain of many errors and much sin. Undoubtedly, many mortals fall into a myriad of offenses that they would avoid if they were not troubled by this fault (Isa. 1:2; Hos. 4:1; Eph. 4:18; 1 Peter 1:14). The second kind is when we neglect or are careless about the public or private duties which we know that God's law imposes on us, and we give ourselves over to leisure, idleness, or cares that have nothing to do with the glory of God, the edification of our neighbor, or concern for our own legitimate well-being and advancement. This is also called laziness, faintheartedness, weakness, or lack of courage (James 1:4; Rom. 12:11).

Thus far we have been discussing the first part of self-denial: abstaining from, renouncing, and eradicating these chief and root vices and everything that the corrupt nature brings with it. Now Scripture calls the virtue that enables this self-denial "repentance," "turning," "coming to one's senses," or "conversion"—that is, switching from vice to virtue, from the world to God, from the power of Satan to Christ, from the darkness to the light (Acts 26:18). If this repentance is holistic, thorough, and such as pleases God (there exists a counterfeit repentance), then it will be accompanied by affection, resolution, and actions. Your affections are involved when you are persuaded of the ugliness, irrationality, and indecency of your vices and the absolutely certain loss and damage that they bring with them, and when you are inflamed with love for the God who made Himself known to you in grace. Your resolution is involved when you purpose and settle in your mind to abstain constantly from every sin. And your actions are involved when you steadily execute this purpose and apply yourself to practicing the opposite virtues.

Jesus calls repentance self-denial. He does this by way of emphasis because the vices we must renounce are so tightly connected to our corrupt nature that they are, as it were, part of ourselves. Christ calls renouncing your sins "plucking out your eyes" and "amputating your feet and hands" (see Matt. 5:29–30; 18:8). How tragic and sad is the condition of sinful humanity! Our inborn nature is full of vice expressing itself in a wide variety of ways. But experience and the witness of our hearts teach us that each person has his favorite vice. Among all the faults stemming from our inner corruption, each of us has a penchant for this or that sin in particular. We can say that this sin does not simply trouble the man but that it inheres to his nature, forming a very part of the man himself. Such vices cannot be taken away except by the power of divine grace. Some people are naturally inclined to deep vices such as ambition, greed, or lust whereas others are slaves to hardness of heart, irritability, anger, or vengeance. These vices are what the Scripture writer calls "the closely-clinging sin" (Heb. 12:1). Each of us feels that when we have to renounce commerce with this sin, we have to renounce our very selves. True enough: when we repent we lose a part of ourselves, but we do it in order to save another part of ourselves.

Now let us discuss a second part of this great virtue of self-denial. Self-denial also consists in laying aside any good thing (something that can be properly loved and possessed) if the glory of God and of Christ, His kingdom, or the truth of the gospel demands it. This is what the Lord commends in Matthew 10:37 and Luke 14:26. Clearly it is legitimate to own and appreciate certain good things that are beneficial to our human nature. A disciple of Christ Jesus may properly possess and enjoy many things, keeping in mind that these things have to do with our exterior and visible condition and may be separated from our highest good. Among these are riches, honors, a wife or husband, children, parents, privileges attached to birth or social status, and lastly temporal life itself. But it may happen (whether in a time of extraordinary testing by God or in a time of persecution publicly organized against the cause of the truth) that believers have to face the grim choice of either denying themselves these good things that they tenderly love or of denying Christ Jesus, the true faith in Him, or the saving communion with Christ which is founded on that faith. Here, indeed, a believer needs fortitude, persistence, and courage of soul. Here the soldier of Christ Jesus is called to the trial of his virtue. Instructed by the divine will in accordance with the example of the Levites, he must not regard father, mother, children, honors, riches, privileges, or any other good thing of this age if it is the will of God (Deut. 33:9; 1 Peter 3:17). Putting all these things behind him shows the entire world that he prefers the communion of God in Christ Jesus to all other good things and that one must subordinate to Christ every favorable external condition distinct from this highest good. This is the law of the kingdom of Christ with its severe demands: "The one who loves father or mother above Me is not worthy of Me; and the one who loves son or daughter above Me is not worthy of Me" (Matt. 10:37). Do not imagine that this is a new law. It is ancient (cf. Heb. 11:8, 10, 24–25). It is no sin to love such people— we love them naturally because they are ours, making up part of our being as it were. The love is placed in us by natural instinct. For just as we become part of our parents, as it were, so our children become part of us. And furthermore, what can more properly be called "ours" than our own physical life? The one who denies himself these good things is indeed denying himself. This is self-denial indeed.

But there is a third and final aspect of self-denial relevant to us all. Self-denial is a virtue that implies the following: We must manifest in all the business of our life that we value nothing in the world above our communion with God in Christ. We must love nothing among all the things of this world (food, drink, proper pleasures) so vehemently that, if necessary, we could not separate ourselves from it except with great bitterness of spirit. And we must use all things temperately and under the government of sanctified reason so that it is obvious that we have been freed from slavery to corruption and transported into the state of the liberty of the sons of God (John 8:36; Rom. 8:21–22). The doctrine of the apostle is "that both they that have wives be as though they had none…and they that buy, as though they possessed not; and they that use this world, as not abusing it" (1 Cor. 7:29–31). This is a mark of the perfection of a Christian: to use moderately the good things of this world that have been provided by divine providence— not indulging the flesh in any way but sharing liberally from our goods with others. Additionally, if a believer feels in himself a greater longing and propensity of soul toward this or that permissible good thing than sanctified reason judges to be balanced, then he will abstain from it voluntarily until the vice of lust is conquered and the use of that good thing can be restricted within proper bounds. This, too, means denying oneself since it involves things that we naturally desire and that are considered to be rightfully ours.

∾

# CHAPTER 6

# Cross-Bearing and Christian Endurance

The life of a man of God involves what we may call spiritual exercises. We have considered the first part of these in our discussion of self-denial. Now we will consider a second part under the rubric of cross-bearing. Cross-bearing is a phrase that our Lord used for emphasis: "If anyone will come after Me, let him deny himself, take up his cross daily and follow Me" (Luke 9:23; see also Matt. 10:38; Mark 8:34). The cross was the torturous and shameful punishment used infamously by the Romans and other ancient peoples. And when our Lord speaks of bearing the cross, it refers to the insults, afflictions, adversities, evils, and troubles that human nature greatly abhors because of its instinct for self-preservation. But according to God's hidden providence, these things are part of God's plan for the believer and bring him spiritual benefit. New Testament writers speak about "taking up" and "carrying" the cross. These metaphorical expressions are taken from the Roman custom of having the condemned carry the cross on his shoulders to the place of punishment and having his hands tied back onto the cross (see John 19:17; 21:18).

Cross-bearing involves patiently and even joyously bearing the reproaches, troubles, setbacks, injuries, persecutions, afflictions, and all sorts of evil decreed by God to test the faith of believers or to perfect their sanctification (1 Peter 2:15; 3:17). During the early days of Christianity and in accordance with His wisdom, it pleased God to transform His church into a more spiritual form. He detached them from carnal things by means of the reproaches and deep afflictions that He had destined for them to suffer. In this way He circumcised, as it were, the new people He was forming. God was forming a spiritual nation that in the desert of this world would feed and be nourished only by the celestial manna—a distinct society that would live by faith and hope alone. He is still doing this today. Along with intermittent periods of public persecution, the common miseries and calamities that constantly accompany the human condition in this sad life obligate each of us (some more, some less) to bear and to endure with great patience various evils and to submit ourselves in all things to the will of God in the hope of the future glory.

It is a fact that Christians are not exempt from evils, setbacks, and troubles. But often it seems that God presses His own (who live by faith in Christ) harder and drills them even more rigorously to test their faith and hope and to bring to perfection their sanctification, which consists in the mortification of the flesh. Believers are less attentive to putting the flesh to death while everything is prospering with them. So through the means of suffering, God often purifies and perfects His people by subduing their carnal affections. First Peter 4:1 is worthy of careful consideration: "The one who has suffered in the flesh has finished with sin."

This virtue of cross-bearing is called endurance in other passages: "If we endure, then we will also reign with him" (2 Tim. 2:12; see also Heb. 10:36). It consists not only in bearing and suffering trouble without grumbling but in taking it up with joy and enduring it gladly. This is implied in the idea of "taking up" your cross. The Romans forced the condemned to bear his cross and forcibly tied his hands to it. But in the spiritual life something more is required of you. When you see the cross that the will of the Lord has destined for you to bear, you must gladly take it on yourself, imitating the example of the Lord Jesus Christ. For no one ceases from sin except the one who has suffered in the flesh (1 Peter 4:1). In this way you will bring glory to God in bearing your cross.

Endurance is a necessary quality for the entire human race. And for the people of Christ, bearing the cross with joy is an outstanding virtue and a true ornament. Such is the character that God loves to see in His people: a godly and calm soul that submits to Him in the most difficult and painful situations of human life with great humility. A person who never abandons his affection for God, zeal for His glory, or trust placed in God's grace, even amid great adversities. The grace of Christian endurance preserves your serenity and tranquility of mind in the midst of the stormy seas and keeps you from blurting out any absurdities or murmurings against God. This kind of virtue protects you even as the winds rage and the tempests roar; it is a virtue that almost overcomes the human condition.

CHAPTER 7

∽

# Following Christ Jesus

We have considered two principal parts of the spiritual life: *self-denial* and *cross-bearing* or *Christian endurance*. The third part or exercise of the spiritual life is *following Christ*. It is commended in Matthew 10:38; Luke 18:22; and 1 Corinthians 11:1. Peter tells us that Christ "left us an example that we might follow (or press hard after) His steps" (1 Peter 2:21). This metaphor is taken from the way a disciple acts toward his instructor: carefully observing his habits, mores, ideas, doctrines, and his entire way of conducting his life in order to imitate it. The disciple copies out the master's example in all his own actions. Or perhaps the metaphor may have been taken from the boy who copies down lines in accordance with the template set before him.

Following Christ is the virtue by which a Christian conforms his mores to those of Christ Jesus his instructor. He seeks to imitate the Master's virtues as much as he can and to translate into his own life the unstained example of Christ. In this quest, of course, it is necessary to know what Christ's virtues actually are.

Christ's attributes that have to do with His distinct office as Mediator are not possible to imitate. But even though Christ is Mediator, He still is a human being. And many of His characteristics and virtues are exemplary for us human beings here below. The virtues perfectly displayed in the life of the man Christ Jesus must be the same as those that ethics (the moral part of philosophy) commends. The inner principles and outer actions involved in virtue are the same for Christ as for every other person since virtue is eternal, having God's own nature as its exemplar. Virtue is, however, accommodated to the various states of man. For example, after the fall many virtues were called into action that would have had no use in the state of integrity.

Just as there are cardinal vices that are the sources of all others, so there are certain cardinal or root [*radicales*] virtues to which all the others can be connected. The ancients often acknowledged four cardinal virtues: prudence, justice, fortitude, and temperance. Obviously they passed over piety, the first of all virtues, and goodness, their perfection. Christian philosophers later remedied this defect, as we saw in the case of John Wycliffe above.

The apostle Paul reduces all virtues to three cardinal categories: piety, justice, and temperance: "Because the grace of the gospel has appeared to all men, they must deny ungodliness and worldly lusts and live temperately, justly, and piously in this present age" (Titus 2:11–12). The apostle summarizes under godliness [*pietas*] all the virtues and duties that have to do with God, under justice [*justitia*] (i.e., righteousness and uprightness) everything relating to our neighbor, and under self-control [*temperantia*] everything having to do with ourselves. Indeed, all virtues can be referred to these three cardinal heads.

As we discuss the true character of Christ, I will discuss the virtues using six terms often employed in Scripture. These dovetail nicely with the apostle Paul's division and correspond to the six cardinal vices reviewed above.

The first of the virtues of Christ given to us as an example is His *reverence and love for God* (which signify ultimately the same thing). "And the spirit of the LORD shall rest upon him…the spirit of knowledge and of the fear of the LORD" (Isa. 11:2). Here *knowledge* should be understood as an acquaintance with and love for God. The fear of God is a holy affection involving the most tender feelings and stirrings that arise from a consideration of God as the kindest Father, the sovereign Lord, the just Judge, the One who possesses the most awesome glory and majesty, and the source of the summum bonum (the highest good). By the fear of God, a believer orders all his actions with devoted care and solicitude so that he might please God in everything, carefully honor and worship Him, and conform his will to the will of God. In Jesus this virtue is very properly called the love of God because of the particular regard that He had for the Father, "But so that the world may know that I love the Father, and as the Father commanded Me, even so I act" (John 14:31). This quality is also appropriately called piety or godliness since Christ is the pious one par excellence (see Ps. 16:10). Christ as a godly man had an intense desire to glorify His Father. This virtue is particularly fitting for Him as pontiff (high priest) since priests were called pious or godly ones—consecrated to God, reverencing Him, and zealously committed to the advancement of His glory.

The second of the cardinal virtues that we see in Christ Jesus is *goodness*. The fruit of this quality is beneficence, doing good for others and expressing charity. It is the opposite of the cardinal vices of malice and injustice. By goodness I mean that Jesus had an intense desire to help others and to promote their interests and their eternal well-being. In Hebrew this is called *hesed*. We may also call this Christ's mercy or philanthropy. He said of Himself, "I am the good shepherd" (John 10:11). People said of Jesus, "He is a good man" (John 7:12)—that is, kind to others—"who went about doing good, and healing all who had come under the power of the Devil" (Acts 10:38). The sense of the Hebrew word for "good" goes beyond being just. Strictly speaking, a person is called just who renders to each the things that belong to him according to established convention. But the good person is moved by an internal concern to promote others' interests and comfort beyond what honest dealing demands (see Rom. 5:6–7 for this type of distinction between the just and the good person.) The good person does good to others liberally, relieving the poor and those who are pressed down. He supports and cares for orphans and widows in their afflictions. He welcomes into his dwelling those exiled because of their faith and gladly supplies their needs. He even helps his enemies if they fall into need. Christ Jesus and His apostles highly commend this Christian virtue. They call it charity [*charitas*] and kindness [*bonitas*], a badge characteristic of authentic Christianity (Matt. 5:44–48; 10:42; 25:36; Heb. 13:2–3; James 1:27). The exuberant charity of the first believers is a striking example of the virtue of goodness (Acts 2:44–45).

The third virtue of Christ is His *purity and holiness* [*sanctimonia*]. This virtue is in opposition to lust [*concupiscentia*]. It signifies the comprehensive and flawless purity of thoughts, will, intentions, desires, and actions in the Lord Jesus. For this reason, He was called "the Holy

One of God" (Mark 1:24; 1 John 2:20) and "that holy thing" (Luke 1:35). He is "the righteous servant" of God "in whose mouth was no deceit" and in whose actions there was "no violence" (Isa. 53:9, 11); "He did no sin" (1 Peter 2:22); "He knew no sin" (2 Cor. 5:21). We in the school of Christ are acquainted with this virtue, but it is not known in the world. It is the complement and crowning grace of all the other virtues. For in holiness (i.e., purity of thoughts, feelings, and actions) there is an imitation of God (Lev. 11:45; 1 Peter 1:16). In Christ we have a perfect example of stainlessness so that by the grace of God we might copy it as much as our present state allows and "purge ourselves of all filthiness of the flesh and spirit, perfecting holiness in the fear of God" (2 Cor. 7:1). The Spirit of God so sanctified and worked this grace into the early believers that on account of it they were called "saints" [i.e., holy ones] (Acts 9:13).

The fourth quality for us to seek is *humility* and *lowliness of spirit.* This is a virtue particularly identified with the school of Jesus Christ. It is directly opposed to the disordered desires that make a person think more highly of himself than is proper. This grace undercuts all arrogance, conceit, self-righteousness, and vanity: "Take My yoke upon yourselves and learn from Me; for I am meek and humble in heart" (Matt. 11:29); "Let this attitude be in you which was also in Christ" (Phil. 2:5). And what attitude was that? As Paul said in Philippians 2:3, "Do nothing because of vain glory, but, in humbleness of mind, esteem others as better than yourselves." Humility involves three things: a modest sense of yourself along with an acknowledgment of your dependence on divine grace; self-control over your feelings, particularly anger, insolence, exasperation, and temper; and patience to commit yourself with a submissive mind and spirit to every dispensation of God's providence. In Christians, lowliness of spirit reminds them that left to themselves they are destitute and unworthy of grace, and subject to various miseries. It also brings a sense of absolute dependence on God's grace regarding the great question of their salvation. This is why they are often called, both in the Old Testament and by the Lord Jesus, "the meek," "the lowly," "the poor," or "the poor in spirit" (see Pss. 37:11; 72:4; Isa. 11:4; Matt. 5:3–5). This virtue is beautifully described in Psalm 131:1–2.

The fifth virtue of Christ, I would suggest, is *the contempt for the things of the world*—that is, wealth, honors, and self-display along with the external splendor and glory attached to one's social standing (Luke 9:58; John 5:41; 8:50; 2 Cor. 8:9). This virtue is particularly connected to that state of humiliation in which the Lord Jesus found Himself while on earth. Christianity does not forbid a Christian to have or to enjoy riches, prestige, or external fashions. What is essential, however, is that a Christian must be so generous and magnanimous that it is clear to all that he does not set great store by these things or seek after them with great passion. His attention is fixed on something greater. He does not love the world nor put his confidence in the flesh or its riches. His concerns are less for visible things than for heavenly and spiritual things. This virtue can properly be called spirituality or a spiritual mind-set. Those who are Christ's imitate the example of Him who has been raised from the dead and exalted in heaven (1 Cor. 2:15–16; 2 Cor. 4:18; 1 John 2:15).

The virtue of contempt for the things of the world is related to self-denial but implies something more. It is greater to contemplate heavenly things, to be inspired with generosity for others, to look down from the heights, as it were, on worldly privileges and to disdain them than it is to simply renounce these advantages when necessity or the ordering of divine providence demands it. "My kingdom is not of this world" (John 18:36). Christianity inspires all those who follow it to a true generosity, large spiritedness, and philanthropy such that the society of Christ is a people of free-will offerings and noble liberality (Ps. 110:3).

The sixth and final virtue in my survey is *diligence*. It is the opposite of sloth and laziness, which I put among the cardinal vices. This virtue, applicable both to Christ Jesus and to His people, involves two particular characteristics. First, diligence implies the desire to find out the will of God and one's own duty. Such diligence was typical of the Messiah (Isa. 50:5; Luke 2:49). It is worth noting that though our Lord was illumined directly by the indwelling Spirit, He did not for that reason give up meditation on the things revealed in Scripture. Second, diligence is the intense desire and zeal to fulfill carefully the duty God requires, according to the knowledge one has of it. Christ demonstrated this earnestness from his heart (Pss. 40:9; 69:10;

John 17:1). He said, "My food is to carry out the will of Him who sent me" (John 4:34). The story of Jesus' entire life testifies to this diligence and zeal if nothing else. The desire both to know and to carry out the will of God are important graces for the disciple of Christ to seek (Luke 12:43; 1 Cor. 14:1). "Do not be slothful in zeal, but serve the Lord with a fervent spirit" (Rom. 12:11).

The virtue of diligence has particular relevance to all the duties that a believer owes to God in keeping with his particular position and callings. Certain duties are common to all Christians. We have been considering the three principal parts of the spiritual life—namely, self-denial, cross-bearing, and following Christ. And in this chapter we have been considering how all believers must seek to manifest the graces of reverence for God, goodness, purity, humility, contempt for the things of the world, and diligence. In pursuing these virtues, they must put off all the opposing vices.

But there are other duties particular and distinct to a Christian's callings in this world. These are relational duties, obligations each of us has in three realms: the civil area, the ecclesiastical area, and the domestic (and economic) area. In the state, magistrates and judges have special responsibilities to those under their authority. And the people in turn owe respect and other duties to their social superiors. In the church, the leaders (pastors, teachers, elders [*presbyteri*], and deacons) owe certain duties to the congregation and the young people committed to their care as well as obligations toward one another. And in turn the people of the congregation and the students have a responsibility to properly respect, obey, and pay attention to their pastors and teachers. Likewise, in the domestic economy and order, fathers have special duties toward their wives, children, and servants. And these latter in turn have duties toward the head of the household. For the sake of space, I will not enter into a detailed discussion of these important matters. On these subjects you should read the teachings of Jesus Christ in the Gospels, all of Paul's epistles as well as the epistles to the Hebrews and 1 Peter. In these you will find your relational duties accurately described, a perfect outline of practical theology and doctrine. In the letters the apostle Paul wrote for the common instruction of the churches, he was always careful to join practice to theory, practical duties to theological doctrine.

# PART 3

# The Challenges of the Spiritual Life

# CHAPTER 8

## Different States and Degrees of Growth

It is pleasant to meditate on the many connections and similarities between the life of nature and the life of grace. Experience teaches that we are born tender infants who are utterly dependent on the care of others, can only be sustained by milk, and are incapable of more solid food. Slowly we grow into children, then adolescents, and we finally become adults in whom the state of natural life comes to its robust completion. This is the state of full strength and virility (beyond which one slowly begins to decline). Not only in man but in most other animals as well, we observe this marvelous and playful display of the wisdom and providence of God. Born weak and dependent on their mothers for care, by steps they come to the stage of perfection that was ordained for them. What shall I say? All living things come to maturity in slow stages. Even trees and plants put forth shoots that take root and gain the strength of life before they are able to produce leaves, flowers, and fruit. So it is with seeds hidden in the earth: they slowly slough off the husks and coverings in which they were wrapped before they burst forth from the earth, produce grain, and richly fulfill the hopes of the farmer.

The same principle, the same order, the same progress takes place in those who live in the state of grace. In grace as in nature there are nursing infants, children, youths, and adults. Those who begin as tender babies become strong boys then mature men in Christ. In the economy of grace, you only attain to the degree and stage of spirituality that has been assigned to you in this life through stages as you mature. God demonstrates His wisdom and kindness as He dispenses His grace in accordance with the age and progress of each. These matters are important and deserve to be discussed carefully. So, first of all, let me make clear the foundational assumptions [*hypothesis*] I will be working from as I seek to describe as clearly as possible the different states of believers—that is, those living the spiritual life.

Throughout the Word of God we find the assumption that there are different stages and states of the spiritual life and that there are attributes corresponding to each state. John expresses this framework and presupposition as he distinguishes believers into three classes: children (τεκνία), adolescents (νεανίσκοι), and fathers (πατέραι—see 1 John 2:12–13). Each stage has its own characteristics. For example, he does not simply call them children but "little children" (παιδία), nursing children, in a way similar to the author of the epistle to the Hebrews who spoke of those who at that time ought to have been teachers but who were still undeveloped, and who still needed to be treated as infants who are fed with milk and not with solid food as adults (Heb. 5:12). Paul in 1 Corinthians 3:1–2 uses the same argument that should be consulted on this point as well. This hypothesis is further proved by the fact that believers are said to "grow" in the spiritual life, a metaphor taken from the fact that all life develops, whether among animals or humans or plants (Eph. 4:15). "In the manner of newborn infants, desire the sincere milk of the word, so that by it you may grow up" (1 Peter 2:2). "Grow in knowledge and in the grace of our Lord Jesus Christ" (2 Peter 3:18). Based on this assumption, Scripture writers contrast believers who are weak with those who are grown to adulthood and are "mature" (Eph. 4:13; cf. 1 Cor. 14:20). The apostles take a metaphor from natural life with its various stages of progress when they speak of believers being "strengthened" (Eph. 3:16) or "established" or "confirmed" (1 Peter 5:10) in the spiritual life. Believers in a weak and vulnerable state are called lambs, still dependent on their mothers' teats. They need to be carried by the shepherds when on long journeys. Robust and mature believers are compared to adult sheep, calves, or even oxen (cf. Isa. 11:5–6 in connection with Isa. 40:11; 28:9; Ezek. 34; Zech. 11:4–17).

Two caveats are in order here. First, though they are discussed with similar metaphors, we should not simply equate the different degrees a believer goes through with the different degrees and states of the universal church. At times Scripture uses the analogy of human development to describe the experience of the entire body of the church as it grows from the foundation of the world to its consummation. The apostle in Galatians 4:1 employs this moving analogy of a person going through stages, passing from infancy and childhood into the strength of adulthood. He metaphorically presents the church of the patriarchs as a human infant. Next, the Jewish church (i.e., the descendants of Jacob) under the law was like a young smart aleck needing to be ruled by a schoolmaster. But finally, under the new economy, the church in its recent liberty is like a young man come into his legal majority and free from the rule of tutors.

It is the case that God has ordered the dispensation of His grace so that the church in this world might grow into the status and strength of adulthood, even as it passes through various epochs and stages (and correspondingly more or less revelation and precious gifts of the Spirit). The New Testament portrays the church in its freedom as a "complete man" who advanced toward his mature state through various stages. For example, in Ephesians 2:14 Paul uses the human metaphor when he says that God has now joined Jews and Gentiles into one new man by breaking down the dividing wall of separation under the old economy. This new man is the complete body of believers in Christ, both Jews and Gentiles, formed by God Himself to grow from weak beginnings into a state of perfect adulthood at the consummation of the ages. As a new man, the church of the New Testament advances toward perfection through stages, like a child passing through infancy, boyhood, adolescence, and then arriving at the state of manhood. And when the church has reached its final state, God will bring on the consummation and the end of the ages (see Eph. 2:21; 4:15–16; 1 Peter 2:5). Here I have been speaking about the body of the church as a unit and a whole. But now I will return to our previous discussion about the individual members of the church.

The second caveat in order here is to underline the complex way that Scripture uses this metaphor of development. Sometimes biblical authors use these descriptions in an absolute sense to describe all believers, but in other texts (such as in 1 John 2:12–13) the terms *little children, young men, fathers,* and so on must be understood relatively—that is, in relation to each other. Such descriptions are used absolutely for attributes of all Christians. For example, all who live the spiritual life are described as children and infants in texts such as "Out of the mouth of children and infants You have established strength" (Ps. 8:2), "I have quieted my soul as a weaned child" (Ps. 131:2), and "I give You thanks, O Father, Lord of heaven and earth, that You have revealed these things to infants" (Matt. 11:25). The qualities of simplicity, purity, and humility apply to every condition and order of believer. All must lay aside foul lust, selfish ambition, pride, harmful prejudices, and other such things. In Matthew 18:2 the Lord Jesus sets a child in front of the disciples to commend to them certain qualities that children have. See also Matthew 19:14 and 1 Corinthians 14:20, which says, "With regard to evil be infants." The basic sense of all these texts is the same. They hold forth as a model the attributes of infants in an absolute sense, characteristics that apply to people at every single stage and state of development in the Christian life. So far my caveat.

But in this book I want to explore the use of these metaphorical terms in relation to each other. We will consider them in a relative sense, with infancy, childhood, and adulthood representing the various stages of growth and completion of a person in Christ. I will now explore where these differences arise from and describe the distinctions between these stages.

The differences in the stages through which a person in Christ passes arise from disparities at the root level of the spiritual life, variations in the fundamental dispositions and capacities [habitus] of a person who lives spiritually. We clearly see differences in the spiritual aptitudes and abilities of each believer. And these arise due to greater or lesser spiritual experience or because of greater or lesser abundance of divine grace. But we must beware of overemphasizing these variances. Indeed, everyone who has been illumined by divine grace in Christ, regenerated, and effectively transferred into the communion of God in Christ Jesus is a "man"—that is, a whole spiritual man who lacks none of the essential components of the spiritual life. For the entire man is renewed throughout all his parts and faculties. Regeneration of a person by grace produces a completely new spiritual man: his intellect is illumined, his judgment is corrected, his affections are purified, all his spiritual abilities are cleansed. The spiritual man receives new eyes to see, ears to hear, a nose to smell and a palate to taste what is from God and what is not, a mouth to speak, hands to work, and feet to walk. He is a new man, shaped into wholeness in Christ Jesus. And the beginning of this spiritual life and renovation is the love of God, which comes from faith, as I have explained above.

A person's spiritual capacity and disposition may demonstrate a greater or lesser degree of perfection. A person is said to be in a state of spiritual infancy, youth, or adulthood according to how perfected are his spiritual capacities. Since the highest degree of perfection is full manhood in Christ (a condition to which the others lead), we should compare the inferior conditions in relation to this highest condition. I will try to account for the various conditions of the spiritual life by explaining the lower states with reference to the highest. Here, then, are the foundational dispositions and spiritual capacities of the spiritual life that should be explained at this point.

1. Purity of understanding that enables a comprehension of spiritual things

2. Vigor, solidity, and experience in judging and properly discerning spiritual things

3. Wisdom and prudence that enable a person to direct his actions to the glory of God and the benefit of his neighbor

4. Spirituality of the affections

5. Experiential practice of Christian virtues confirmed by established habits and long-standing custom

6. A disposition [*habitus*] of trust as one walks with God and the experience of relating to God in a manner worthy of Him

7. Growth in self-denial, along with vigor and strength of mind to resist the temptations of the world and of the flesh

8. Finally, the experience of afflictions that test us and that must be borne with patience

A proper estimation of the spiritual state of a person can be made in accordance with the affections listed here. To the degree that these qualities are evident in a person's life, to that degree they have progressed in spirituality. The first three capacities are part and parcel of faith itself, and the others are dispositions and capacities [*habitus*] that flow from faith.

The first two of these are *purity of understanding* and a *solid judgment.* These enable a person to rightly comprehend and discern the things of God. Though distinct, I join these abilities together because they can hardly be separated but instead mutually support each other. When a person is first led to faith in Christ, he requires a clear understanding of the foundational articles of the faith. But this perception (which is the basis of his faith and is needed at every stage in a person's spiritual life) is found in different degrees. It may be clear and distinct; it may be more confused. It may be restricted, limited to the first principles of the faith, or it may involve a wide understanding of all the corpus of divine wisdom. A person's perception may be purer (cleansed and freed from fleshly prejudices) or it may be weakened and tainted with erroneous and worldly preconceptions and misjudgments. This latter condition is often the case with those who come into the state of grace as adults. God gives eyes of the soul to those who were spiritually blind. He has indeed illumined them, but this does not mean that in the state of grace they immediately see and understand all things clearly and distinctly at once. On the contrary, many things are still obscure to them. Spiritual things, such as the kingdom of Christ and the preeminence and demands of that kingdom, they never see without various fleshly prejudices that obscure their understanding and often mist over their eyes from seeing the glory of God in Christ.

The Lord sets this very thing before our eyes in the striking and emblematic tale of the healing of the man born blind in Mark 8:23–24. For when the Lord spit on his eyes and asked him if he could see anything, he said he saw men like trees who were walking. And when the Lord touched his eyes again he said he saw all things clearly through the faculty of sight common to all. This took place in a poignant way when Jews and Gentiles were being converted to faith in Christ at the outset of the time of the new economy. The Jews were hindered by many fleshly prejudices, and their understanding was not entirely cleansed from these things even when they entered into the kingdom of heaven. How much worse was the situation of the Gentiles, who until then had been sunken in idolatry and every kind of base lust. It is no surprise that when they managed to come into a state in which they had a purified understanding of spiritual things they nevertheless remained in the condition of "infants," as the apostle puts it in 1 Corinthians 3:1–2. There he calls them "babes in Christ" and "carnal"; that is, they had not yet been purified from their fleshly affections and preconceptions. The writer of the epistle to the Hebrews complains about the slow progress of the Hebrew believers in grasping the mysteries of the faith (Heb. 5:12; 6:1). Like infants needing to be fed with milk, they still required instruction in the first articles of the Christian religion.

Therefore, the "adult in Christ" is the person who, having been regenerated by the grace of God, has put away fleshly preconceptions and prejudices. Such a man perceives the saving truths of the faith, and particularly the things pertaining to the spiritual economy of the New Testament, in all their connections and proper order. He has a strong and practiced faculty of judgment that enables him to reason from solid principles and to draw just conclusions that are based not on a limited understanding but on a wide knowledge of the content of Scripture and of divine wisdom. The person who fails to attain to this state, whether to a greater or a lesser degree, is considered to be an infant or a child. It is proper to note at this point that there is no real knowledge of the mysteries of the faith apart from the sanctification that is found among those who are regenerated. Knowledge and learning are of little value in the kingdom of heaven when separated from holiness and virtue.

The third foundational characteristic of the spiritual life is *wisdom and prudence* in ordering all our actions and regulating all our affections toward the goal of the glory of God and the benefit of our neighbor. Practical wisdom and prudence, which involves governing our affections and actions toward their proper end, can never be separated from true faith. For faith moderates, calms, and settles one's turbulent bodily affections and is always joined to prudence, which implies the circumspect management of our feelings (see Prov. 1:4; 2:10–11). But this wisdom, too, increases and comes in various stages. Although human weakness does not allow one to attain perfection in this area, such wisdom, when a person possesses it to a notable degree, is one of the principal ornaments of a man in Christ, as the apostle suggests in Colossians 1:9 and Ephesians 1:8. It is useful not only for properly ordering the common affairs of human life but also for governing the church of Christ. It enables one to determine when brothers are walking inappropriately, and it is useful in the councils and courts of the church when matters of great importance are being decided. Wisdom and prudence characterize adulthood. "With regard to evil be infants, but in prudence be adults" (1 Cor. 14:20).

The fourth characteristic by which one's progress in the spiritual life can be determined is the *spirituality of the affections*, to which I would add the seventh, which is closely connected to it: the *vigor and strength of mind to rebuff the temptations* of the world, of Satan, and of the flesh. This notable ability distinguishes the various ages, in other words, how much improvement believers have actually made. The grown man in Christ is called πνευματικὸς (spiritual) (1 Cor. 2:15), not just in his capacity for judgment but even in his affections. This spirituality shows itself particularly in two things: First, in the regulation of our actions related to our outward conditions in this world—for example, external things that are pleasurable or comfortable to us, useful to us, or advance our honor in society. Second, in the subjugation of those carnal and twisted affections of whatsoever sort that dominated us before when we were in our natural state. Both of these involve the self-denial that the Lord Jesus requires of His disciples (Matt. 16:24) and that we discussed above.

In his natural state, man has within him the leaven of every kind of corruption. He is besieged by all sorts of twisted affections that drag him in different directions and subjugate him to the various types of worldly or fleshly lusts in accordance with the bent of his temperament. Envy, selfish ambition, and inordinate longings of all sorts reign in him. Passions like pride and wrath produce in him fruits such as disputes, jealousies, outbreaks of anger, and partiality as the apostle describes in Galatians 5:19–20 and Titus 3:2–3. Through continual use these passions are so joined to the nature of man that they virtually become part of his nature.

But when God by His grace renews a man in keeping with His own image, these twisted affections are suppressed, subjugated, and cast down from their privileged position. Sanctified reason takes the upper hand, and as it comes to rule over all the affections, thoughts, and actions of the regenerated mind, it begins to exercise its sway over the man. God establishes His throne in the person's soul, and the Spirit of God instructs and fills him with His gifts and fruits, such as love, joy, peace, patience, goodness, self-control, and moderation (Gal. 5:22–23). Nevertheless, the flesh (i.e., those carnal affections not yet completely driven away and extinguished) often resists the rule of the sanctified mind and stirs up the affections to rebel against the rule of the Holy Spirit (1 Peter 1:14; 2:1; and James 4:1 are notable texts on this matter). And surely from time to time when the opportunity presents itself, Satan stirs up the subdued passions of nature so strongly that they would overpower the mind unless the powerful grace of the Holy Spirit sustained it. And this is exactly what happens to those who are spiritual infants. But the person who has come into spiritual adulthood either no longer fears the power of carnal passions or overcomes all such temptations easily being armed with strength in this kind of combat, having cast off or subdued the fleshly affections. John expresses this beautifully in 1 John 2:14: "I have written to you, young men, because you are strong, and the word of God dwells in you, and you have overcome the evil one." To the extent to which a person makes progress in purging his soul from faulty and corrupt affections, in regulating his actions toward external things that serve our pleasure or utility and in repelling the temptations that the flesh continually presents, to that extent he is to be considered as having progressed in his spiritual "age" and condition.

There is the same gradation in all the other characteristics of the spiritual life that I listed above, and it is not necessary to go through them all in detail. Consider with me briefly the spiritual abilities and dispositions involved in practicing the Christian virtues, praying confidently, speaking clearly about the mysteries of the faith, and patiently enduring the testing afflictions that God sends us (see 2 Peter 1:5–7; Rom. 5:2–5). These are inseparable characteristics of the spiritual life. There is no one in Christ Jesus who is not active in the practice of all kinds of Christian virtues to the glory of God and the edification of his neighbor. This ability clearly arises out of the principle of new life within that person, expressing itself by faith joined to hope. There is no one in Christ Jesus who has not received the Spirit of adoption by which he is taught how to bring his prayers with faith and confidence to the throne of grace. There is no one in Christ who is not prepared to endure the afflictions that divine wisdom and providence has ordained for him. But all such characteristics may be strengthened or weakened, more or less confirmed in the life of a spiritual person. Development depends on the larger or smaller experience of the person, which in turn arises from his spiritual practice and exercise. To the extent a person progresses in these things, the more his mind is cleansed, the more his spiritual judgment is sharpened, the more his faith is strengthened, the more his hope is solidified, the more he bears afflictions with fortitude, and the more practiced he becomes in repelling the temptations of Satan, to that extent he will be reckoned to have advanced in age in the spiritual life. To the degree that these characteristics appear in our lives, to that extent we may be an "infant," "child," "adolescent," or "full adult" in Christ. As you pass from lesser to greater stages, you grow in the spiritual life. As you advance in this journey, you "go from strength to strength" (Ps. 84:7).

CHAPTER 9

⁓

# Illnesses and Pitfalls

We have been speaking thus far about the different states and degrees of progress in the spiritual life. And we have seen that these differences arise from the quality and quantity of spiritual dispositions and abilities [*habituum*], which are the sources of that life. But even those of the same age and maturity in natural life do not all enjoy precisely the same health and physical condition. Natural life is subject to various sicknesses, infirmities, indispositions, and a wide variety of diseases whose symptoms disturb or often even destroy it. Some people seem to enjoy a vigor that wards off sickness. But there are many types of disease (the precise knowledge of which can escape even the physicians), and no one enjoys the health and strength to ward off every illness and bodily weakness.

The same principle operates in the spiritual life. Just as in God's providence no one's physical life is constantly robust, so our life as believers is exposed to a variety of internal sicknesses, infirmities, and diseases. When believers are healthy, they are strong, vigorous, full of hope and faith. They glory in divine grace and are able to defy Satan and all his infernal temptations. But when they feel cast down, anxious, lacking consolation, and are full of fear, then they complain bitterly and moan like the turtledove. As physical diseases and complaints afflict the lives of the most robust and healthy people, likewise no attainments in the spiritual life ever free us from the experience of spiritual diseases and afflictions. There is no man in Christ (no matter how mature, how masculine the strength he has achieved through long exercise, or how developed his spiritual sensibilities) who dare boast that his condition is so strong that he is beyond falling into any illness.

I assert this as a foundational principle for my views on the spiritual life. And I expect that everyone who is a participant in this spiritual life has learned it by experience. But if there is someone who has not yet understood it experientially, he can be convinced by the Word of God, the true looking glass of the spiritual life, where the different conditions of the spiritual life are painted in their true colors. I have in mind particularly the psalms of David and the odes of the saints in the Psalter, which were bequeathed to the church for this purpose: so that both the church as a whole as well as each of its members might observe all the variations of their own condition in these complaints, that they might compare their own affections and weaknesses with the sentiments and ailments of the saints of ancient times, and that they might obtain for themselves the remedies for the healing of the same spiritual infirmities. In this book of the Bible you will see believers explain at length the inequalities and variations of their spiritual states. In Psalm 30:7–8, for example, the holy man, when he found himself confirmed in the state of grace, had said about his prosperity, "I will never be moved" (Ps. 30:6); but then, "when God hid His face, I was troubled" (Ps. 30:7). Psalm 23:3–4 shows the mind of a holy person liberally supplied with gracious influences and divine consolations. He explains his confidence about his condition and status with certainty, even though he may walk through darkness and the shadow of death. On the contrary, in Psalm 42:7 we see a soul thirsty for divine grace, devoid of consolation, and crying out under the heavy trials to which it is exposed: "All the waves and breakers of God" have gone over this person. Psalm 88:15–16 presents us with a touching picture of a saint who describes himself as afflicted, laboring under evils, fainting in spirit, and near to death unless the powerful help of divine grace intervenes. This is the same experience as Psalm 119:25, "My soul clings to the dust; enliven me according to Your word," and as Psalm 138:7, "When I walk in the midst of anguish and troubles, You make me alive"—a portrait of a soul, sick and exposed to death, needing a strong influence to give it life and health. In Psalm 73:2 a godly person is set forth who was exposed to a violent temptation that he only overcame with difficulty. He said he was reduced to a state where his "feet almost slipped and his steps nearly strayed." He teaches us how he had been sustained and fortified. Finally, note Psalm 147:3, which, in a way similar to Psalm 103:3, says that God "heals the broken in heart and binds up their griefs."

Many other scriptural writers have the same foundational assumptions and point of view. They depict the saints in all the variety of their state. For example, as Isaiah describes the flourishing state of the church, he notes, "No one will say, 'I am sick,' for the people that dwell there will be forgiven their iniquity" (Isa. 33:24). But the same prophet (in 42:3) calls believers "bruised reeds" and "smoking wicks" since they are disturbed by various trials of their faith, which, though it survives, becomes so weak that it is near to spiritual death. Compare Ezekiel 34:4 and Zechariah 9:16, in which the afflictions of the lives of believers are set forth under the metaphor of flocks of sheep with their weakness and neediness. The entire Song of Solomon sets forth the various states of the spouse of Christ Jesus: at times languishing, cast down, mourning the absence of her beloved, at times burning to have him or joyfully resting in fellowship with him.

Although spiritual life under the New Testament economy is more perfect and stronger than before, this does not mean that it is exempt from the changes and illnesses of which we have been speaking. The writers of the New Testament speak of the health, sickness, and strengthening of believers just as we have (cf. Acts 20:35; Rom. 15:1; 1 Thess. 5:14; Heb. 12:12). Since this material is worthy of our serious attention, I propose to set forth the following: the differences or types (*species*) of these spiritual illnesses, their nature, their causes, and finally, the remedies by which spiritual diseases must be cured.

Regarding the first of these headings, it seems to me that the *differences or types of these diseases* can be reduced to three subcategories: *Feebleness* or slowness in carrying out the activities of the spiritual life (as opposed to strength, confidence, and vigilance in carrying out all the functions of the spiritual life); habitual *weakness* (as opposed to the vigor of those who are living in a state of grace), a condition close to serious illness; and finally, *disease* and sickness (as opposed to health and well-being).

In contrast to *feebleness*, the *strength* or well-being of the spiritual life is that laudable quality by which a person, having been provided with a healthy faith in God and an integrity of affection, carries out all the functions of the spiritual life. That is, he speedily and diligently fulfills all the duties required of a Christian man by the law of God and Christ Jesus. He does this with the support of the consolation of the Holy Spirit and the enabling influence and experience of divine grace. In this way he is able to resist manfully all the temptations of the world and of Satan, and by the power of faith and of divine grace he conquers and overcomes. It is this strength that the apostle John attributes to "young men," for whom it is particularly appropriate, though this quality should not be lacking at any period in the spiritual life: "I have written to you, young men, because you are strong, and the word of God remains in you, and you have overcome the evil one" (1 John 2:14). Similarly, the psalmist writes, "Wait on the LORD: be strong and let your heart take courage" (Ps. 27:14).

This state of *strength* is opposed to the first vice of the spiritual life, which I have called feebleness, torpor, drowsiness, or slowness. The apostle points out this vice in Romans 12:11, "Do not be slothful in zeal, but be fervent in spirit," and in Hebrews 12:12, "Lift your drooping hands and strengthen your weak knees," which refers back to Isaiah 35:3 (see also Heb. 5:2; 6:12). Slowness is the vice-ridden and faulty disposition of a man who, though he is in the state of grace, does not show himself sufficiently diligent, careful, or quick to fulfill the duties corresponding to the state of grace. He is less attentive to making progress in his spiritual condition than he was at the beginning when God graciously called him into His communion in Christ Jesus. This is a common vice that, if not overcome early on, may slowly settle into the habitual weakness, which I will shortly describe.

Indeed, experience teaches that those who attain to adulthood in the communion of God in Christ must in their early days put forth a zealous effort to carry out the duties of their state scrupulously and carefully. They should give themselves to prayer and to the reading of and meditation on the Word of God attentively and intentionally. They should frequent sacred assemblies gladly and find consolation for their souls and find as much pleasure and benefit in every holy exercise as a starving man finds in food or a thirsty person in drink. After a proper and serious preparation beforehand, they should approach with great reverence the most holy mystery of our religion set before the eyes of believers in the Lord's Supper. They should anxiously seek out the company of the saints, that they might edify and console one another. They must not neglect practicing the duty of charity toward the poor or of benevolence and love toward all. They should continually seek to demonstrate a humble attitude of mind that is devoted to Christ Jesus in everything.

But such a display of first love is not always long lasting. Too often lukewarmness, apathy, and spiritual coldness creep in. These may not extinguish but they certainly hinder the love and care for true religion that stem from the love for God. When the Lord Jesus sees in a person a marked reduction in the love and zeal they showed in the beginning when called by grace, He has to pronounce against this slack and careless soul the rebuke He gave to the Ephesian church, "I have this against you, that you have abandoned the love you had at first" (Rev. 2:4). We have another picture of this in the bride of the Song of Songs, who had fallen into a deep languor and listlessness when the groom came knocking for her to open the door (Song 5:2–8). Christians reduced to such a state do not observe the public or private duties of religion with the same care, attentiveness, or joy. They do not apply themselves to seek after God in the means established for that purpose as they once did. They are not as careful to avoid falling into communion with the world as before. And bit by bit, without any spiritual struggle, they accustom themselves to the habits of worldly people that are inappropriate to the spiritual life. Entirely opposed to this vice are the virtues that Scripture calls diligence, vigilance, and zeal, as we saw from Romans 12:11 (see also Mark 13:33; 1 Peter 5:8).

Although this is only the first of the vices a spiritual person may fall into, the importance of the vice of *feebleness* should not be minimized or its impact underestimated, both with respect to the honor of God and its consequences. Feebleness dishonors the divine name and is injurious to the state of grace. For it is as if a man brought into communion with God found less benefit than he had hoped. It seems as if the heavenly food and drink that he desired were a deception. God had not been able to fully satisfy the hungering and thirsting desires of his soul for true joy and consolation. Instead of finding happiness, such a person seems to be grieved for having been brought into communion with God. Who does not sense that this is an insult to the Lord? Additionally, feebleness has many negative consequences on one's spiritual life. Through this vice, believers deprive themselves of the solid consolation and true joy secured only through communion with God. They sadden the Holy Spirit and open the door wide to all kinds of temptations. Note the Lord's words in Revelation 16:15: "Blessed is the one who is vigilant and takes care of his garments so that he may not walk naked, and they see his shame."

A second spiritual disease birthed from the first is *weakness* (Rom. 15:1; 1 Thess. 5:14). Ezekiel 34:4: "The weak ones you have not strengthened." Let us first carefully observe the meaning of this term. In Scripture the meaning of the Greek term ἀσθένεια repeatedly denotes a serious illness or a disease with little hope of cure, such as dropsy, stones, or consumption. In this sense the Lord Christ is said to have healed τοὺς ἀσθενεῖς (the weak/sick). And in Romans 5:6 a man in the state of nature is said to be ἀσθενής (infirm). But the sense in which we are using the word *weakness* is not so strong and has two distinct meanings. It means either weakness of judgment, by which a person makes improper use of the liberty that we enjoy under the gospel (see 1 Cor. 8:9), or it denotes the faulty and reprehensible trait in a person in a state of grace who has trouble resisting (or after a slight struggle easily gives in to) the serious temptations and scandals set before him even as he is urged toward them by those aspects of his corrupt nature not yet subdued by the grace of the Holy Spirit. It is this latter meaning of the word that we are using: that it is properly a weakness in one's state (though we can include weakness of judgment here as well). In terms of natural life, we sometimes speak of "the weak" as those whose condition lies halfway between a state of perfect health and strength and a state of serious illness. You cannot say that they are gravely ill, but neither do they enjoy solid health. They are not strong enough for great labors; and lacking strength, they easily succumb to the buffeting of other people.

The same is the case in the spiritual life. In the state of grace, "the weak" are those who easily step away from the way of truth because of

public scandals, disputes, or other conflicts. Their progress in the race
of piety is checked. Or they quickly succumb to the remnants of native
corruption within and are not sufficiently resolved in mind to resist the
temptations of the world and of Satan. In the state of grace, sins that
fully dominate and spread themselves throughout the entire being of
a man find no place. But the state of grace does not exclude the vice
I am referring to here: the tendency of letting oneself be seduced and
the powerlessness to resist—not to every kind of temptation or sin
but those less severe types of sins that are dear to the remnants of the
old man not yet completely eradicated by grace. Certain people are
led by their corrupt natures toward pride, selfish ambition, anger, or
the vanity of this age, others toward laziness or life's pleasures and the
immoderate use of those things that serve the interests of lust, luxury,
and self-indulgence. It is wrong for a person in a state of grace, having been admitted into the communion of God, to succumb to these
vices habitually. And those who do so do not deserve to be enrolled
in the assembly of the saints. But it still happens that a person in the
state of grace, due to a certain laxity of mind or disposition of character, may be overcome by the impact of these temptations in such
a way that he does not resist these vices as strongly as Christianity
demands, especially if he does not properly fortify himself and diligently guard himself from occasions that lead into temptation. But it is
always the case that when those who have participated in divine grace
find themselves vanquished by the flesh, they feel a profound grief and
shame. And if they feel this way having succumbed to weakness after
a single fall, how much more if they fall a second or a third time. Let
me repeat: this vice of weakness is the corresponding opposite of the
believer's condition of strength, constancy, and firmness. By these he is
able (like a robust youth, veteran soldier, or courageous lion) to stand
firmly against all types of temptations and to repulse them forcefully,
as the apostle has said in 1 Corinthians 15:58: "Therefore, my beloved
brethren, be steadfast, unmovable" (see also Ps. 31:24).

The third and final malady of the spiritual life is *disease* (i.e.,
sickness and illness properly). Disease develops out of weakness as
weakness comes from feebleness. In nature, disease is a widespread
influence that affects a person's entire constitution. We might say it

is an offense against the natural condition of the constitution of the body and tends toward its destruction. The vice of the spiritual life that we call disease or illness is analogous, as we see in Isaiah 33:24, "No one will say, 'I am sick' or 'I am distressed by grief,'" and Ezekiel 34:4, "You have not healed the sick person." This defective [*vitiosa*] quality, directly opposed to health and strength, violently upsets the condition of the spiritual life. It so weakens one's entire spiritual constitution that it puts one's spiritual life in grave danger. Those in this condition are indeed spiritually diseased.

There are three chief characteristics of this condition of disease. The first is that the feelings, capacities, and dispositions [*habitus*] of the spiritual life (which, as I said, are its source and fountain) not only do not grow or become strengthened as happens in a state of spiritual health, but they diminish and decline, as often happens with the symptoms of diseases such as fever. In this condition one's faith weakens by being exposed to various temptations: the intellect becomes darkened, hope wavers, and love toward God and neighbor becomes cold if perhaps not entirely extinguished. And this state of indisposition spreads itself over every exercise of the spiritual life. Over a person's prayers, meditations on the Word of God, and participation in public and private worship there reigns a sluggishness, a numbness, an inactivity, a nonchalance, and an impotence. Weakness debilitates one's entire spiritual constitution.

The second characteristic of this state of disease is that the entire temperament of a spiritual man is disturbed. All the good dispositions and affections that accompany the state of spiritual life cease, such as tranquility of soul, rest in God, peace of conscience, present joy from a sense of divine communion and future hope, and joined with these things, the contentment, satisfaction, and consolation received in carrying out each duty. And if these are not completely lacking during this unhappy period, at least they are expressed coldly and weakly whereas sadness, weariness, and torments occupy and vex the soul.

The third and final characteristic of this state of disease is a weakness that makes a person fear that his spiritual life is at the point of disappearing unless God intervenes to help the afflicted soul with His grace and saving medicine. This is when we see the "bruised reed…and the smoking wick" (Isa. 42:3), the man near to spiritual death, in whom only a little breath of life remains, which must be diligently nursed. Nowhere is this sad and disturbing feeling described more clearly and distinctly than in Psalms 32 and 88. This last poem should especially be applied to Christ Jesus as He was struggling in His mind and spirit with these extreme and deadly pangs. Our Lord, though He was free from all sin, became for a time the personification and representative of His suffering and miserable people. And He bore their sicknesses and miseries to the utmost extent that His holy nature would allow. And so He was deprived of all the consolations that ordinarily accompany the spiritual life, all its joy and comfort, and He was for a time afflicted with the deepest sufferings: "My life draws near the grave" (Ps. 88:3). His soul drew near the gates of death and was nearly extinguished as He played the part and was invested with the character of another (though, of course, in His sovereign person He did not experience the least alteration in the condition of His spiritual life): "I have become a man without strength" (Ps. 88:4); "My eye dries up because of weakness" (88:9); "From my youth I have been afflicted and near death. I have suffered Your terrors and feel utterly abandoned" (88:15). Psalm 30 furnishes us with further things to be noted on this matter.

Additionally, in the order of nature each illness has its own characteristic symptoms, and the situation is the same regarding spiritual maladies. I do not intend to press the comparison too far. But each spiritual sickness has its own nature that we should seek to discover and understand.

We generally discover three causes when we inquire into these illnesses and their symptoms: the more serious sins or scandals that disturb the condition of the spiritual life, the temptations of various types to which a person in the state of grace is exposed, and the economy and administration of divine providence that God graciously dispenses either more or less liberally.

Regarding the first of these, it is certainly the case that if a person who has been brought into the state of grace happens to fall into some great sin, then his entire interior constitution is disturbed. His mind is clouded, and he is reduced to the saddest and most lamentable condition. So it is that whoever wishes to maintain his state in Christ amid all the evils and adversities of this life ought to beg God to keep him from this as the most serious of evils in accordance with the prescribed formula that the Lord Himself dictated to His disciples. A believer ought to watch with supreme vigilance so that when tempted by Satan or the flesh he might not commit any serious scandal, disturbing and troubling his soul, because repentance from such sins only ends with life itself. In the penitent David we have an example of this in Psalms 32 and 51. One should carefully examine and ruminate on such passages. For experience teaches that people who are in communion with God almost never fall into these sorts of serious sins without first having indulged in idleness or in pleasures more than is proper. Or, having been inflated with pride and spiritual arrogance, they felt superior to their betters and had a higher opinion of their spiritual state and stability than was proper (2 Sam. 11:2; Matt. 26:33). Those who keep themselves from such pride deserve (by divine grace) to be kept from great falls. "The wise person fears and departs from evil" (Prov. 14:16).

But among the causes that we are exploring, by far the most common is the second: that is, the temptations to which the spiritual life is exposed in this world. They come in many forms, including the adversities of life (particularly poverty); long-lasting persecutions in opposition to the faith; the corruption of the age and a certain apathy and listlessness that commonly reigns in the church; notable public scandals on the part of certain people; the injuries that believers suffer at the hands of others from which, in accordance with the reasonings of divine providence, they can expect no resolution or satisfaction; riches and long-lasting prosperity (whether temporal or spiritual); and spiritual trials to faith and hope, not simply through heresies but also through the philosophizings and speculative reasonings of unstable and impious persons, which are intended to disturb the minds of unlearned people and do often cast them into doubt.

The spiritual life is subjected to all these types of temptations, which often combine to harass vehemently a man in the state of grace. James calls these diverse and variegated trials and temptations, since one temptation or cause is frequently mixed together with others (James 1:2). The race of this life is a course of trials and temptations, a time of ordeal and battle during which the godly must at all times be prepared, maintaining the armaments by which they can repel the weapons and the flaming darts of Satan (Eph. 6:16). These include the adversities by which individuals and entire families are often for long stretches of time afflicted and weighed down, one following the other as wave succeeds wave. Public calamities involve entire peoples in which no particular distinction between the good and the bad can be observed. Such are times of war, famines, weather that produces sterility of the fields, plagues, and the deep injuries by which the poor and helpless are frequently oppressed by the rich, influential, and proud.

Such trials (whether coming one at a time or all together) would overwhelm the godly, whatever their status, if they were not powerfully sustained by divine grace. But if God indeed loves them, elected them from eternity, and singled them out over others, then why can the effects of this love not be seen in the order and ways of divine providence? Why do they bear the brunt of public evils and calamities along with the others? Why does God allow them to be oppressed by proud people who are more powerful than they are? This seems a legitimate and indisputable deduction. But it must be resolutely denied since God does not neglect His own. His providence does indeed involve a particular care for them. He never ceases to watch over them, even when it does not seem so (such as in the case of public calamities). An infinite variety of examples of this can be produced from Holy Scripture. Here I wish people would study and consider Psalms 38, 52, 73, and 119 (as a whole). The laws of the kingdom of nature and of grace are wisely mingled together according to the order of divine providence in such a way that their effects are never opposed to each other but rather sustain each other mutually. And so it is that even events that appear to us most random and unforeseen are actually directed to the end that God intended for them and always work together for the true benefit of the elect (Rom. 8:28).

All the above causes are able to drive believers to fall into feebleness, weakness, and spiritual disease (when lukewarmness and coldness take the place of charity—a most lamentable and sterile condition for a person's soul). But with good reason I maintain that among all the causes of spiritual feebleness there is none more serious than long-term prosperity in one's temporal or spiritual condition, unless it is handled with particular moderation and good sense. In speaking of "spiritual prosperity"

I understand a long-term unruffled condition in which a man in the state of grace experiences not simply divine grace but consolations without any mixture of adversities or deep temptations. Such a condition invariably brings with it a certain security. And from that security comes negligence, sluggishness, and a wide door open to temptations unless God supplies the man with particular grace and an appropriate measure of wisdom, prudence, and watchfulness. Furthermore, from such a condition comes spiritual pride, which (among all the vices) is particularly displeasing to God (cf. Ps. 30:7; Prov. 30:8–9; Song 5:2–3).

*The economy of divine providence* I consider the third cause of spiritual illnesses and symptoms. God administers His providence and dispenses grace, joy, and consolation to believers in a wide variety of measures. Although as He distributes His grace, God is a most generous householder, He does not always use the exact same measure in dispensing it. As His divine providence judges best, at times He gives more, at times He gives less. He may suddenly hide His face from a soul, not comforting a person accustomed to His consolation, not allowing him to experience the same vivid sense of His presence as before that filled him with joy and enlivened his spirit (Ps. 119:25; Isa. 57:15). While clouds and darkness besiege this soul (and the person himself is not able to account for what is happening), he may not dare to persuade himself of God's paternal favor, to glory in the hope God gives or to lean on God with filial confidence as was his former experience. And for a time that soul may languish like a flower thirsty for the water that so often provided it with life. An outstanding passage expressing this is Psalm 30:7: "In my state of prosperity I said, 'I will never be moved.' It is You who make my mountain firm. But when You hid Your face, I was troubled."

A final note: the fourth major subject that I have proposed to explain in this book deals with the remedies that can properly be administered for the cure of these spiritual diseases. Now, of course, this is closely related to the means for promoting sanctification. I do not intend to confuse and collapse these topics, however, and so I will indeed follow the order of subjects I set out at the beginning: we will deal with the remedies in chapters 10 and 11 and the means in chapters 12 and 13.

# CHAPTER 10

# Remedies That Should Be Applied to Spiritual Sicknesses

In the order of nature, two things are important for the person who enjoys good health. The first is that he must look after his health diligently. He must preserve it, strengthen it as much as is possible, and carefully avoid whatever would disturb his healthy balance. The second is that if he should fall into some situation that disturbs his constitution, he should put forth all possible efforts to recover this condition of health. The same thing takes place in the spiritual life, and that is what we must discuss in this place. For having spoken briefly about the mishaps and setbacks to which the spiritual life is subject, it is now necessary to set forth the remedies that one should apply to them. And after that, we will explain the means of strengthening the soul's health once one has recovered it.

Let us continue to develop the comparison between physical and spiritual well-being. People who have lost their physical health (to which all mortals are prone) tend to do three things to recover it in accordance with that instinct for self-preservation which we have by nature. The first is to diligently make an examination of the reasons that have caused the illness and to endeavor to understand its causes. The second is to make use of the most appropriate remedy for the sickness in question. And the third is to call in an able doctor, to ask for his help, and to trust the state of one's health to him. The same courses of action should take place in one's spiritual life.

With regard to the first duty, no healing can reasonably be expected to take place if one does not understand first where the illness comes from. Such a thing might possibly happen in the natural state, but it can never take place in the state of grace. No one can be healed of any kind of spiritual infirmity if he does not first examine and seek its causes. This is where the beginning of healing comes from.

The first act of a spiritually sick person who wants to recover his health, therefore, should be to reflect on his condition, to consider himself, and to examine seriously in the presence of God (in the sacred place of his own heart) what can be the cause of the spiritual malady by which he finds himself afflicted. Old Testament believers spoke in this way in Jeremiah's Lamentations 3:40: "Let us test and examine our ways; let us explore, study, and return to the LORD" (cf. Zeph. 2:1). When a person does this, he calls himself before the tribunal of his conscience. He becomes his own judge. He carefully reviews all the circumstances of his past life. He asks questions: What may he have done that has distanced God from him or alienated him from his God? What can have been the reason that has brought His anger on him and has made him unworthy of the influx of His graces and the light of His previous consolations? In this state a man plays two roles. He himself takes action against himself. He is at the same time the judge and the criminal. For whenever anyone finds himself guilty at the tribunal of his own conscience, he condemns himself in spite of the desire he has to be absolved. He who wishes to press ahead toward his healing in a proper way must proceed with good faith and without hypocrisy. He must not deceive himself through negligence, for that could be deadly.

However, since *philautia*, or "self-love," is so natural to man, so constantly leads him to excuse himself, and so often confuses the judgment that he ought to have of himself, it is necessary that a man apply himself to this examination with all possible care. He must prostrate himself humbly before God who is the true Physician of souls and ask Him to open his eyes and expose in him whatever might displease Him. David, the holy king and prophet expresses himself in Psalm 139:23, "Search me, O God, and know my heart. Test me, know my thoughts, see if there is in me any harmful way, and lead me in the eternal way."

When a person has done this first thing and come to know the true cause or causes of his spiritual sickness (called in the style of Scripture "knowing oneself" [cf. Jer. 31:19]), reason teaches that a person should take the second and third steps and search for a cure and seek out a capable physician who is able to prescribe and apply a proper remedy. These two things naturally go together, even more in the order of grace than that of nature, because the Physician is at the same time Himself the medicine for our languishing spiritual estate.

Our Physician, then, is none other than God. As a moral healer He teaches us by His Word the remedies that a spiritual person should apply to his illnesses if he truly wants to find healing. And as a physical healer, He Himself condescends to apply to us the remedies that He commends in His Word. *Physician* is a title that the saints in all ages have attributed to God. He makes Himself known in this capacity and wants His people to acknowledge this, as He says in Exodus 15:26: "I am the LORD who heals you." The prophet Jeremiah speaks similarly: "Is there no balm in Gilead; is there no physician there?" (Jer. 8:22). The Psalms speak likewise: "O LORD, heal me, for my bones are terrified" (Ps. 30:2); "I cried to You, LORD, and You healed me" (Ps. 3:4; cf. Pss. 103:3; 147:3). These passages all serve as models of a heart penetrated and broken by a sharp remorse for its sins, a heart that has turned to God and humbly implores His help to apply to its wounds the appropriate measures—that is to say, in order that it might receive the grace of the remission of sins and of the gift of the Holy Spirit, which alone is able to relieve this burdened soul, to give it life, to purify it from its filth, and to reignite in it the desire of finishing the course and arriving at the goal of sanctification.

Those who are spiritually sick should pass on from this general prayer to a more particular one, accompanied by a humble confession of their faults, where they honestly and forthrightly lay out their condition to God: "I acknowledge my sin to You. I said, 'I will confess my transgressions unto the LORD.' And You forgave the iniquity of my sin" (Ps. 32:5). Nothing is more logical or more necessary than this course of action. For if in the case of corporal illnesses a person cannot find healing without exposing his condition to a physician from whom he must not hide any of the circumstances in which he finds himself, how much stronger the reason for doing this in the case of spiritual illnesses where the consequences are so much greater? God is the master; He is the sovereign who has the right to command us.

And He demands the repentant sinner to profoundly humble himself before Him and to make a sincere confession of his faults to Him. As in the case of corporal sicknesses, those who hide their true condition deceive only themselves and not the doctor. And since the majority of spiritual illnesses have been contracted by a person's own failure in his course of living, nothing is more fitting than the obligation for him to turn to God (whom he has offended and from whom he had refused help) in order to make to Him a humble and sincere confession of his disorderly conduct. In this he glorifies God by giving Him what He deserves, and thus gains for himself rest and perfect tranquility.

A second remedy is to flee and to separate oneself completely from all the causes and occasions that have led one into sin and have brought on the sick state in which the soul finds itself. Psalm 18:23 expresses this in the following terms: "I was upright before him, and I kept myself from my iniquity." If anyone finds in himself that the corruption of the world is strong or that bad company, the temptations of the flesh, or the stumblings of others have troubled his soul and made it lose its innocence, he should, without wasting any time, have recourse to this remedy. The first step toward healing oneself is to avoid the cause of the evil. Nothing is more advantageous than flight: separating oneself from occasions for sinning. It is also useful not to be overly liberal in making associations to which neither duty nor charity call. The prophet suggests such counsel for a person afflicted by the hand of God: "Let him sit alone and be silent" (Lam. 3:28). Solitude calls the soul back to itself and away from the distraction of exterior objects. Solitude gives the soul time to consider itself and to reflect on its state. This is a sure remedy for recovering one's lost spiritual health.

A third remedy for spiritual illness is the reading of the Holy Scripture, truly a special balm which by itself may heal a soul that is languishing, sick, and near death. As Psalm 119:92–93 says, "Unless Your law had been my delight, I would have perished in my afflicted state. I will never forget Your statutes, because by them You have given me life." Psalm 119 is an excellent song that focuses entirely on this point and can rightly be called a rule for the spiritual life. It recommends reading and meditating on the Word of God as the balm and true remedy for a sickly soul. It considers the divine Word as in the following three ways: (1) As a word of grace that produces hope and consolation. It is a word of promise and of good news that announces Jesus Christ to us as the Mediator and Physician of the penitent soul. He has obtained redemption and the remission of sins by His blood for all who have faith and repentance. How sweet and how life-giving is the consolation of this divine Word to a wounded and afflicted soul, damaged by sin! With what reverence, with what sharp sense of joy will not the soul receive this good word of God and apply it for the healing of its hurts! Provided with such help, the soul approaches God with confidence and brings along with it the very words of God (in which it is impossible that He would deceive or lie). And in deep humility, the soul asks God to grant grace that it might be allowed to experience the truth of these things. (2) As a word that contains the precepts of life—that is, the rules that we should follow if we would be settled and established in whatever state we find ourselves. (3) As a word that provides us with the examples of the saints, particularly appropriate to encourage us and to serve as models for us—those who have passed as we have through all the conditions and all the vicissitudes that we now experience. Let me add a few more thoughts on this extremely helpful practice of benefiting from the example of the saints in Scripture.

The examples of the saints and the experiences of help that they received at various times by the grace of God are an important fourth remedy for spiritually sick souls, providing consolation, comfort, and strength. This type of meditation provides a firm foundation for holy reasoning (or what we could call reflecting "in accordance with the rule of the sanctuary"), such as in Psalm 27:14: "Wait for the LORD. Be strong and let your heart take courage." By following such an example of thought, the crushed and weak soul, after a sincere and faith-filled repentance, will surely be raised full of confidence and hope, which will cause it to return to its original state. This is what the apostle Paul, following Isaiah, calls "lifting weary hands and strengthening tottering knees" (Heb. 12:12; cf. Isa. 33:24: "No one will say, 'I am sick,' for the people that dwell there will be forgiven their iniquity").

These are, briefly expressed, the main remedies that a soul struggling with spiritual illness should make use of. There are, of course, many others, but they can be considered among the means of preserving the spiritual life, regarding which we will speak shortly. I will only add that nothing is more useful in cases of spiritual malady than the wise and prudent ministry of pastors, established in the church by the gracious providence of God. They serve as spiritual physicians applying these remedies at the proper times to the people with necessary care (by way of contrast see Jer. 6:14; 8:4). For example, when pastors find sinners hardened and given over to immorality, they must stir them to contrition and true repentance. When they find those who are crushed and afflicted by a vision of their sins, they should be able to encourage them by words of consolation so that they do not fall into desperation. When they find those who are doubting and uncertain, they must be able to lead them to examine themselves so that they might know their true spiritual condition. Pastors should be able to fulfill all the duties their ministry demands of them on such occasions, which make up, as Scripture calls it, the art of winning souls (Prov. 11:30; cf. Zech. 11:16).

When a spiritually sick person on his part engages in good faith to do the things that depend on him, God by His grace will supply what is lacking. He Himself, the sovereign doctor, will do what none of His ministers can do. When the favorable time of His grace has come, He will lay His hand on the wounded and penitent soul. He knows a person's internal state and is not unaware of any of the soul's needs. By His Holy Spirit, He reveals to a person his own condition; He enlightens and teaches him what he should do to get out from his spiritual troubles. The consolations that He pours into that person's soul, like a balm full of sweetness and power, restore health to him little by little. They enable him to recover his strength. As God stirs in that soul the same zealous actions for which it was formerly known, He makes the person run along the paths of the divine precepts with greater ardor than ever. The godly soul expresses itself this way in Psalm 30:2: "I cried to You, LORD, and You healed me."

# PART 4

# The Development of the Spiritual Life

# CHAPTER 11

## Promoting Sanctification and Guarding against Temptations

In the spiritual life it is not sufficient to simply enjoy good heath or to have recovered it after a loss. Just as in natural life, you must go on to preserve your health after having recovered it. And you must work at strengthening it as much as possible. This responsibility is our topic in this chapter.

In natural life everyone who is eager to keep and strengthen his health is very careful about his diet and lifestyle since according to the laws of nature the preservation of our state of health depends on such things. A healthy lifestyle and regime consists principally in two things: (a) carefully abstaining from anything that could damage our health and (b) taking good nourishment at the right time and engaging in proper exercise to refresh and revive the body and mind.

There are two types of means for supporting the spiritual life and for promoting sanctification. The first kind is under the power of man according to the laws of nature and of grace. The other kind depends directly on God. Of course, a person has no power of this. We will give particular attention to the first kind. It too can be divided into two categories: the first dealing with things that we must avoid, and the second dealing with the things we must put into practice.

The duties of the first kind involve vigilance and appropriate prudence so as to avoid carefully anything that can damage our constitution. This sentiment is so natural to man that certain things, without conscious thought, produce disgust and aversion in us. We carefully avoid poisons or anything that causes death since they go against our very nature. In the spiritual life (where one needs to employ just as much circumspection), unfortunately, such is often not the case. Not only do people fail to avoid things that can be detrimental to the soul, but it often happens (an effect of the corrupt nature within) that the soul has a distaste for good and healthy food but avidly seeks out the worst and most dangerous.

We can describe in a general way the things that a person in a state of grace should avoid, but some aspects need to be treated with special concern. In general, one must flee from vices of any kind or type. For just as the virtues give rise to and sustain each other mutually (and certain virtues lift a person up by degrees to greater virtues), so also vices have a deadly connection among themselves. They give birth to each other and mutually support each other. But we will not prolong our discussion of our need in general to flee vices since we have already spoken of it in dealing with the matter and substance of the spiritual life. Let us pass on to things in particular that we should avoid: the occasions for sin and the means by which vice is contracted. In this chapter I will deal with eight major areas under this category.

## 1. Luxury, Excess, and Drunkenness

This is the vice in which a disordered appetite leads a person to drink or to eat more than he really needs or than is suitable for a soul in communion with God. The Savior Himself gives this advice to His disciples in Luke 21:34 where He says, "Take care of yourselves so that your hearts might not be weighed down through overindulgence and drunkenness," as does the apostle Paul: "Do not get drunk on wine, which is an indulgence, but be filled with the Spirit" (Eph. 5:18). These two passages are sufficient on this matter since it would be easy to produce a limitless number of others from both the Old as well as the New Testament. I cannot believe that a true disciple of Jesus Christ needs a long list of reasons to strengthen him against such a vice. Propriety itself condemns it, and even the more refined among worldly people take care to avoid it. It is certain that nothing stupefies the spirit more than eating or drinking too much; nothing is more opposed to the exercise of spirituality. How can a drunkard be apt for spiritual things if he cannot even accomplish the duties required of him by society?

It is true that there are movements of the Holy Spirit in which He fills the soul in transports of generosity, trust, joy, and consolation. He stirs in the soul motions of supernatural life that make a person sing the marvels of God and celebrate His immortal praises. The ancients referred to this stirring as "prophesying" since it is somewhat analogous to the affections and motions produced in a person by the effects of wine. That is why the disciples of Jesus Christ, when they were affected and prophesying by the divine Spirit, were said by worldly men to be "full of new wine" (Acts 2:13). Similarly, it was said of the heroes of the people of God who were to receive the Holy Spirit that they would "be stirred up" as if they were "drunk with wine" (Zech. 9:15). And the same prophet compares the gifts of the Holy Spirit to an excellent wine that makes the virgins flourish (9:17).

However, all who have an experience of the spiritual life know that these effects which may seem the same are actually opposed to each other. The transport that comes from sensual drunkenness wipes out the positive effects and good movements of the Holy Spirit. It chases Him away, so to speak. The fullness of one spirit necessarily excludes the fullness of the other Spirit. So the more a man is given over to intemperance, the more he becomes inept and incapable of fulfilling his spiritual duties.

In setting forth this principle, it is not my purpose to condemn the moderate use of wine, which, far from damaging the body, serves to strengthen it and to put it in a state of readiness. But in light of the scriptural texts cited above, the abuse of wine should be considered by Christianity to be among the worst vices. Certainly, all people of every sort should be ashamed of succumbing to this vice, which takes away his use of reason, the quality that distinguishes man from the animals. Drunkenness reduces an elevated and excellent creature to the condition of a brute beast.

## 2. Idleness

Here I mean laziness as opposed to honest rest and proper relaxation. Everybody knows that "idleness is the mother of all vices." It opens the door wide to all kinds of sins and temptations, whereas work and honest activity puts them to flight. This kind of idleness I want to oppose here. I do not tend to treat idleness in general here—that is, the person who neglects the duties to which reason and law obligate him, or the person who does not make use of his talents, energies, or time (he must give an account to the judgment of God for these). Such laziness belongs to the general category of vice that we reviewed earlier and is opposed to the virtue that we have called diligence. The idleness that I am critiquing here is similar to indulgence. It consists in not avoiding the opportunities for sin and in opening the door to the vices and temptations to which an idle person exposes himself through negligence. Such idleness is similar to luxury in its effect. The mind that is not occupied and deliberately active suffers the attacks of various lusts. Since the person incautiously neglected to protect himself, these desires take advantage to set his mind on fire. Experience teaches us this in an even more dependable manner than all the outstanding warnings of the prudent and ancient philosophers (which the limits of this short work do not permit me to cite). The sage of Proverbs 19:15 said, "Laziness makes a person fall into a deep sleep." Such sleep is the spiritual stupor brought on by serious sins. Jesus Christ condemns precisely this vice when He recommends vigilance: "What I say to you I say to all, stay awake!" (Mark 13:37). Be busy in honest activities and labors lest Satan take advantage of your idle and careless condition. "Blessed are those servants whom their lord will find awake when he comes" (Luke 12:37; see also 1 Thess. 5:6; 1 Peter 5:8). When a demon finds a soul idle and unoccupied, he enters and finds a dwelling place there (this is one application of the parable of Matt. 12:44).

This matter is quite clear. Paul says, "For we have heard that certain persons among you are walking disorderly, doing nothing" (2 Thess. 3:11). These are slothful and lazy people who are not working and do nothing useful for society. There are, of course, pastimes and recreations for the mind that are not only proper but even necessary. Brief pauses from our labors are condemned by no law of Christ Jesus. The point is that the soul should be continually busy and constantly involved in exercise and activity like metal tools that can only be polished through continual use. When neglected and not pressed into service, they get eaten up by rust.

## 3. Bad Companions

It is a very common maxim (much confirmed by experience) that "bad company corrupts good morals," as the apostle Paul says in 1 Corinthians 15:33 following Menander [Greek dramatist ca. 342–290 BC]. And Proverbs 13:20 says, "The person who walks with the wise will become wise, but the companion of fools will be shattered." Note also Psalm 1:1: "Blessed is the one who does not march in the counsel of the godless, nor stand in the way of sinners, nor sit together with mockers." This precept is universal. No one doubts that to be frequently in the company of a person of a profane mind and corrupt heart (whose mores are scandalous and whom everyone sees as a violator of the laws of society) must be detrimental for a believer who desires to advance in virtue and to show himself pleasing to God in Jesus Christ. It is indeed impossible that a person who has entered into communion with God and has learned to distinguish the light from the darkness can take pleasure in such company.

But I want to talk about bad company in a more general way: not the company of the worst people but the companionship that does not lead to edification or profit. I have in mind those social connections where vanity, ostentation, and worldly pomp reigns and where people are caught up, if not in sinful things, at least with silliness and trivialities: in short, where people are caught up in tasteless, risqué discussions that are thoroughly unprofitable. At times it is only manners and basic sociability that force us to be in such company. I do believe that when necessity or service to one's neighbor demands it, a man who is considerate of his salvation can engage in such meetings without sinning. But I do suggest that you should not seek out such company. Avoid it as much as possible, as long as you do not shirk your duty or violate the principles of politeness and honest sociability.

Through worldly company there are two principal things that often hinder a man from his spiritual duties, stain his conscience, disturb his interior state, turn him aside from good works, and hinder his search for godliness: vain discourse and the bad example of people engaged in questionable activities. These are both difficult to avoid in common interactions. In such society a person tends to say all kinds of things that are fruitless, lack focus, and are neither dictated by prudence nor seasoned with grace. One says things out of keeping with the care and accuracy demanded by Christian discipline. I would add that there is no one so prudent and circumspect, no man so thoughtful and judicious who has not had a rash, imprudent, or misspoken word escape from his mouth that he would not have said if he had the time to reflect beforehand. If you get in the habit of such conversations, they will turn you away from serious matters and accustom your mind to laziness, inertia, and pleasure seeking.

In all the above, however, my intention is not to criticize honest conversation or proper social interactions. Quite to the contrary, these are very laudable, as we will see when we soon deal with the means of bolstering the condition of one's Christianity.

### 4. Overly Free Jesting and Lascivious Witticisms

Since human spirits are oriented toward pleasure and merriment, it comes to pass that some people, even among those who do not lack divine grace, have a natural tendency toward unbridled witticisms and jests that their fertile minds provide for the gratification of others. If they notice that their pleasantries meet with favor, they try to shine even more brightly in such displays by spouting forth vanities. But the prudent person ruled by the dictates of his conscience carefully guards himself from this vice since it quickly degenerates into a shameful habit unworthy of a person in Christ.

It is not only permissible but profitable at times to put in a bon mot to stimulate the conversation, however. A statement "seasoned with salt" may prick and awaken others' spirits. But it is the role of prudence to set limits to such sallies. One should learn moderation and not give in to the intemperance of the tongue. We must not become accustomed to a spirit of scoffing and jesting that is out of keeping with the dignity and beauty of Christianity. Additionally, we should not jokingly put forth opinions that on other occasions we would say seriously. If we make fun of others and take pleasure mocking at their expense, we run the risk of being mocked at by others in turn, which would be a just judgment by God. A Christian man should maintain gravity and seriousness in the common interactions and commerce of life. The apostle commends this: "May your speech always be seasoned with grace and salt, so that you might know how to respond to each person" (Col. 4:6); "No corrupt communication should come forth from your mouth, but only that which is good and useful for edification, bringing grace to the hearers" (Eph. 4:29). Or as the Lord Jesus said in Mark 9:50, "Have salt in yourselves." Wisdom, prudence, moderation in judging, gravity, decorum, circumspection, and the principle of incorruptibility are nothing other than true and sincere faith. All these things are properly represented under the image of salt. But one must in particular read the proverbs of that wisest of kings to see how he depicts mockers, wits, and wags as being people absolutely destitute of true wisdom (Prov. 1:22; 9:6). We list this vice among those that the spiritual man ought to carefully avoid since it troubles the soul's tranquility, puts it out of sorts, and leads it away into levity; nor is it in keeping with the works and influences of the Holy Spirit, which require a settled and circumspect state of mind.

**5. Conformity to the Corrupt Mores of This Present Age**
If you consider the matter in a general way, nothing could be more clear and distinct than the warning of the apostle in Romans 12:2: "Be not conformed to this age." However, it is one thing to dash off a theoretical description of the vice and another to define precisely what this admonition refers to. And even if you manage to meditate in detail on these things and can define them accurately, it is very difficult to put this precept into practice since it is so easy to sin in trivial matters. At the time in which the apostle gave this precept, all the practices of pagan peoples were influenced by their religion; Gentile mores stemmed from pagan spirituality. Almost all public ceremonies served the flesh with all its corruption. Every area of life was marked by superstition, luxury, lust, vanity, display, and idolatry, though the government, courts, and military discipline restrained the decay somewhat. The leaders of the people felt the need to invent all kinds of vain amusements to occupy the populace and gain their favor: corrupt entertainments such as gladiator combats, circuses, feast days, theatrical presentations, and comedies and banquets in the temples of their gods.

But there were social duties, civil laws, matters of Roman justice, and municipal duties involving many things that were innocuous or at least *adiaphora* (matters of indifference) and in which a person could "conform to the age" without any risk of sinning. It would be fruitless and boring to enter here into the details regarding the mores and practices of the Romans (to whom the apostle wrote this epistle) or of the Greeks, Syrians, or Egyptians. Under the general expression "this present age," Paul understood the pagan manner of living: mores centered on idolatry, superstition, luxury, vanity, pomp, ambition, and sensuality—all the lusts of the flesh that have their origin in such values and causes. There is a certain worldly style that shows itself in outward things: a way of living characterized by pride, display, vanity, and fleshly desires—a secular spirit far removed from the simplicity, purity, and modesty of a Christian. Anything of this sort and everything that has its origin in these kinds of carnal lusts is what the apostle calls "the present age" or "the course of this world" (Eph. 2:2). Certain of these things have faded away with the destruction of pagan idolatry, superstition, and the ancient way of life that sustained these vices. While paganism was dominant, Tertullian [ca. 155–ca. 240], Cyprian [ca. 200–258], and the canons of the ancient synods took great care to promote Christian purity and warned the faithful against many scandalous practices. But although many of the behaviors castigated by these zealous men still continue, they cannot be defined with precision by anyone. No one is able to describe precisely how far a Christian is permitted to give himself over to the pleasures of the table. No exact rule can be set as to how far one may indulge in outward things such as matters of dress when it has nothing to do with necessity or utility but only questions of fashion, comfort, or beauty. We should keep in mind that custom might make something (e.g., a form of dress) necessary for one person, whereas for someone else it might not only be unnecessary but simply pomp and display. We must consider social differences: people differ in wealth and resources, in rank, in the honors and tokens of social status that are customary among men. Such is life. These distinctions stumble no one and are not sinful in themselves.

In all situations, the critical thing is to recognize up to what point something is in keeping with the principles of Christian discipline and modesty or is not. If our conscience is well instructed and if our reason (judgment) is pure, holy, and uncorrupted in what it approves or condemns, then we will have a sense of how the principle of moderation applies to this or that particular instance. Worldly values and secular mores have particular characteristics by which a Christian can recognize them. If your conscience is pure and unaffected by worldly lusts, it will readily teach you to recognize worldliness. And if one mistrusts his own judgment, here is a sure guide that each can follow and not go astray. Keep farther away rather than closer to the things that worldly people use and twist to indulge their pride, vanity, self-display, and lust. I refer, of course, to things not sinful in themselves. The more that you study modesty and the more restrictedly and cautiously you use your liberty, then the more surely you will walk, the more tranquil will be your conscience, and the less you will sin (or at least give sins and vices less occasion). The way of a man in Christ is the way of modesty and self-restraint. Such is the way the saints follow who are always on their guard to avoid falling into sin. As we read in Isaiah 35:8, "A highway will be there and a way that will be called 'the holy way.' No impure person will walk along it." No matter how great one's self-restraint, who is not alarmed at the view of so many dangers? It is indeed incredibly difficult to resist the torrent of worldly lusts and to keep oneself from being dragged off by the violence of the waves of temptation. On the raging sea of this world, we often face crises on every side and frightful vortices.

## 6. Heavy Cares and Anxieties That Disturb the Soul

Everyone will understand that I am speaking here about the cares, worries, and excessive anxiety that we sometimes have for the temporary and perishable things of this passing life: worldly things that have to do with our temporal condition. These anxieties arise on the one hand either from an excessive love of things such as wealth, honors, health, our social standing, or our posterity, or on the other hand from a lack of confidence in God's favor, protection, and providence. This is a dangerous vice because it disturbs the life of a man in Christ, which, where truly lived, is joined to peace, serenity, consolation, and joy. Anxiety stifles the progress of sanctification. This is why the Lord Christ and His apostles always took care to warn their disciples against this vice and to guard themselves against its noxious effects on their spiritual condition: "Take care of yourselves so that your hearts might not be weighed down…with the cares of this life" (Luke 21:34). The Lord warns against having too many cares and excessive worries about the needs of this bodily life (cf. Matt. 13:22). "Therefore I say to you, do not be worried about your lives [that is your animal life], what you will eat or what you will drink; nor be concerned about your bodies, what you will wear, etc." (Matt. 6:25). Again we read, "Be anxious about nothing, but in all things, through prayer and petition with thanksgiving, let your requests be made known to God" (Phil. 4:6) and "Cast all your worry upon Him, because He is concerned about you" (1 Peter 5:7). This is an allusion to Psalm 37:5, "Commit your way to the LORD; trust in Him, and He will bring it about" (cf. Ps. 55:23).

There is, of course, a proper solicitude, a necessary and praiseworthy care that each must have for the preservation of his life and the maintenance of his family. Reason, nature itself, and the links of our social life demand such concern from each of us. Christianity is not opposed to a man fulfilling his own needs through the honest and legitimate means established by nature and civil laws. Such is the duty of people of every social status. But this concern must not exceed its proper limits, which are (1) when you have carefully and diligently done everything that can be expected of you, you must leave the rest to God; (2) you must not carry these anxieties for an overly long time; (3) you must not worry about things that God has reserved exclusively to His own providence; and (4) take care that your concern not become excessive, not disturb your mind, and not involve too great an attachment to the goods of this age or too little trust in God as I warned earlier. Overmuch concern for the things of this life disturbs the entire condition of the soul, draws it away from God toward earthly things (which entirely occupy the mind), and allows no place for any spiritual exercise. The overwhelming weight of these cares depresses the soul, making it incapable of rising up toward things that are spiritual and heavenly, drawing it toward earthly things as if by a magnet. Spiritual exercise and training demands a free soul that does not neglect temporal matters but is not overmuch attached to them—one that trusts God and His providence toward His own. An unencumbered mind esteems spiritual and celestial things more than perishable and passing matters and regards some things as worthy of no attention whatsoever. This state of mind is particularly appropriate to the new spiritual economy: "Therefore if the Son will set you free, you will be truly liberated" (John 8:36); "We do not look at the things that are visible but those that are invisible, for the visible are temporary while the invisible are eternal" (2 Cor. 4:18); "Occupy yourself with the things above, not the things of earth" (Col. 3:2).

Established by the laws of providence, the order of nature teaches prudent people that it is useless to fret ourselves into anxiety. On the one hand, it happens again and again that in our most desperate situations something unforeseen happens to make a way of escape. And on the other, even when we take the most vigilant measures in keeping with human caution, it regularly happens that an infinite number of unforeseen incidents befall us and dash our hopes. How much better to entrust ourselves entirely to the care and goodwill of our heavenly Father, who continually watches over the needs of men and who never lacks tenderness and perfect affection toward His own!

### 7. Rivalries, Quarrels, and Disputes, Especially with Christian Brothers

Such is the unhappiness of our human condition that it is difficult to avoid disputes and contentions with our fellow citizens. And it often happens that in a doubtful matter each one views things in his own favor, and the matter must be brought to a judge for an equitable decision in accordance with the laws of civil society. It is possible, however, for a person to engage these things with such moderation that the soul is not troubled and the parties are not alienated nor come to have bitterness, animosity, or hatred for each other.

Something similar happens in church affairs and spiritual matters. Differences of doctrine and of convictions can give birth to schisms, divisions, and controversies. And from these in turn arise disputes, accusations, and wranglings. Brother may cause injury to brother through bitter words, disrespectful gestures, or hurtful publications against the other, which results in the cooling of love, hatred, strife, and contention, during which it is very difficult to maintain a peaceable and equitable condition of spirit. In serious disputes about religion, even those made necessary and unavoidable, it is almost impossible to take part without a perturbation of the soul, a disturbance that causes the mind to lose its tranquility, joy, and consolation—the gentle and placid influences of divine grace that are comparable to the blowing of a light breeze (1 Kings 19:12). I would add that even in a just cause this agitation of soul often brings with it depraved affections such as envy, jealousy, or ambition. These and other such affections darken the light of the soul, covering it in mist and shadows, and often open the door to great sins and enormous scandals. It follows, therefore, that for a person to be protected in the communion of God, three precautions are necessary.

First of all, except for those that the glory of God, the cause of truth, or the defense of our honor or rights unavoidably demand of us, we must abstain from all disputes in civil or spiritual society that are not absolutely necessary.

Consequently, we must forgive all the wrongs and injustices that people do to us, unless the public good or our own interests necessarily require us to call for an accounting. We must pardon without seeking any vindication or even the desire for vengeance; we must rather put to death and extinguish any such affections springing up in ourselves. This is the perfect law of love, the royal law of the kingdom of Christ that the Lord Jesus prescribes and demands so strongly of all His disciples as the "bond of perfectness" (to use the apostle's phrase in Col. 3:14). For this is the order that the divine Savior has established and settled in His house, His school, His kingdom: all those who are members must constantly provide to other people a continual example of love, concord, unity, and perfect equity and fairness, which is of the greatest possible benefit to human society. Such is the pure and perfect reasonableness that rules in all Christ's teaching and is of much greater merit than the principles of the Pythagoreans, so vaunted among the ancients. Inquire and judge for yourself if God's instructions have any goal apart from this (Matt. 5:38–48): "Let all bitterness, rage, anger, strife, and cutting speech be put away from you along with all malice. Be kind to one another, merciful, and forgiving one another even as God in Christ has forgiven you" (Eph. 4:31–32); "Bear with one another, and pardon each other if anyone has a quarrel with another" (Col. 3:13). This, too, is the model that the Lord Jesus has set for us in the form of prayer that He gave us in Matthew 6:12.

We must also diligently guard against giving others reason to hate, quarrel, or dispute with us. Rather, both in word and deed we must bear ourselves and treat others with sweetness, charity, and moderation. And we must do nothing against the honor or reputation of anyone. Ministers and other teachers must keep themselves from the vile and harmful affection of ambition. They must not put on airs of superiority or mastery over those whom the Lord has put in their care or seek to subject to their own particular opinions those who are the Lord's freedmen. Let them carefully avoid teaching novelties and paradoxes for the sake of vainglory. Such only stumble the brethren and come off as absurd to those who disagree. In teaching they must avoid trying to distinguish themselves from a principle of vainglory but gladly think and speak as others do. Paul warns, "Let no man put down or take advantage of his brother in any matter [i.e., usurping mastery, rule, primacy, or dominion over him]" (1 Thess. 4:6); "Do nothing because of vain glory, but, in humbleness of mind, esteem others as better than yourselves" (Phil. 2:3; cf. James 3:14; 4); and "I beg you, brothers, in the name of our Lord Christ Jesus, that you all might speak the same thing, and that there might be no divisions among you, but you might be joined in the same mind and the same point of view" (1 Cor. 1:10). Similar things exist everywhere in Scripture.

Second, we must carefully examine ourselves whenever we would engage in a dispute for the glory or the truth of God. If necessity calls us to defend the fundamental principles of the faith or the teachings of the church that have been recklessly attacked, or if our reputation has been ravaged unjustly, we must examine ourselves. With what spirit and attitude are we engaging these things? What are our real concerns and affections? It is not fitting for a minister of Jesus Christ to be quarrelsome, pugnacious, or contentious, engaging in disputes and debates not required by God's honor and the church's need. All agree that at certain times a person cannot remain silent without being one of the "dumb dogs" Isaiah speaks about (Isa. 56:10). But we must take care not to substitute our cause for the cause of God or mix in our cause under the pretext of battling for the truth. We might want to seem to be battling for the truth but be deluded by our own desires. Ambition, envy, rivalry, and self-love are so often involved in such matters! Those who do this consciously fall into hypocrisy, that serious vice abominable to God and the saints. But those who do it thoughtlessly or ignorantly are not for that reason free from blame. Indeed, they expose themselves to the just judgment of God, who at the proper time will demand a reckoning for the injuries committed against the brethren: "Those who make a man out to be an offender for a word [i.e., small thing]" (Isa. 29:21); "Against an elder do not receive an accusation unless it be with two or three witnesses" (1 Tim. 5:19); "Let us not be desirous of vain glory, provoking one another, envying one another" (Gal. 5:26); "For he [i.e., Pilate] knew that it was out of envy that they had delivered Him [i.e., Jesus] up" (Matt. 27:18). The history of the church in every period teaches that this has been not only a very serious but a very common sin.

Third, if absolute necessity calls us into disputes and proceedings, we must go about it with such moderation and in such a restrained fashion that it is obvious to everyone that we are enemies of the cause and not of persons. Whenever we combat errors, we must always show consideration for the honor and reputation of their authors, seeking their repentance, conversion, and welfare. We must not make lesser errors seem great nor serious errors worse, but we must use the "balance of the sanctuary" in weighing every matter, using as much restraint as the matter permits. "The servant of the Lord must not strike out, but be gentle with all people, able to teach bad people with tolerance and to instruct with gentleness those whose minds are opposed" (2 Tim. 2:24). What then? Did the apostle forget this when he wrote to Titus, "Rebuke them sharply [or severely], that they may be sound in the faith" (Titus 1:13)? Certainly not. If we are dealing with impudent, proud, ambitious, slanderous, false, mocking, blasphemous, and obstinate people, those whose intentions are clearly evil, Christ's minister may indeed sharpen his pen and with severe and weighty words restrain and rebuke the arrogance, pride, insolence, recklessness, and all the other vices of the hotheads who contradict (Titus 1:9).

Therefore, if our disputes are carried out within such limits, they will disturb our souls much less, and they will not wound our consciences. But if we go beyond these bounds there is no doubt that our spiritual life will suffer considerably. Those who breach these limits will surely fall into some scandal or vice.

## 8. All Occasions for Sinning Whatsoever

The believer living in the world of this age must view himself as a man walking through thickets of brambles and thorns. If he does not carefully watch himself, they will easily stick to him and do him harm. Similarly, spiritual prudence means being attentive carefully to avoid all occasions for sinning. No one is such a stranger to himself that he is ignorant of the type of wanderings and missteps his corrupt nature inclines him to, a nature subdued by grace in regeneration but not entirely eliminated and extinguished. Each person knows the weakest point of his flesh, that susceptible place where Satan aims his most powerful stabs and attacks. The most certain way to protect and uphold the state of your spiritual life is to constantly be on your guard, carefully noting and prudently avoiding any occasion that would stir up the remnants of your old and vitiated nature. This is the "prudence of the saints," of which I have already spoken above (cf. Job 28:28; Prov. 9:10; Matt. 10:16).

The Lord Jesus Himself advises this when He teaches us to pray in the prayer He gave us, "Lead us not into temptation" (Matt. 6:13). This means the following: (1) Give us grace by Your Spirit so that we might not expose ourselves recklessly, foolishly, or carelessly to be tempted by Satan, but that we might prudently flee from all occasions of wandering or slipping into sin. (2) If it so happens that in keeping with divine providence we find ourselves, through no fault or vice of our own, in certain places or with certain companions where we cannot avoid being exposed to temptation, sustain us by Your grace that we might not succumb, but rather, roused, inspired, and armed by divine grace, that we might come forth not just victors but "more than conquerors through Him who loved us" (Rom. 8:37). As the apostle says in Ephesians 5:15, "Be careful to walk circumspectly, not as fools, but as wise." The truly strong man is not the one who proudly seeks out a duel or a battle, trusting in his own abilities and vainly displaying his strength; the truly courageous Christian is the one who with a firm mind is ready for the enemy's attack, and when duty or necessity calls, he endures the assault, parries the blow, and triumphs.

# CHAPTER 12

## Prayer and the Word of God

In the spiritual life it is not enough for a person to carefully avoid temptations, vices, and sins. It is the duty of a man living in communion with God to progress in the race, to confirm and promote his spiritual standing, and to bring his sanctification to completion in the fear of God. Many things are involved in a person's progress in the spiritual life, and we have already considered many foundational matters. We have seen how God in His grace gives to believers a knowledge of spiritual things, prudence of judgment, the ability to pray, the appreciation for preaching, the capacity to moderate their affections and to pursue good works. In this chapter I want to consider in detail the means of promoting sanctification, which consists particularly in the purity of one's affections and actions: "Since we have such promises, dear ones, let us purify ourselves from all uncleaness of the flesh and the spirit, perfecting sanctification in the fear of God" (2 Cor. 7:1); "Not that I have already achieved or become perfect, but I seek to take hold even as I have been taken hold of," to which he adds, "forgetting what is behind I focus on what is before me" (Phil. 3:12–13). He reaches forth with his full attention on the things which are in front of him: "Meditate on these things. Give yourself to them so that your progress might be manifest to everyone" (1 Tim. 4:15; cf. 2 Peter 1:5).

As we consider what Scripture teaches about our sanctification, we will begin with the following presupposition about all the saints on this earth. Though Christians are regenerated by divine grace, even when they have been solidly confirmed in their faith by much practice, none of them attains to such a stage of perfection that they may dare to glory of being freed from all sin and vice or of having arrived at the spiritual summit. Indeed, nowhere in the Word of God is the stage of perfection for saints in this life defined or set forth. Rather, each has the duty to strive and stretch toward the summit.

Among the saints both in Old and New Testament times [*œconomiae*] there have been outstanding persons, utterly filled with the Spirit of God, upright men, consecrated to God, and devoted to divine matters by long practice who have made great progress toward holiness and spiritual perfection. But who can persuade himself (mindful of his human condition and weakness) that he has attained to that state which Paul himself denies ever having attained? Continual experience in this life confirms what the Lord's apostle says clearly: "We all stumble in many things" (James 3:2). If we measure the purity of our actions in the presence of God, how difficult it is in the business of our lives to regulate just our tongues so as not to sin with our words! How truly difficult it is to control the direction of the internal thoughts of our minds so that they are not besmirched by any vanity, lust, or sinful affection so that we can offer them to God as pure sacrifices.

Furthermore, we sin not only by commission but by omission. The duties that each person has toward God and toward neighbor depend on one's circumstances. These demand such careful attention and continual vigilance that who without arrogance can say, "I am pure and there is no iniquity with me" (Job 33:9)? Job comes close to speaking in this way, but even he does not claim the perfection we are speaking of. Indeed, none of the saints is so keen-sighted so as to perceive all his faults (Ps. 19:13). All of us fall short in our duties. We all have very many flaws and defects, both accomplished Christians and beginners. The greatest among us is the one who seeks to purge himself from all impurity of the flesh and to progress daily in true sanctification. He employs the necessary *means* that serve this purpose. Though almost everyone knows what they are, it is beneficial to review them.

As is proper, I put *prayer* in the first place among the means of promoting sanctification: that most holy exercise by which the godly soul joins itself to God, ascends to God as by stairs to heaven itself, and (as from a flowing watercourse) draws for itself divine grace. Surely there is no more glorious exercise for a man (who is mortal, ashes and dust, a sinner from the womb) than to dare appear before the very throne of God on the basis of the divine grace that is offered to him in Christ Jesus, by the merit of His obedience and the support of His intercession. In prayer the believer both brings his requests to God with confidence as to a good father and joins in the choirs of the angels to celebrate the mighty works and the benefits that he has received from God's divine majesty. I understand *prayer* in a broad way. It refers to everything we communicate to God. This includes our petitions for the good things necessary for this life and for piety, our appeals for God to avert the threat of bad things, our intercessions for others, our thanksgivings for the benefits He has bestowed, and our glorifying and celebrating the divine excellencies, perfections, grandeur, and majesty. Such is the teaching of the apostle in 1 Timothy 2:1 and Philippians 4:6.

The holy exercise of prayer makes up the first part of rational religion (which is to say *spiritual* religion), and it is not only recommended but indeed commanded throughout Scripture as the means of perfecting and completing our sanctification. Prayer is recommended by our conscience and demanded by our needs. We could almost say that apart from this means of prayer there is no grace that God communicates to human beings. The Lord opens to the one who knocks. He is found by the one who seeks. The first of all things the Holy Spirit teaches a person by secret grace is this very thing: to knock and to seek. Such is the first spiritual movement of a person who has been alienated from God. The response of prayer opens the door to communion with Him (cf. Matt. 7:7; Luke 18:1–14; 1 Thess. 5:17; James 5:13).

There are various types of prayer. Public prayers are spoken to God in the assemblies of the saints. Domestic prayers are the appointed times that the head of the household leads. Private prayers are when each person by himself worshipfully honors God and asks for His strength and His grace. We can also speak about our fixed and ordinary prayers (carried out in the presence of God at certain set times of the day such as morning and evening or also midday, as was the practice of the ancients; see Ps. 55:17; Dan. 6:10) and our extraordinary prayers. These occasional prayers are when a person is persuaded to pray from his pressing need or a strong sense of the benefits he has received from God and casts himself on God as the Holy Spirit stirs up good and noble feelings in his mind. With regard to private prayer in particular, I have in mind those times when the godly soul exercises the freest relations and most intimate commerce with God, experiencing the large influences of His grace.

Prayers, made with requisite devotion and in keeping with scriptural principles, are the most useful means for promoting sanctification because they never lack effect if they are offered in accordance with the will of God. It is a characteristic of God to "hear prayer" (Ps. 65:2). The Lord Jesus emphasized the importance and effectiveness of prayer as did the apostles after Him: "But I say to you, ask and it will be given to you; seek and you will find; knock and it will be opened to you. For whoever asks receives; and whoever seeks finds; and whoever knocks, it will be opened to him" (Luke 11:9–10); "Truly, truly I say to you, whatever you ask My Father in My name He will give to you" (John 16:23); "If any of you lacks wisdom, let him ask it from God who without reproach gives generously to all" (James 1:5).

Prayers, supplications, and thanksgivings poured out before God from a sincere heart have an excellent effect on a person's spiritual life. They mold and dispose the soul toward all kinds of good affections and praiseworthy actions. Nearness to God sanctifies the soul. A person is never nearer to God than when in prayer he rises up from earth to heaven and stands before the very presence of His throne. Speaking to God in prayer, a person holds intimate communication and exercises a secret commerce with Him. As you pray you are sanctified through nearness and communion with the glory of God, even as the face of Moses shone after he had spoken with God (Ex. 29:43; 34:29). You feel and experience that it is "good…to draw near to God" (Ps. 73:28). Your thoughts are purified. Your love for God is stirred up. You are led to contemplate His glory. Your mind is drawn away from earthly and perishable things and inspired to nobly seek out and generously expend itself for the great things that please God. You are able to calm yourself and restrain vain lusts and the rush of turbulent affections. In sum, a light extends through your mind and sets it aflame for the cultivation of all godliness and every virtue.

But if prayers and praises to God are to produce such salutary effects, one must perform them in accordance with the will of God and the rule of the heavenly sanctuary. It is not as though any prayer offered is automatically pleasing to God. The Holy Spirit in Malachi 2:3 calls the prayers of ungodly, impure, and hypocritical people "dung." Isaiah calls them an "abomination" (Isa. 1:13). Even those who are in communion with God and the church can pray improperly and "ask amiss," as James 4:3 reminds us. There is an art to praying well that can only be learned in the school of the saints. "And this is the confidence that we have with God, that, if we ask anything according to His will, He listens to us" (1 John 5:14). This art, so different from those that can be attained through human brilliance and cultivation, is set forth in the precepts of Christ Jesus, the examples of the saints, and by spiritual prudence. The apostles understood this well and so asked the Lord Jesus to teach it to them (Luke 11:1).

A detailed discussion of prayer is not possible here. There are, of course, well-known principles about prayer that I cannot develop, such as the importance of the interior attitude and disposition of the one who would engage in this spiritual duty (i.e., that prayers must be offered from a pure heart and pure hands—that is, with no evil clinging to hands or thoughts). One must pray in faith, in the name of Christ Jesus, with filial trust (the confidence of a child before his father), with a reverent attitude, without hypocrisy, without showiness, and in spirit and truth. Also, our prayers must be adapted to the promises of grace that God has made to us: we are to ask nothing but what God wants us to ask. That is, we are to ask only what He has promised.

Taking for granted such basic matters, I would like to write briefly about a particular kind of private prayer, when a person closes the door and directs himself to God in friendly intercourse and familiar exchange, as the Lord said in Matthew 6:6, "But when you would pour out prayers, enter into your chamber and close the door. Pray in secret to your Father, and your Father who sees you in secret will reward you openly."

The first thing necessary in this type of praying is that the person should set forth all his needs frankly and intimately before God, just as they are, with proper reverence and submission, not concealing anything. In the school of the saints, this is called "pouring out the heart," laying out one's mind entirely in the presence of God. "O you people, pour out your heart before His face!" (Ps. 62:8; cf. Ps. 42:4; Isa. 26:16). The godly soul, alone with God and regarding Him as a caring father, comes humbly before His throne and takes no great care with what words to speak or the arrangement of what to say (as one must do in public prayers) other than that which easily comes to mind. He simply prays, humbly and with confidence, using whatever words his own affections suggest as he is standing before God. Does his supplication require a confession of his sins? The believing soul will not be silent, lie, or cover his faults (Ps. 32:5). He will not justify or minimize his wrongdoings but fully and frankly set them forth before God with all his heart. In his requests, he will tell God his every need and lack, all the pressing circumstances he finds himself in, his temptations, dangers, and fears. He asks God what he should seek or not seek, and what he should prioritize for the glory of God, the public good, or his own benefit. Even though the heavenly Father knows all these things, He wants to be asked before He responds. He loves to see childlike confidence in His people, the filial affection characteristic of His own.

The second thing necessary is that these prayers should be poured forth ardently and seriously, not weakly and carelessly. "The effective prayer of a just person is very strong" (James 5:16)—that is, a prayer expressed with focus and zeal. No one among mortals is exempt from having his inward state of mind influenced by a diversity of affections that impact what he does, including his spiritual activities. It is not always possible to say with the holy man in Psalm 57:7, "My heart is prepared, O God, my heart is prepared. I will sing and give praise." The lessening of zeal and focus, as often happens in prayer, may arise from one's temperament, a lack of divine grace, or from sinful emotions and dispositions that stifle and repress a person's appreciation and desire for spiritually good things. But wherever this weakness and carelessness of spirit stems from, everyone should realize that to get an answer from God he should pray for it zealously and seriously. James reminds us of the same thing: "Let him ask in faith without hesitating" (James 1:6)—that is, not uncertainly or in a doubtful or unfocused frame of mind. He must ask ardently and in such a way that it is obvious that he is persuaded of the urgency and necessity of the good thing that he wants to gain from God.

The third and final thing I want to underline about prayer is that when we are praying and making supplications (assuming we are doing so in good conscience and for good things necessary for our condition), we must be insistent with God; we must not give up making request of Him until He has answered our prayers. This is beautifully expressed in Luke 18:1, where the Lord told a parable, "that it was necessary to pray always and not to grow sluggish." Such is the teaching of the apostle in 1 Thessalonians 5:17: "Pray without stopping." Paul illustrated this doctrine with his own example, as he often remarks in his letters (Col. 1:9; 2 Thess. 1:3).

This kind of importunity, incessantly continuing in a petition, might seem inappropriate with fellow humans. If a person has been denied two or three times but continues to insist and repeat his request, he might be considered shameless, lacking in honor and civility. But the reception hall of the court of heaven does not take it so. It is proper not only to pray but to plead, to demand, to request insistently and continually, even as a beggar does. This is not displeasing but pleasing to God. When God puts off responding to His people's first and second requests, He is provoking them to more ardent prayers and deeper desires. He tests and uncovers the internal affections of their minds and persuades them of their great need and misery. And He confirms and strengthens their trust in His grace, goodness, and paternal care for His own. The remarkable example of the Canaanite woman in Matthew 15:22–28 underlines this. She turned her initial sharp rejection by Christ to her own advantage. The holy man prayed in this attitude: "O LORD, God of my salvation, I cry to You by day, and my prayer is before You at night" (Ps. 88:1); "Continue tenaciously in prayer; be attentive in it as you give thanks" (Col. 4:2); As Peter was in prison, "prayer was made for him by the church intensely and tenaciously to God" (Acts 12:5); Cornelius was "a devout man…who assiduously interceded with God in supplications" (Acts 10:2). If you seek divine grace in this way, if you implore His strength, and if you insistently press your case while prostrate before His throne, you will triumph. Through prayer you will receive a hearing. You will overcome, and by assaulting and wrestling after the example of your father Jacob, you will conquer the unconquerable One.

We will now consider the second means for strengthening and promoting sanctification and the spiritual life: *reading, meditation*, and *rumination* on the Word: "'My Spirit which is upon you and My words which I have put in your mouth will not depart from your mouth nor from the mouth of your descendants, nor from the mouth of your descendants' descendants,' says the LORD, 'from this time and forever'" (Isa. 59:21); "Your words were brought to me, and I ate them. And Your words were the joy and happiness of my heart" (Jer. 15:16); "Let the word of Christ dwell in your hearts with all wisdom" (Col. 3:16); "And from boyhood you have known the sacred Scriptures which can bring you wisdom for salvation" (2 Tim. 3:15; cf. Isa. 34:16; John 5:39; Acts 17:2; 2 Peter 1:19; Rev. 1:3).

It seems to me that this holy exercise can be considered in two ways: either as a duty to which all are called by God's command or as a very useful means for promoting the spiritual life. Here I focus on the latter. The reading of God's Word is a means for illuminating our minds, for growing in knowledge and wisdom, for strengthening our faith and hope, for promoting our sanctification, for purging our affections, for gaining comfort and consolation, and for directing all our actions with true spiritual prudence. These are among the many purposes for which the Word of God has been given to the race of mortals—truly a benefit of infinite price (cf. Ps. 19:8–11; 2 Tim. 3:16).

All those gifted with healthy judgment and persuaded of the divine origin and authority of the Word have recognized it to be a treasure whose value is impossible to conceive. Though God had instructed the human race about the way to live through reason, man willingly plunged himself into the most profound darkness from which no one could ever expect escape. How good of God to make the light of His Word shine into the world and under the new economy to disseminate it to all nations, so that now no mortal should lack a guiding light as he makes his way through the gloomy darkness of this life. Assuredly the Word of God is the light of God (Ps. 119:105). He who reads it hears God speaking to him: he converses with God and with Christ Jesus Himself. He recognizes in the voice and writings of the prophets and apostles the very voice of the Holy Spirit. This Word is the fountain of life for him. It is medicine for his mind. It is food for his spirit. He finds here the delights of the celestial paradise.

In Scripture there is nothing inferior or cheap, nothing fictitious or far-fetched, nothing false or mistaken, nothing dry or sterile. Everything is valuable, pure, solid, and nourishing. If the meaning of certain texts is profound and difficult, this only serves to stimulate our curiosity, deepen our meditations, and sharpen our reflections on Scripture. In short, the Bible expresses divine wisdom in every part and is worthy of its author, the most exalted and most rational God. "The sayings of the LORD are pure, silver refined in a tile oven, purified sevenfold" (Ps. 12:6).

Reading the Word of God is a means for advancing in sanctification and holiness and is a practice established by God Himself. It affects one's entire spiritual life. Experience itself teaches that everyone who gives himself to meditating on the Word of God comes away from the exercise a better person—more knowledgeable, humbler, more holy, better prepared for the conduct of life. For the presence of God, which he hears speaking in the Word, affects him and inspires him with reverence for God. The glory of God shines out to him. As a person reads and meditates on Scripture, the Spirit of God who inspired it influences him. Through the Word, the Spirit sanctifies such a person, strengthens him, comforts him, confirms his faith and hope, represses his vain lusts, and quiets his turbulent and wandering feelings. The Spirit stirs up every good affection in that person and furnishes him with the prudence and self-control necessary to face the attacks of Satan and the temptations of the world. The excellent Psalm 119 celebrates this universal experience of the saints.

But these fruits should not be expected from merely opening up and perusing the Bible. The divine Word must be approached conscientiously in keeping with its distinctive qualities. The spiritual discipline of reading Scripture must be approached according to the "rule of the sanctuary," as God Himself requires, just like the exercise of prayer. The reader should apply himself to this exercise carefully and with reverence for God: approaching the Scriptures with a pure mind free from prejudices and preconceptions; ardently desiring a true understanding; having his mind composed, calm, and humble; and submitting himself to God in faith and love. He must take up the reading not unwillingly but gladly, with pleasure and delight. Reading Scripture is not just pronouncing words aloud but carefully considering and reflecting on what is said. Many passages of Scripture will arrest us, and we should suck the sweetness from the flowers as the bees do.

What we read from Scripture should be ruminated, carefully recalled, and compared with other parts of the divine Word so that we may grow solidly and securely. We must meditate on the text, inwardly digesting it and turning it into part of our own substance. To read in this way is to eat the word of the Lord (Jer. 15:16; Ezek. 3:1; Rev. 10:9). It is to "drink from the fountains of salvation" (Isa. 12:3), to "feed in luxuriant and green pastures" (Ps. 23:2), and to "eat pure food" (Isa. 30:24). Text after text affirms that those who chew on Scripture will never come away empty, because the Word of God truly satisfies and fills its readers.

CHAPTER 13

Holy Singing, Public Worship,
the Fellowship of the Saints,
Self-Examination, Solitude, and Fasting

The *singing* of God's praises is a third means of advancing sanctification, an excellent and salutary practice that we can properly call
psalmody. *Holy singing*[1] is a practice highly recommended in the books
of both Old Testament and New Testament economies, both as a duty
owed to God (being an aspect of spiritual worship) and as a means of
promoting our spiritual condition. As with prayer and the reading of
the Word of God, we can consider holy singing under both of these
categories. But I will focus on it here as a means for growing in the
spiritual life: "Sing to Him; sing psalms to Him; consider and tell all
the amazing things He has done" (Ps. 105:2); "Speak to one another
[he uses an expression from Ps. 145:11] in psalms [the songs of the
saints often sung in ancient times with the accompaniment of musical
instruments] and hymns [often sung a cappella in praise and celebration of God] and spiritual songs [carefully composed choruses on a
variety of subjects], as you sing and chant in your heart to the Lord"
(Eph. 5:19); "Let the word of Christ dwell in you richly with all wisdom, as you teach and build up each other through psalms, hymns and
spiritual songs, singing with grace in your hearts to the Lord" (Col.
3:16); "Is any among you sick in spirit? He should pray. Is any in a
healthy mind and happy? He should sing psalms" (James 5:13).

Although there is no explicit reference to the practice of singing in
the precepts of Christ Jesus, it was established as a religious observance
in His day. Not only during the time of the Old Testament sanctuary

---

1. This is rendered "le Chant des Psaumes" in the French version.

but also in the period of the synagogue, even the reading of Scripture and prayer were generally cantillated or chanted. The Lord left in place earlier practices that did not conflict with the economy of the church that He had come to establish. He Himself, when He was celebrating the Passover with His disciples, sang the Great Hallel (Matt. 26:30). It cannot be doubted that Christ customarily took His part in the other religious festivals of the time. His practice of singing was in keeping with the state of humiliation of Christ Jesus even as was the practice of prayer and supplication.

Do I really need to list the examples of the saints of ancient times in support of what I am saying? Do we not have the example of the angels themselves? Nature itself impels us to lift our voice and sing when our minds have been freed from grief, sadness, or anxiety, or when we are affected by a strong sense of some benefit received. The very capacity to sing, forming sounds and modulating our voices in a thousand ways, is an invitation for us to do so. So excellent is the divine nature; so outstanding are His perfections, powers, and works; and so many are the benefits He has showered on the human race, that we never lack reasons for putting forth the greatest, most glorious, and most excellent praises, celebrations, and thanksgivings possible. The things said in Psalm 145:3 on this subject are magnificent: "Great is the LORD, and greatly to be praised; and His greatness is unsearchable." If certain species of birds, having been instructed by the author of nature, know how to make sweet and delightful sounds purely from instinct and without rational thought, they are setting an example for us in carrying out this duty. How much more should a human being, using the rational part of his nature that the Holy Scripture calls his "glory," employ his mouth and tongue to celebrate God and to tell of His marvelous deeds? "Awake, my glory; awake, psaltery and harp!" (Ps. 57:8).

Holy singing, whether public or private, is a most beneficial means for promoting sanctification and furthering one's spiritual condition. One author said about singing in church,

> Through a type of pleasure, singing arouses in the soul the burning desire to possess what is being celebrated in the song. It calms the boiling affections of the flesh. It banishes the evil thoughts that our invisible enemies inject into us. Singing irrigates the soul for the

production of the divine fruits of good works. It makes us noble conquerors and encourages us to constancy in the face of adversity. It provides a medicine for the godly in the face of all the sad and grievous things that befall us in this life.[2]

Let me illustrate a few of these useful thoughts.

First of all, singing calms the condition of our minds. We all know that holy songs are composed on a variety of topics. And whether we are celebrating the praises of God and the benefits that He has lavished on us, expressing our supplications to God, praising Him for freeing the godly and judging the godless by means of crises throughout the experience of the church, or setting forth in song godly doctrine, singing composes our turbulent affections and produces all sorts of good, bright, and grateful feelings in us. I am speaking, of course, of songs that are not irreverent but serious, not effeminate but strong, not bawdy or wild but well composed. Such singing brings our minds peace and soothes and comforts our spirits. It pushes out the boiling feelings of sin and puts an end to the soul's wearying restlessness.

Each of us knows how songs powerfully stir our feelings. For this reason, singing has been practiced among all peoples everywhere from ancient times. Songs produce a variety of feelings according to their varied subjects and kinds and can either be beneficial or injurious to us. Since songs cannot be composed or performed without feeling, singing stirs our feelings more than reading does.[3] If a song is vapid, mushy, superficial, crude, or lascivious, it excites the lusts of the flesh and the vices that dominate one's corrupt nature. Such pieces inflame a person's bodily appetites, self-indulgence, wrath, desire for revenge, impudence, shamelessness, and similarly twisted affections and impulses. On the other hand, if a song is well-composed, serious, noble, masculine, and well-themed, it composes the mind and brings serenity to a person. It stirs in him an emotion of love toward God, a reverence for His majestic greatness, a sense of gratitude for all His benefits, a humble and modest acknowledgment of His own

---

2. Vitringa cites this source anonymously.

3. The French reads, "Since therefore one cannot compose songs without a certain flame that has something of enthusiasm in it, from this it arises that singing stirs one's feelings much more than reading."

unworthiness, and a confidence in the goodness of God. Singing inspires and inflames the person with zeal to practice virtue and good works. If a person prepares himself and has the proper attitude, singing to the Lord reforms the mind and disposes the soul toward God, as the inspired writer has said: "O God, my heart is prepared; I will sing and give praise, even with my glory" (Ps. 108:1). That is, may the rational part of me express itself in intelligible sound through the use of my tongue (Ps. 49:3).

Second, I think that holy singing, more than almost any other spiritual exercise, serves to mold the mind and impress it with good affections, emotions, and intentions, which very much support the quest for sanctification, purity, and virtue. Many people have the vice of not reflecting or meditating on what they read or hear. Too many people's thoughts wander off topic when they read or listen to preaching. They do not focus or use their imagination attentively. This fault may be a question of temperament. It may arise from a lack of practice in thoughtful meditation. This defect very much hinders solid progress in the spiritual life as people lightly skip through what they are reading or listening to, give it only cursory consideration, and hurry on quickly to new objects. But the best remedy for this shortcoming is singing, especially worthwhile and well-composed songs. This is an excellent means of getting the singers to carefully consider what they are expressing in song. The singers meditate on the content, which embeds itself in their minds. Hebrew words for singing often suggest meditating, humming, or carefully reviewing something. "I will meditate on Your amazing acts" (Ps. 145:5; see also Ps. 105:2).

In the early and wilder ages of the world, when people wanted to keep alive the deeds of famous men and notable occurrences, they would put these accomplishments into songs or chants and commit them to memory. This is how all the ancients transferred things to posterity, and the Hebrews were no exception. History shows that Arius composed songs to popularize his doctrines (opposed to the commonly held faith of the church) and that Augustine followed the same example in carrying on his dispute with the Donatists. When the perfections, excellence, dignity, and majesty of God are set forth and the benefits He showers on mortals are proclaimed in song, our souls are stirred toward godliness and filled with strength and constancy. The imprint of great things remains fixed in the mind for a long time. Since it makes such a lively impression, holy singing is a most useful means for advancing one's spiritual condition.

Third, I would add that holy singing is especially helpful for disentangling our thought life. The person taken up with psalmody is freed from vain, frivolous, useless, and sinful thoughts that often upset our state of mind when we are not on our guard, and from the new inducements to stumble that present themselves to our minds almost continually. It is hard to regulate and govern the thoughts and lusts of the mind. Only with difficulty can even those who are experienced in the ways of God and have made some progress in the spiritual life guard themselves so that disorderly thoughts and lusts do not get aroused in the mind and put down their roots there. But it is extraordinarily challenging to eliminate these irregular longings and wandering thoughts when free time and leisure open the door. Therefore, it is a very useful practice to keep your mind occupied with solid thoughts when it is free from other business or when you are engaged in manual labor or things that require no special mental attention. A spiritual exercise such as singing helps the saints to distract their minds from futile, false, and petty things and to fix them on God.

Holy singing has been an extremely ancient practice in the school of the saints. Although it may be the first recorded, it is not necessary to believe that the thanksgiving song by which Moses and the Israelites sang in choirs responsively to celebrate the benefit of their liberation from Egypt was the first of its type (Ex. 15). Throughout the entire period of the old economy, saints of both sexes have provided us with praiseworthy examples. And from the collection of these songs in the histories and the book of Psalms, we of the present period gain immense benefits and comforts. For in the book of Psalms we learn how strong the spiritual life was in them, how solid was their faith and hope, and how lively their ardor and zeal for God. We understand the inner affections and movements of their good hearts and their experience of His ways—all from this book as from a treasure chamber of infinite value.

Even as the Old Testament period was coming to an end, the practice of holy singing was strongly established among the Jews. Philo supports this by referring to one group who "not only make time for contemplation but compose songs and hymns of praise to God in a variety of meters and tunes, producing melodies of a serious and majestic tone as is appropriate." The Christians of the first centuries customarily composed hymns in praise of God and of Christ Jesus along with instructive songs explaining the hope of the godly and the unhappy destiny of the godless, and had skilled singers present these songs a cappella. Often one would begin and then the others would join in (a custom to which the apostle refers in 1 Cor. 14:26, "Each of you has a psalm"). From the epistles of Pliny [ca. 61–ca. 113], Tertullian, and Eusebius [ca. 262–ca. 340] (not to mention many others) it is certain that singing was admitted as a regular part of early Christian worship services.

It would not be proper to omit those outstanding men of the Reformation who gave themselves to the work of restoring religion (which had nearly collapsed). In this effort they used the exercise of singing to stir up true life in the souls of men that were not only lukewarm but frigid and nearly dead. This is what Jan Hus [ca. 1369–1415] did, that notable and true martyr of Jesus Christ. He composed hymns and lyrics of various kinds, which he taught to the people and connected to particular tunes. His hymns were not only doxological but didactic, and through them he taught the people the foundational points of religion. He often used melodies taken from Gregorian chants since the people were accustomed to this means for expressing holy things. Among all the congregations that separated themselves from the Roman communion, none have been more diligent in developing the use of singing than the praiseworthy Bohemian Brethren, true sons of Hus. In the sixteenth century, when their congregations were in a flourishing condition, 743 songs for pious purposes were in use among them. The use of spiritual songs would thrive wherever they took up residence. It was a widespread practice among all these people to praise God. And in Bohemia, Moravia, or wherever they found themselves, and despite all the discrimination and afflictions they endured, they never lost this comfort, and they were never abandoned by God.

What more shall I say? Many of the men called by God to purify religion and reform the church in the century after Hus did not neglect this salutary means. They employed singing with equal success to instill the people with spiritual teaching, sanctify their affections, and lift them out of the spiritual torpor and frigidity so common when Christianity was corrupted and had fallen to pieces. Ulrich Zwingli [1484–1531], Leo Jud [1482–1542], Wolfgang Capito [1478–1541], and Justus Jonas [1493–1555] were outstanding men in this regard. Luther deserves great praise for the promotion of holy singing, along with all the churches of the Augsburg Confession following his discipline. In addition to the psalms of David, they composed a great variety of songs on holy subjects. These hymns were accommodated to the temper of the people's minds and to the state of the particular churches, but the goal was always to encourage piety.

It is proper to honor the great achievements of the Germans, but they are not the only ones to be praised in these matters. Once the pure gospel had spread its light over the vast and flourishing kingdom of France, no historian could pass over the incredible zeal and devotion with which people promoted this holy exercise and the benefits it procured for the godly. Clement Marot [1496–1544], one of the chamberlains to King Francis I, turned the first book of the Psalter into French meter with great success by the help of the learned François Vatable [d. 1547]. The rest were versified by Theodore Beza [1519–1605]. Claude Goudimel [ca. 1517–1572], a man of eminent ability in the art of music, provided outstanding tunes perfectly adapted to these songs. In this way the lyrics can be sung melodiously, not to weak or effeminate tunes but in a manner consistent with true religion—that is, strong, manly, well ordered, majestic, and dignified.

From the mid-sixteenth century, Reformed believers of France were moved to great joy by these psalms and began to praise God publicly. They sang not just in the holy assemblies but also in their homes and wherever they went: at work, on journeys, at table, and at bedtime. But this stirred up such hatred on the part of those who followed Roman superstitions that even if these melodies had always been sung with proper seriousness, the singers were oppressed and persecuted wherever possible. The blameless practice of singing psalms inspired by the Holy Spirit came to be regarded as a peculiarity of being (as the singers were called) heretics. In reality, the matter was quite different.

These were people affected by the truth of the gospel and zealous for purity in religion.

This practice carried over into Flanders, Belgium, and the Low Countries, where French verses were adapted to the local language so that the same tunes could be used. All I have described required an unbelievable amount of effort, but it was the undertaking of people who had stepped forth into the light after having been sunk in darkness. And they delighted in this type of holy singing as something that would contribute to the progress of the gospel and the benefit of others. The indifference of their posterity and the coldness of Christians today is deserving of censure: such singing is almost only heard in the public assemblies. If in treating this subject of holy singing I have gone beyond the proper limits of this short book, it is to stir up in lukewarm souls and frigid minds a pious and sincere desire to follow the outstanding example of our ancestors to whose prudence, godliness, and zeal (having been ignited by God) we owe the precious benefit of the Reformation—that is, purified religion.

All the means for promoting sanctification that I have considered thus far in our discussion are involved in *public religious worship*, which I will now consider as our fourth subject. The components of what an individual does in private worship are not very different from those of public worship. The worship offered is of the same kind and nature in both. (The matter was very different in Old Testament times. Under the old economy the role of external, ritual, public worship was much more important. And it was so tied to the tabernacle or temple that it was forbidden to be offered in another place.) From whatever point of view you consider it, the public worship of the true religion (celebrated properly in accordance with the divine law) is something holy, grand, and admirable. This is true whether you look at public worship as a duty owed to God and required by the law, as a symbol of the confession of our faith and hope, as a means for obtaining God's favor, or as a help for promoting sanctification. This last perspective will take up our attention now—public worship as a means for promoting holiness. Christian worship (if performed as it should be) is outstandingly holy, pure, sacred, reasonable, and spiritual. And the conscience of all mortals who have any remnant of religious affections in them approves and commends it. Even outsiders coming into the holy assemblies are moved to worship God and to confess that God is indeed among Christian worshipers (1 Cor. 14:24–25). In what follows, I will now briefly consider divine worship strictly as a means for advancing sanctification.

First of all, the Lord Christ has promised to those who gather in His name not only an abundant outpouring of His grace but His very presence as well. "I say again, if two of you agree on earth regarding any matter you ask about, it will be done for them by My Father who is in heaven. For when two or three are gathered in My name, there I am in their midst" (Matt. 18:19–20; this saying is confirmed in Luke 24:36; John 20:19, 26; and Acts 2). Such an outlook was shared by the saints under the old economy who had the very same hope: "Blessed are those who frequently come to Your house; they will continually be celebrating You" (Ps. 84:4). Where Christ Jesus is present, He is there with His Spirit and His grace. There He illumines minds. He lifts up souls. He sanctifies them, and they are consoled. He hears those who call on His name. There in grace He reveals Himself to a person. He stimulates in that soul an affection for Himself. There in public worship He offers Himself to the believing soul to be contemplated in all His glory and to be marveled at in all His beauty. "When I saw You in the sanctuary, I was looking at Your power and Your glory [God's power here refers to His grace by which He gives righteousness to sinners]" (Ps. 63:2). Do not doubt that Christ is speaking and testifying to the pious soul in public worship. There is no one who has not experienced the truth of Christ's promise to be in the midst of the brethren as they come together in His name. All believers are acquainted with this. On the other hand, why be surprised if a person not seeking Christ does not find Him? Or if a person turns away his eyes and does not see Him? Or if a person not extending his hands does not receive the benefits of His grace? Should it shock you if a person who knowingly and willingly stops up every portal of his soul against the light and the divine grace so accessible in public worship does not receive Christ's gracious influences?

Second, in public worship the principal means for confirming the spiritual life and promoting holiness are administered. For this reason (among other similarly beneficial purposes), public worship was instituted, ordained, and commended to the saints (Heb. 10:25). It is here that ministers and pastors, who are (if they carry out their duty properly) the overseers and healers of souls and the "stewards of the mysteries of God," distribute the bread of spiritual life in accordance with the needs and troubles of every person. Here in public worship they teach truth and refute error, they convict and reprove, they appeal and warn, and they console. From time to time, if the topic and occasion demands, they thunder and strike like lightning. But weak, heavy-laden, and afflicted souls they nourish, encourage, lift up, and support with comfort and consolation. Those who are presumptuous and proud they expose and restrain. They stimulate those who are inactive. They strike fear into those who tenaciously indulge themselves in vice and depravity. They push forward those who are sluggish and lazy. The thoughts of the heart and the inner workings of the conscience they expose to view the deep workings of vanity and malice and the corruptions that lay hidden in the inmost chambers of the heart. They call the minds of their listeners to the tribunal of God and of their own conscience. To the unresponsive they expose their own deformed condition and everything that they are trying to hide from themselves, even if they hate listening. But pastors lead those who are convicted and broken by the message, submissive and reverent toward God, and concerned about their duty to the fountains of gospel consolation, the springs of living water from which they can drink abundantly.

Here in public worship the pious soul, having come to know God as He is revealed in Christ Jesus, celebrates His benefits with purity of affection and sings His praises with sincerity and gusto. Here the believer brings his prayers, thanksgivings, and supplications to the very throne of God. He presents himself before the Lord in the holy of holies, pouring out all the concerns of his soul before Him as to a loving father, with filial confidence and childlike trust. Here the sacraments (marks and symbols of grace that remind us of the benefits that we have received from the Lord and of our duties to Him) are set forth publicly and distributed to believers as confirmatory signs in order to strengthen their faith and hope. They were instituted to fortify our trust and assurance. And last of all, if the sacred acts of public worship are carried out with appropriate order, reverence, care, and the mutual love that binds the brethren together, then each believer furnishes an example that benefits his neighbor, and each one enjoys communion with the other. Each one acts to arouse and enliven others, and this greatly fosters the godliness and sanctification of each participant. For we humans are more quickened and stimulated by example than by instructions and warnings. Jacob provided an exemplary attitude for us regarding public worship when he said, "This place must be treated as holy! This is certainly the house of God and the gate of heaven" (Gen. 28:17).

Here is a third benefit of public worship: when a soul is occupied with sacred things, it is freed to be taken up with God alone. It is disengaged from the affairs of the world and particularly from the vanities of this present age, which are difficult to avoid in the busyness of human life. The assembly of the saints (properly ordered and reformed in accordance with the discipline of the kingdom of Christ) has an air of the heavenly communion in it, particularly now under the new economy. A person in the congregation of believers is taken into the chamber of the heavenly sanctuary and has a communion in the sacred things prefigured by that first room in the temple that was called the holy place. And since the veil between the holy and the most holy place has now been removed, all things shine out clearly in our services of public worship. The believing soul finds itself in the very presence of God and comes under His influence. Separated from the world, it forgets its vanities. Separated from the world, it is no longer polluted by the world. Brought away from earth to heaven, that soul now is taken up with heavenly things. Those who are in public worship see the glory of Christ and say with Peter in Matthew 17:4, "Lord, it is good for us to be here," and with the holy prophet in Psalm 133:1, "Behold, how good and how enjoyable it is when brothers dwell together!" We cry out that God is certainly "the fountain of life, and in His light, light breaks forth" (Ps. 36:9).

In public worship we are in school for the study of salvation. Here we find the bath of regeneration. Let me particularly emphasize this point: God often gives to His people in worship a foretaste of the celestial delights of paradise. He affects and moves them by a powerful and intimate influence of His grace so that they find themselves carried outside of themselves and transported to the heavenly realms.

Forgetting all concerns for worldly things, they find in God their all in all. They are taken up with Him, filled with comfort from Him, and inflamed by a love for Him: "Blessed is the one You choose and make to come near You so that he may live in Your courts. We will be satisfied with the goodness of Your house, Your holy temple" (Ps. 65:4); "They will be irrigated by the richness of Your house, and from the torrent of Your pleasures You will give them drink" (Ps. 36:8). This is the reason why the people of God (those concerned about finding salvation and true comfort), when forced to be absent from the public meetings of the saints where the pure religion is set forth, have such a burning desire to return and share again in this communion of the saints. Among many other texts that show this attitude, Psalm 84 depicts it clearly. But let no one approach public worship without a fitting attitude: a pure mind and a proper respect for God and the holy exercises.

Let me not neglect writing something about a fifth means of great usefulness for progressing in sanctification: *the fellowship of the saints*. This sharing and partnership can be very helpful for piety and growing in holiness if one goes about it properly and does not turn aside from the ends for which it is intended. I am not referring here to the public meetings that are a part of all believers' participation in worship together. Nor am I speaking about the variety of normal social contacts we have with our fellow citizens because of our mutual duties, social customs, and common interests. I am talking about the friendly fellowship that takes place between two or more persons who have similar characteristics, a like frame of mind, and shared interests, and who begin to pursue praiseworthy goals together.

It is, of course, true that because I am a Christian I have a strong and indissoluble bond to all those who are in the Lord. All of us who are in Christ are members of the same body and stones in the same house, and therefore none can refuse to extend to another any honest duty of charity and humanity required by this bond. But the intimacy of private friendship is a different matter. No one is required by force of the law of Christ Jesus to develop familiar personal relations with everyone indiscriminately. For entering into this kind of close communion, it is not enough to be members of the same city or church or even to have the same faith and hope. What is clearly required is to have similar temperaments, to be like each other in character, to share a common disposition and spirit, and to be in a similar status.

Many close friendships come about from having the same needs and pursuing the same goals. The more things people have in common, the tighter the bond between them will be. What is particularly necessary is commonality of character and attitude joined to an equality of status and condition. Perfect friendship generally exists between those who share the same rank and privileges; it is rarely found between people of widely varying social status. Even among people of the same status and who have the same interests, perfect likeness of character and mind is very rare, owing to the fact that the most-wise Creator delights to display diversity in all the individual products of His work. Even between those who seem similar and have comparable gifts, it is difficult to find a person whose spirit resembles your own or who is a true analogy to yourself. And so, with those in civil society and even with those in the state of grace, it is difficult to find people with whom one can develop close friendship. We are restricted to those who share the same disposition and judgment as ourselves. And this limits us to a few close friends since being in the state of grace amends and purifies but does not destroy and remake the natures and minds of men.

Beloved, if you find a friend who is good, sincere, faithful, honest, gentle, humble, godly, similar to you in temperament and spirit, sharing with you in Christ's grace, seeking the same goals as you, committed to sharing the same responsibilities, and oriented to the same pursuits as you are, then foster this friendship. Cherish this friend and hold close to him (though, of course, sensibly and in accordance with your circumstances). Attach yourself to that friend with such constancy and propriety that he may never have cause to blame you or doubt your faithfulness. In sum, treat him as Jonathan did David. This will profit you greatly as you run your race in the Lord. It is enormously beneficial both from the pleasure you will have from this kind of honest fellowship as well as from its usefulness, which is not paltry.

Just as bad company is damaging, so good company is edifying. Inasmuch as the one harms your sanctification, so the other results in your growth and progress in sound doctrine and virtue. The wise man in Ecclesiastes 4:9–12 says beautifully, "Two are better than one, because they have a good wage from their labor [i.e., they can do more by aiming at the same goal]. For instance, if they fall, one will lift up his partner [i.e., by mutual admonition, correction and faithful exhortation to repentance so that a person does not remain in the state of sin into which he has fallen]. But woe to the one who is alone when he falls and has no other to lift him. Also, when two lie together they keep each other warm. [They stir each other up to good work through holy jealousy and honest competition, and through their exhortations and mutual help they chase away any spiritual coldness and lukewarmness.] And if one alone is confronted by a stronger one, two shall stand against him [If Satan comes upon them through temptations and worldly lusts, they will drive and keep him away, overcoming him through their united watchfulness, prayers, and efforts. And how much stronger will they be if they take Christ Jesus Himself as their partner and ally!]. And a threefold cord is not quickly broken." How great is the fruit of fellowship and familiarity with friends who are striving for the same goal as we are! This is why the godly man says, "I am a partner with all who reverence You and keep Your precepts" (Ps. 119:63; cf. Ps. 122:1).

I consider *self-examination* to be a sixth means for advancing in sanctification. The daily survey of one's conscience is so beneficial for progress in virtue that it was often commended by the pagan sages. What is more useful than self-examination after the labors and occupations of the day are finished? What is more in keeping with reason than a person composing his mind in the presence of God and concluding the day in a pious exercise in which he reviews not only what happened to him that day but also his own accomplishments and actions? Here you subject yourself to examination: Where did you make progress, and where did you fall back? What in your words and deeds tended to the glory and praise of God, the benefit and edification of others, or your own true benefit? Where did you hold back, and where did you fall? If you failed, to what do you ascribe the failing? Where did you make greater or lesser use of the grace of God? If you find that you have left a duty undone or utterly failed at some point, then do not be slow to repent. Diligently seek cleansing for this fault and make a firm

resolution to be more attentive in the future, to avoid this temptation, and to flee from this occasion for sinning. You will never regret
this practice of self-examination. "I will meditate with my heart in the
night, and my spirit will search carefully" (Ps. 77:6). "Let us search out
and make a careful investigation of our ways" (Lam. 3:40; cf. Zeph.
2:1; 2 Cor. 13:5).

I would include *solitude*[4] as a seventh means of promoting sanctification. I will say a few words in support of retreating from society
from time to time for holy exercises. But I am no way in favor of the
practices of those called hermits or solitaries, who withdraw into unin-
habited deserts and inhospitable mountains where they try to work
out their own salvation through fasting and prayers. They may have
obtained a grand reputation for holiness among the masses, which is
perhaps what they were seeking. But before the third century (and
starting with Paul of Thebes [ca. 227–341], who entered into such iso-
lation by necessity as he fled from persecution) there are no examples
in the church of this type of life. The example some take from John
the Baptist, Elijah, and Elisha is not truly germane to the discussion of
solitude. God did not create men to live for themselves alone but with
the goal of benefiting others. He always wants men to work out their
salvation in such a way that human society benefits through the virile
efforts of each. Each person is to "put out at interest" the talents committed to him (see Matt. 25:27). The gifts that divine providence has
given to each man should be employed for others, resulting in thanksgiving. It is more authentic to exercise humanity by living among men
than to cast off humanity, live among beasts, and benefit no one.

The solitude I wish to commend as an aid for progressing in sanctification is not only that one should abstain from too frequent and
unnecessary dealings with worldly people but also to be temperate
in spending time with praiseworthy people. Solitude means that a
believer loves to be with himself, to dialogue with himself, to always
have honest business to occupy himself, to make use of faithful friends
as necessary, but never to be burdensome to them and never to waste
time (our most precious resource according to the ancients) that

---

4. "La Retraite" in the French version.

should be spent on weightier matters. The notable saying of the sage is relevant here, "The one who separates himself seeks that which is desirable. He gives himself over to every good thing" (Prov. 18:1). How blessed is he who can be free from the press of business to give himself to pursue true wisdom!

A bad conscience flees solitude and seeks out society in order to block out its own accusations. It seeks to distract itself through company and to fend off the inward stings. But the person whose mind is good and upright does not fear being alone since he has no reproach to make against himself. He has no need to search outside for a tranquility that he can find in himself. He has within something to refresh and renew himself. Solitude and silence are dear and pleasant to him. He enjoys a peace and tranquility of soul that easily overcomes all the sought-after pleasures of the world. Solitude is certainly necessary if you want to give yourself to prayers, holy exercises, and humbling yourself and the state of your mind before God. The Lord Jesus Himself retired by night into an inner chamber or a deserted place in order to pray (Mark 1:35; Matt. 14:23). The prophet too commends this: "It is good for a man to bear the yoke when he is in the age of youth. Let him sit alone and be silent, for He [God] has laid it on him" (Lam. 3:27–28).

Finally, and in the eighth place among means for advancing in sanctification, I would recommend the spiritual practice well known since ancient times: *fasting*. This religious exercise can be considered from two points of view. It can be considered either as part of public religious practice or as a means of fostering an individual's spiritual growth. When there is a time of public calamity, the magistrate or the leaders of the church may call for solemn fasting. As presented in the scriptural histories and writings of the prophets, such fasting is a public religious duty. The church humbles itself before God with a confession of sins, and by abstaining from food and drink, it makes supplication before God and testifies that it is not only unworthy of all the supports of this temporal life but of life itself. Those who wish to commend themselves to God humbly and reverently will not neglect to observe this religious practice when called to it.

But this is not really the type of fasting I would emphasize here. I suggest that fasting (i.e., a religious abstaining from food or drink) can be a means of living more freely and easily in the state of grace and of helping us carry out our religious duties in a more perfect and natural manner, as the Lord would have it. Those who abstain from food and drink or use them more sparingly are better prepared for prayer, meditation on holy things, and every other religious duty. This is how the saints at the beginning of the new economy made use of fasting. Luke says about the prophets and teachers of the church at Antioch (including Paul and Barnabas) that "as they carried out their religious duties and fasted, the Holy Ghost said…" (Acts 13:2); "When they had ordained elders in every church, and had prayed with fasting…" (Acts 14:23). And the apostle Paul says, "Do not deprive one another except by agreement so that you might have free time for fasting and prayer" (1 Cor. 7:5).

It is true that neither consuming nor abstaining from food or drink commends us to God (1 Cor. 8:8). And since fasting should be a spiritual exercise where a person humbles his mind before God and sincerely seeks cleansing from his faults, when a person engages in fasting with detestable hypocrisy, it provokes God's indignation greatly (Isa. 58:3–14). But if you engage in fasting with the proper attitude and goal, at the proper times and places, without seeking witnesses, and as a support in carrying out your private or public religious duties, then there is much in the practice that is praiseworthy. Our fasting is an outward demonstration of the deep respect that we have for God and the practices by which we honor Him. Fasting helps restrain and check the lust of the flesh. It helps compose the soul, curb our sinful passions, and settle our twisted emotions. It woos our mind away from fleshly things, draws us closer to God, and makes us more prepared for contemplating spiritual things as they really are. It helps make us more open to receiving the enlightening influence of the grace of the Holy Spirit. Separated from the flesh, our frame of mind comes closer to God. Such a state of soul is extremely profitable as we come and pour out our prayers before God. This is why the ancients rightly connected the practice of fasting to praying.

CHAPTER 14

Celibacy, Voluntary Poverty,
and Obedience to Superiors?

The various means of advancing in sanctification that I have taken up thus far are not complex, hard to understand matters. Anyone in the state of grace is acquainted with them. It is also the case that every act of virtue, every duty carried out in accordance with the law of Christ, becomes a means of obtaining a higher degree of perfection and sanctification. Just as those who cling to and live in vice do not stay at the same level but proceed "into worse ungodliness" (2 Tim. 2:16), so also those who run the race of virtue are always making progress. And from one act of virtue they find persuasion, help, and encouragement for another one.

But during the time in which Christianity had already begun to degenerate from its early simplicity and purity, and as the church began to be governed more by zeal than by prudence, the opinion insinuated itself into the minds of men that there were certain distinctive means for obtaining the very highest state of spiritual perfection, and that these means were different from the ordinary, common means for progressing in holiness. They taught that there is a state of highest completion and accomplishment, which they called the state of evangelical perfection, and that this is distinct from the common state of perfection that is required of every Christian in keeping with the precepts of Christ Jesus and the apostles. Then they made this state of highest perfection consist in celibacy, voluntary poverty (in which one distributes all his goods to the poor or to the public), and obedience to one's superiors in the monastic life (which they appropriately but forebodingly called blind obedience). This opinion became very

strong after the establishment of the monastic orders in the fourth
century from the example of Anthony (ca. 251–356), and it took such
strong hold of people's minds that it almost became (indeed, it did
become) a rule of faith. One cannot say that in the third and even in
the second century there were not examples of people who abstained
from marriage (e.g., certain bishops as well as virgins who consecrated
their virginity to God). And there were those who practiced severe
self-denial in giving away the goods and advantages of this life. But the
example of Anthony was not immediately followed, and there was no
system in place to manage this particular way of living. (Paul of Thebes, as I mentioned above, did not enter on this way of living in order
to gain merit but out of necessity.) This lifestyle was not widespread
until the fourth century.

The hypotheses on which this system has been constructed seem
impressive but are specious. The foundational assumption is that there
are two distinct kinds of moral perfection. The first is common: this is
the ordinary state that involves faith, sanctification, and regeneration.
It is required of all people by the law of Christ Jesus. Without it no one
can hope for communion with God or a share in His salvation in this
life, nor expect to obtain eternal glory in the life to come. The second
moral perfection is special, particular, higher, and more sublime: this
they call *evangelical*. It is commended not as a requirement of the law
but as a recommendation of Christ Jesus and the apostles for those
who aspire to enter into the highest level of perfection. God wishes to
honor and remunerate those who attain to this degree of perfection by
giving them a fuller measure of glory than that which will be enjoyed
by the mass of believers in the future state of bliss. God has left it
completely to the free will of each whether or not he wishes to aspire
to this higher stage. Any person can refuse without sinning or losing
his salvation. But those who strive for the highest stage will shine with
well-deserved preeminence in the eyes of God and of the saints and
will have greater praise and greater hope.

In this conception there is something similar between the spiritual
life and the experience of a servant or day laborer. When he completes
the work that was agreed, a worker has the right to demand the salary that was promised to him. But he would be counted worthy to

be praised and honored more fully if he were extra diligent and went beyond what was expected of him. The one who willingly goes further and does what he knows is pleasing distinguishes himself by his greater obedience to his master. We see the same thing with the schoolboy. To be considered among the good and diligent students, it is enough to do what is required by the teacher. But the one who, moved purely by his own free will, continues to love and advance in his studies particularly pleases his teacher and deserves his greater affection and the widest possible recognition and praise for his diligence. Among the teachers of the Western church, none has so often or so strongly urged these hypotheses (i.e., foundational ideas) than Jerome [347–420, translator of the Vulgate], who imbibed them from Eastern teachers (having spent the greater portion of his life in the East).

It comes as no surprise that so many people filled with religious zeal followed this path. They gave all their goods to the poor or for the strengthening of the church. They abstained from marriage, bid farewell to the world, and went away into deserted places where they could devote themselves exclusively to work out their salvation in a place hidden away from society. Others went into monasteries where they could be free for holy exercises, earning just what they needed by manual labor, donating the rest to the poor, living under the rule of a spiritual director, dwelling with others in a community under certain laws, and vowing to obey in all things the one whom they had chosen. Such was the origin of the communal monasteries.

Given the assumptions about evangelical perfection, it is no wonder that people acted this way. Now, what person concerned to make progress in the spiritual life would not want to arrive at the highest degree of perfection if he were shown that the way to gaining that high status was not beyond his own abilities? In other areas of life, people often refuse to undergo the struggle necessary to enter the front ranks, whether in the sciences or careers that lead to political power and economic wealth. People turn their backs on the labors that one must undertake and the burdens that one must bear in order to be successful in gaining such fame. People may feel that they lack the necessary abilities to achieve these high positions in the world. They remain skeptical that one can entertain hopes of such glories through easy and comfortable means.

But now they hear that that state of "evangelical perfection" can be obtained by a minimum of inconvenience and without great difficulty. All of these means to achieve it are of a negative nature, and each involves some self-denial or sacrifice that almost anyone might consider to be within his power. Is there a person who desires glory from God and longs to enjoy His favor who would reject standing in such an exceptional and high place? This belief that would assign us the first rank among those who share in the communion and grace of God is so sweet and soothes the mind so pleasantly! It assures us that we will have a greater position and a larger share of the heavenly glory than the common herd of believers.

Who is surprised then that men would choose such a lifestyle and make themselves outstanding by austere habits and discipline (particularly the hermits)? In this way they are lifted up and celebrated everywhere as divine, great, wondrous, saintly, and perfected. Even in the best of men such titles would serve as fodder for self-importance and the inducement to prideful ambition. Of course, it had that effect in people inclined toward vanity and a lust for glory (such as the Greeks and particularly the Egyptians). Having said this, I do not intend to cast suspicion on the motives of all the early practitioners of this discipline indiscriminately. Judgment belongs to the Lord and not to us.

You may ask, by what reasoning were the ancients led to these hypotheses about a dual status in the Christian's perfection? What induced them to make such assumptions about a distinct "evangelical perfection"? Two passages in the writings of the New Testament were particularly brought forward in support of this understanding: The first is the Lord's statement to the young man in which He gives him, or so it seems, counsel about how to obtain the highest perfection (Matt. 19:21). The second is in 1 Corinthians 7:25–40, where the apostle distinguishes between the conditions of the celibate and the married life, compares them, and clearly makes his preference known for the former. The apostle says about the unmarried state, "It is good for a person to remain in that condition" (1 Cor. 7:26).

Additionally, this hypothesis seems to be supported by the progressive nature of Christian perfection. For the state of moral perfection under the economy of grace admits degrees. One man can be holy and another holier. One man can be accomplished and another more accomplished. Some are more just than others. There are greater or lesser stages of perfection. Surely the one who is weak could become stronger, the one who labors could do so more vigorously, and so forth. In Christ Jesus there are children, young men, and adults. And since the glory of the future life will be dispensed by the just judge in strict proportion with the degree of perfection and the measure of grace attained in this life, there is a certain logic in believing that those who seek a higher perfection (who have chosen to deny themselves, renounce temporal goods and marriage, and embrace what seems the more perfect state of poverty and celibacy) will obtain in the life to come a more abundant recompense. Because of their outstanding efforts and example in this life, should they not receive a crown in the life to come beyond the glory to be given to believers in common?

To my mind, these arguments concerning degrees of moral perfection carry more weight than the questionable interpretations of passages from Jesus and of Paul put forward in defense of this doctrine. Let us examine the text in Matthew first. To anyone examining the context of the saying in the gospel where the Lord gives counsel to the young man regarding perfection, it is obvious that Christ is not speaking of any superior degree of perfection distinct from the common perfection that He requires of all His followers. He is in fact speaking of that common, evangelical (i.e., gospel-derived) perfection that, stemming from the decree of divine grace, is connected to eternal salvation. This is precisely what the young man had asked: "What good thing shall I do, so that I might have eternal life?" (Matt. 19:16). The man did not have in mind some greater degree of glory in heaven. And the Lord told him that he could have no hope of eternal life at all if he rejected His counsel (or to express it more accurately, the precept that He laid down for him). This is what Jesus underlines as He immediately says to His disciples in verse 23, "Truly I say to you that a rich man will enter the kingdom of heaven difficultly." So, is it necessary for everyone who aspires to communion in the celestial kingdom to sell everything and give it to the poor, which was the law for the obtaining of salvation that the Lord imposed on the young man? Certainly not. This precept was given privately to the young man as a test. It was accommodated to the state of his soul, which the Lord knew intimately. Having been imbued with the principles of the Pharisaical system, he boasts in verse 20 that he had kept all the precepts of the law from his childhood on. Because he thought that he had already attained to that state of complete perfection that the Mosaic discipline required, it pleased Jesus Christ, who perceived his inner state, to rebuke his pride through revealing his inner condition to himself. He showed him the state of his own soul and declared clearly to him that it was impossible to hope for any share in the kingdom of God or to have any dependable hope of entering into eternal life unless he was healed from the sickness of his soul that he was laboring under—that is, the vice that controlled him: his excessive love toward earthly things. Jesus showed him that he could not be healed of this sickness unless he completely renounced not only all his goods but even his very self and submitted himself completely under the discipline and direction of Christ. From this we can deduce the following principle: that an excessive desire or lust toward the good things of the earth is inconsistent with the state of the spiritual life; that is, no one deserves to take his place among the disciples of the Lord Christ who, when convinced of his duty, is not prepared to let go of his riches and expend them for clearly required uses and needs.

Now let us examine what Paul says. In short, it is ignorant and prejudiced to use what the apostle says about the married and celibate conditions of life in support of the doctrine that celibacy is a means to "evangelical perfection." It should be obvious to a person reading 1 Corinthians 7 that Paul is not speaking about higher or lesser states of moral good but of physical states or conditions. He is speaking about what condition of life was easier or more suitable to the stressful times in which Christianity found itself—what social condition was more or less fitting "in view of the approaching crisis," as he puts it in 1 Corinthians 7:26.

He is not at all suggesting that there is more or less perfection in either state of life; it is not a question of virtue or vice in either case. He is addressing which form of life is easier and which more difficult—what are the advantages and disadvantages in both the celibate and married conditions. He says something very similar to the widows at the end of his discourse in verse 40, "She is more blessed [that is happier] if she remains as she is," because, as he says in verse 28, "Those who marry will have worldly troubles, and I would spare you that." By remaining a widow, she will free herself from the many troubles and burdens that come with married life.

On this point Jerome loses himself in vain subtleties and is, one might almost say, beside himself. As he disputes with Jovinianus, he cites 1 Corinthians 7:1, where the apostle says, "It is good for a man not to touch a woman." And he draws out the following consequences: "If it is good for a man not to touch a woman, then it must be an evil to touch her. For there is no good except what is contrary to an evil. If therefore it is an evil but permitted and pardonable, then it must be allowed in order that nothing worse comes about."[1] This is as if you were to say that it is good (or not good) to govern the republic, that it was good to consecrate oneself to God in the service of the church, that it was good to make voyages to faraway regions, or six hundred other such assertions of this sort, and then conclude with the learned man that it was an evil not to do these things, and furthermore, go on to assert that this evil is a vice! This argument is like taking the apostle's saying in 1 Timothy 3:1, "Those who aspire to be an overseer aspire to a good work," and then making the inference, "If a person does not aspire to become an overseer he desires an evil thing." O Jerome, has God, who is the author of the conjugal union of husband and wife, so ordered things that the entire human race is obliged to engage in sin in order to reproduce itself?

The apostle says that it is a good thing for a man not to touch a woman because the celibate state of life has its advantages. And if a person can remain in that state without sinning, it permits an ease and usefulness greater than that of the married state. But the conjugal state is by no means condemned as an evil thing, much less as a vice. We should notice that as the apostle speaks in 1 Corinthians 7:25 of the condition of virgins, he says that he has no command from the Lord

---

1. Jerome, *Contra Jovinianus*, book 1, section 7.

but gives his opinion. So what does this imply? If the Lord Christ had indeed laid down a doctrine or given recommendations regarding a supposed state of perfection that should be desired above all things, sought with the utmost care, and part of this was celibacy, would the apostle be ignorant of it? Surely not! It follows, therefore, that all these hypotheses about a supposed double state of perfection for the Christian of which the ancients boasted so much were absolutely unknown to the Lord Christ and the apostles since there is no trace of it in their writings. And it is impossible to doubt that if this hypothesis of a double state were true, it would appear in their writings since it was the goal of all their teaching to bring people to holiness and the highest moral perfection.

Now I will respond to the arguments set forth for this doctrine from the progressive nature of Christian perfection. And I will need more than a few words to handle this debate accurately since there are implicit questions that need to be explained and resolved. I regard the following as proven: (a) that the state of moral perfection under the economy of grace admits of degrees, not with regard to the source and origin of the spiritual life (which admits no degrees or variation) but with regard to the circumstances and accidents of this life; and (b) that the state of glory in the future life is in keeping with the state of grace in this life (i.e., in the divine judgment, one's condition in glory will be in just and equitable proportion to the grace one has received in this life). Furthermore, I deny the following (though others regard them as true): (a) that there are different types and categories of moral perfection in the economy of grace; (b) that there exists (or even can be conceived) a state of human perfection in the economy of grace that falls outside the precept and law of Christ; (c) that celibacy, voluntary poverty, and obedience in all things to a spiritual director are properly to be commended as certain and universal means for attaining the highest stage of moral perfection (the first stage of which is attained by all true disciples of Christ Jesus).

In contrast, I maintain and defend the following hypotheses (foundational assumptions) in accordance with the pure doctrine of the Lord and His apostles: (a) That moral perfection is of a single type and category rather than diverse and distinct types and categories. The kind of perfection to which all the saints are called indiscriminately is of a single type, in keeping with the saying of the apostle in Hebrews 6:1: "Let us go on to perfection." (b) That every step and stage of this single type and category of perfection falls under the law of the Lord. Every Christian is obligated to keep Christ's precepts: to strive as much as he can to gain the highest wisdom, to strive for the strongest faith, prudence, and holiness. Each believer is to seek as much purity of soul and moderation of his affections as possible. All of his actions must be equitable, constant in virtue, and free from vices and offenses against all others. Will you deny that everyone must keep himself from sin and vice as much as he is able? That each Christian must devote himself to the work of purifying his soul as much as he is able? Loving, worshiping, honoring, and glorifying God with all his strength and utmost effort? Pressing forward toward the highest degree of self-denial? Since it is true that all believers without distinction are under such an obligation by the law of God and Christ, what shall we say about nuns, monks, and hermits seeking to elevate themselves to the highest stage of the spiritual life through celibacy, voluntary poverty, and obedience to superiors? There exists no highest degree of perfection other than the kind to which all believers are commanded by the law of Christ and to which all are obligated to aspire and strive.

(c) Up to this point we have been able to define things based on solid reasoning. Now it remains to be determined whether or not celibate life, chosen poverty, and blind obedience to superiors can be properly recommended as a means of attaining to that highest grade of common perfection—that is, to that stage of holiness and self-denial to which every believer in Christ is obligated to aspire and to struggle manfully to reach in accordance with the law of Christ Jesus.

First of all, I hold that what is called "blind" obedience toward superiors, abbots, priors, and other spiritual directors in the monastic orders can be dismissed as a means of sanctification. Blind obedience is a sad practice (and even the name is inauspicious if you take it literally). It is absurd and certainly contrary to the state of Christianity, which is a state of light and liberty. It is necessary to obey our leaders (that is, the overseers of the church) as the apostolic writer instructs us in Hebrew 13:17. And it is proper and reasonable that some Christians, particularly those of weaker judgment, may choose someone to serve as their spiritual director and to be guided by their counsel in religious practices. There were numerous examples of this in the ancient church, particularly in Africa. But to give blind obedience is appropriate only for the blind, those who are ignorant of the excellence and dignity of what it means to be a free human being. The apostle said in 1 Corinthians 7:23, "You were bought with a price. Do not become slaves of man." How is it that you, a man who boasts of being set free by Christ Jesus and of being by His precious blood in a state of light and liberty, can submit yourself to utter obedience with your eyes closed to the directions of another mere man like yourself?

*Blind* obedience? Let us take away this word *blind*, and let obedience remain. But it should be a bright, clear, and rational obedience. You must discern whether the counsels suggested by the directors of your spiritual state are rational, in keeping with the Word of God and reason, fitting to your situation, and appropriate for purifying your soul. If so, you will obey them not as a slave but as a freeman, not unthinkingly but intelligently, not blindly but being able to see. In this way you will be rendering complete obedience and submission to Christ Jesus alone who illuminates you by His Spirit and through the preaching of the ministers of His Word. The cry of the saints is, "Send forth Your light and Your truth to lead me and bring me to Your holy mountain and Your tabernacles" (Ps. 43:3); "You will lead me with Your counsel" (Ps. 73:24); "Your word is a lamp to my feet and a light to my path" (Ps. 119:105). Or as Christ Jesus said to the young man, "Follow me" (Matt. 19:21). Let those who follow another take care lest they willingly blind themselves, commit themselves to blind leaders and teachers (the number of whom is tragically great), fall with them over a cliff, and perish miserably (Matt. 15:14). So, we can set aside this matter of blind obedience since it is based on false and dubious interpretations, and now go on to debate the questions of celibacy and poverty.

I do concede that celibacy and voluntary poverty in certain cases and particular circumstances may be means of growth in holiness, but with the following caveats: (a) They do not inevitably produce this effect nor are they infallible, constant, or causal means for progressing in sanctification, but rather they are accidental, occasional, and auxiliary means. (b) They are not universal means, accommodated to the condition of all believers, but rather they are particular and restricted to certain cases. (c) Far from being the most outstanding means of perfecting holiness, they are much inferior to those I have mentioned above if you consider closely what they are. For a person can devote himself to the celibate life and freely chosen poverty and still be outside of Christ; he may lack the love and living faith that characterize the Christian (1 Cor. 13:3). There have always been sects of philosophers within paganism that devoted themselves to this way of living. The same is the case among certain groups within Islam today. None of these, however, have entered into the state of moral perfection that true spirituality demands. (d) Though there are certain things in this way of living that are or at least can be good and commendable, experience has taught us for the most part that its consequences have harmed and blackened the state of Christianity. This lifestyle has caused more scandals and brought more serious shame on the church as a whole than it has benefited individual members. History could furnish me with a myriad of examples. To go into detail is not permitted here, so I will limit myself to the following reflections.

The way of the anchorites (hermits) is not consistent with reason or the law of Christ, as I have suggested above. I have no doubt, however, that in the early years of the movement many entered into it from a good and praiseworthy intention, out of a desire and love for true holiness. But in a short period of time this way of living became corrupted and turned aside from its origins. Great ambition, envy, spiritual pride, trust in the merits of this way of life, contempt for others, absurd practices of every sort, detestable superstitions, and the hypocrisy that cloaks itself best in devotion worked their way in. This lifestyle actually fostered such vices. Being a hermit encouraged men to be lazy, to love leisure and shameful sloth. Loafers and men who had no serviceable talent but who loved public praise found a way of life that suited them rather well. They could just do nothing! Without putting themselves to much trouble, their friends and neighbors would abundantly provide for their needs. And furthermore, they would gain a fine reputation in the minds of the people. Being free from any proper service for the benefit of civil or ecclesiastical society, they found themselves free to join in the factions that have caused so much trouble to the church.

With regard to the monks who live in communities (i.e., ceno-bites), I have a rather different opinion. There is no fault, as I see it, with free cloisters (i.e., open convents or unrestrained monasteries). In such an arrangement, celibate brothers or sisters who are confident that they can remain comfortably in a state of self-control [*continentiae*], following certain rules, dwell in community under the care of a wise and prudent spiritual director. They choose to live together, separated from unnecessary dealings with the world, so they can give themselves to honest work and certain pious exercises for their mutual edification and profit. But in this community they continue in a free condition and do not bind themselves with any vow. A monastic vow is a human invention that restricts Christian liberty too narrowly and thus provides much material for Satan's temptations.

I see no vice in this lifestyle; it could contribute much to a person's advancement in holiness. But experience shows just how difficult it is to maintain this living arrangement in a holy and unpolluted way. How many abuses have crept into monastic living! How many scandals have arisen and crimes have taken place! Though the people may have started with good and serious intentions, much superstition became mixed into cloister life, as can be seen in the majority of monasteries before the breaking forth of the light of the gospel in the time of the Reformation. Though designed by their founders for the intense culti-vation of holiness or the study of sacred literature, they became dens of impurity, indulgence, libido, and laziness. They often became factories for training in vice of all sorts in which the men who lived there had the name of being spiritual, but in their hearts they were carnal. They stuffed themselves and indulged in every lust without restraint. And the reasons for this are not hard to understand. I gladly recognize, however, that the monasteries of the Benedictine Order were better able to maintain their good condition and have served the interests of Christian and of secular literature very well. But if you place against this all the other monkish orders that were founded on superstitions, if you compare this with all those monasteries that later became cor-rupted in remarkable ways, you will become amazed at the capacity of human nature to produce vanity, wantonness, foolishness, and abuse. How subtle are the ways of Satan—drawing men away from the simplicity of the gospel under the pretext of leading them to a more perfect type of life!

Here is a summary of what I have argued in this section: that there is a single type of perfection prescribed for all the disciples of Christ, and toward this each one must bend all his strength. The celibate life may be of help in pursuing a holy life, but only if one can remain in it without exposing himself to temptation. Celibacy itself, however, plays no essential role in perfection or sanctification. It is an accidental and auxiliary aid, not an essential, necessary, or outstanding means for advancing in perfection. Indeed, in the state of marriage one may please God just as much (or often even more) as in the state of celibacy if he manages it honorably and makes use of the truly necessary means for promoting holiness. Consequently, each one should examine his condition with prudent judgment and consider long and hard which state is best suited to his temperament. And I would say the same thing about voluntary poverty. I will not continue further, but if the matter may seem to have been insufficiently discussed, a person may consult what I have written in the "Moral Perfection of Man" and "The Evangelical Perfection of the Christian" in my *Observationum sacrarum.*

CHAPTER 15

# The Chastening Rod of God

To this point I have discussed the means that God has prescribed for the elect to use in advancing the work of sanctification. These means are, so to speak, under believers' own control. But there is a means for correcting and purifying believers of a different kind, which I have only briefly mentioned above. It is a means that God Himself employs toward His own beloved elect to stir them up, reform them, and purify and perfect them if they fail in their duties. It is the *chastening rod of God*. By this rod He restores them to Himself. By this rod He warns His people where they have fallen short and where they have strayed. By this rod He reminds them of their duties and callings, and He humbles, sanctifies, protects, and strengthens them against worse sins and evils. In the school of the saints this type of warning and correction is known as παιδεία (discipline): the reproving switch by which God calls His beloved sons to order and whisks them into shape. We see this in Psalm 89:30–32: "If his sons forsake My law, I will visit their desertion with the rod and their iniquity with blows." This applies not only to David's literal sons but metaphorically to all believers. "My son, do not despise the discipline [παιδεία in Greek] of the LORD. And do not turn away or grow tired of His correction; for the LORD corrects the one He loves, even as a father corrects the son in whom he delights" (Prov. 3:11–12). Note Job 5:17, where Eliphaz says, "Behold, happy is the man whom the LORD corrects. So do not despise the chastisement of the Almighty," and 1 Corinthians 11:32, "When we are judged, we are being taught by the Lord, so that we might not be condemned along with the world" (cf. Heb. 12:5–11).

You may ask, "What kinds of evils does God use to chastise us?" In my view, He employs every kind of affliction and suffering that can be experienced in this life—even the most serious hardships—anything except for eternal destruction and those afflictions connected to a person's everlasting ruin. These sufferings include all kinds of sickness, maladies and diseases of the mind and body, griefs, anxieties and mental illnesses, and weaknesses of every sort. Added to these are the loss of reputation, honor, and the goods and comforts of this life, including those misfortunes God allows our enemies to inflict on us. Additionally, the death of our children and dear family members; setbacks in our finances; all losses and troubles in our persons, families, and estates; all havoc wreaked by our adversaries; war; exile; drought; barrenness; plague; and even temporal death. The rod of chastening may employ all these sorts of calamities (cf. Num. 20:12; 2 Sam. 12:10–11, 14; 24:10–25; Isa. 38 [esp. note v. 17]; Ps. 99:8; 1 Cor. 11:30). In scriptural fashion these are often called "visitations" or "judgments" (1 Peter 4:17), "vengeance" (Ps. 99:8), or "plague" (2 Sam. 24:21). Owing to the overlap in terminology, it is important to distinguish between what may be called probatory or testing hardships (which have been discussed above under cross-bearing) and castigatory or rebuking hardships. At least three of the causes that provoke the chastising rod of God can be demonstrated from Scripture.

1. Sluggish, feeble, and lukewarm attention paid to religious worship; lack of care and diligence in carrying out the duties to which we are obliged since we are called by grace; a less than adequate concern for purifying and perfecting ourselves than the greatness of our redemption demands; and an indifference toward the things of maximal importance in our spiritual and religious life that should be attended to with the greatest care—God does not put up with these things in His own. And they are unworthy of those who call themselves the people of God, as can be seen clearly from the Lord's letters to the churches in Asia (cf. Rev. 2:5, 18–20; 1 Cor. 11:30–31). I have already dealt with this vice above in the section on spiritual languor and its causes. Not the least of the reasons for this failing is more traffic with the world than is in keeping with being in a state of grace, too

many dealings with worldly people, and neglecting to use the means for preserving our spiritual life.

2. Among the things that provoke God's chastisement I include those great, public sins and serious falls into which people who are in the state of grace sometimes plummet (and against which every one of us should be on our guard with the utmost diligence). Believers may stumble into such sins, pollute themselves, dishonor the name of God, and cause great scandal and offense to their brothers because they become overly confident, remiss in keeping watch over themselves, indulgent of their passions for wrath and their fleshly appetites, or self-satisfied and arrogant in times of prosperity. In such cases it is the individual's duty to pray and seek God's forgiveness with tears, contrition, self-humiliation, and repentance in order to be restored and kept in God's favor and not lose the hope of eternal life.

However, God—the Father and also the sovereign and judge of His own—"who without respect of persons judges the doings of every person" (1 Peter 1:17)—does not always withdraw the rod when He sees these inward changes. Internal contrition does not sufficiently satisfy the offense against His public honor nor sufficiently cleanse away such public sins. He will sometimes make an example so His people might see that He puts up less with vices in His people than those among outsiders. He often chastens His own more severely than He does strangers since, indeed, "judgment begins with the house of God" (1 Peter 4:17). This is how He explained His harsh treatment in the case of David (2 Sam. 12:14). And we see the same thing in the notable examples of Moses, Elijah, Uzziah, Hezekiah, and even that most holy man, Zacharias (Luke 1:20).

3. Third in this list of provoking causes are those injuries that believers commit against their brethren and those with whom they do business. If they do not repair the damage they have done in keeping with the law of God and Christ Jesus, the Lord Himself may take up the case of the innocent and demand a reckoning. His reprisals may often be severe, but they are always in accordance with the laws of justice by which He governs the human race as its great governor. The Lord Christ summarized the guiding principle and canon of providence and of divine judgment (which has been proved by ten thousand examples

and will be validated in yet more to come) when He said, "You will be measured by the measure that you used" (Matt. 7:2). Even the pagan moralists and historians have all acknowledged this principle. Among the ways of divine providence, nothing is more conspicuous or well known. People have no need to seek proof from others; they themselves are living examples of this rule. Although it is very common for people to injure each other, whether in word or in deed, how few observe the law of Christ Jesus (which is a law of the purest rationality) and say to their companion, "Forgive me. Have mercy. I have erred. I repent" (see Luke 17:4). The Lord's words are applicable here: "Make up with your adversary quickly while you are with him in the way [i.e., while you are still alive], so that your adversary will not turn you over to the judge, and the judge put you into custody, [i.e., the brother or person you have harmed may die and leave God to take vengeance for the injury]. Truly I say to you that you will never get out of there till you have paid up the last penny [i.e., until you have satisfied divine justice completely]" (Matt. 5:25–26). I am fairly sure that many believers are under the chastising hand of God for their wrongs against others. If you carefully observe the ways of divine providence, you will see that in this life God punishes this type of sin against others more quickly and more severely than the sins people commit against God Himself through error, impaired judgment, or poor discernment.

I will add no more under this heading. What the apostle says in 1 Corinthians 11:31 is universally applicable: "If we would judge ourselves, we will not be judged by the Lord." Therefore, it is the duty of everyone who feels the rod of the heavenly Father to diligently examine the state of his soul, his habits, and all his actions. And if he grasps his fault, he should turn to the God of the rod in repentance and make supplication as David did (2 Sam. 24:10), or as Micah said, "Give attention to the rod and to the one who appointed it" (Mic. 6:9).

From what I have already said, you can perceive that the principle according to which God punishes and chastises believers is always justice. (We should note again that in God's probatory or testing hardships He has another purpose in mind.) But God's justice in dealing with His own is not a naked, impartial justice such as the judges at court should measure out. It is rather the justice that a tutor, master, or head of household dispenses. God's justice is personal and depends on His discretion. It is tempered by grace, and grace always overcomes justice. The principle for God's dealings is easy to discern if you consider the goal and end that God intends through these castigatory or censuring hardships. He chastens those He loves, not to destroy them but to save them. God wants to save His elect from eternal destruction. Therefore, even the censures He sends are an act of supreme love and grace. The words of the apostle here are well known but contain golden consolation: "But when we are judged, we are being instructed by the Lord, so that we might not be condemned with the world" (1 Cor. 11:32). Those whom God punishes to the point of destruction are said to be punished in His "wrath" or "hot displeasure," which the psalmist begs to escape (Ps. 6:1). Indeed, God's worshipers do not always pray against divine chastisements and corrections, since they understand them to be healthy, profitable, and even necessary for themselves. For those whom He loves He reproves and disciplines (Rev. 3:19; Heb. 12:5–11). As Proverbs 13:24 puts it, "He who spares the rod hates his son." On the other hand, one of the notable characteristics of reprobate men is that they do not experience the rod of God during the time of prosperity that has been decreed for them in this world (Job 21:9–16). In the proper time, however, a weightier calamity will overtake them.

In the chastising afflictions that believers experience, there are κρίματα (judgments) but not κατακρίματα (condemnations). The censures that Christians experience are arguments for the fatherly love of God and have nothing of condemnation in them. It is true that God does not overlook the demands of justice, but what He has most in view in His dealings with His own is to secure their salvation and perfect their holiness. The goal and intention of God in chastening is evident from the effects it produces. As the godly man said in Psalm 119:67, "Before I was afflicted, I would go astray; but now I observe Your word," and in verse 71, "It is good for me that I have been afflicted." Experience teaches that certain afflictions are more burdensome than others. The most grievous sorrows produce a sharp sense of pain (1 Chron. 4:10). Such adversities require an uncommon measure of the grace of the Holy Spirit to receive with patience and to convert and use such experiences profitably.

This is the true and solid reason why, within our understanding of the doctrine of salvation, these chastising afflictions cannot be called or considered expiations, judicial afflictions, or compensatory sufferings (for the system of redemption is not the invention of men but has the Holy Spirit as its author). Compensatory penalties and expiatory punishments properly considered are inflicted by God as a judge, in keeping with strict justice, and they lead to eternal destruction and loss. In contrast, chastising hardships are administered by God as a father for a brief time to His own for their benefit and eternal well-being. The great difference between these two kinds of afflictions and hardships should be clear. The person who properly discerns spiritual things should not reduce these evils to a single category. Furthermore, in chastising afflictions the grace and goodness of God as our father overcomes His justice as our judge (for such indeed is the true character of the terrible troubles that believers experience). So is it not more accurate for us to consider them as chastisement and discipline rather than as judicial or expiatory punishments? Reason demands this conclusion.

Along the same lines, Scripture tells us we have received the "remission of sins," but we have not been freed from chastising evils (cf. 2 Sam. 12:13–14; Luke 1:77; Col. 1:14). God is said to have "remitted the sins" of a person whom He transfers from the state of His wrath to the state of His grace. This frees such a person from condemnation— that is, from the eternal destruction he deserved. Is there really any comparison between eternal destruction (and the evils that accompany that condition) inflicted by a severe judge on those whom He has adjudicated worthy to be condemned and the temporary afflictions that God as the father of His children has decreed in order to promote their sanctification, their eternal comfort, and their welfare? The difference between the two types of suffering is immense. Almost no comparison can be made between them at all. When we are in heaven, I believe the Holy Spirit will set out for us most clearly the significance of the evils we experienced in the present and how they promoted our welfare.

Making profitable use of this means for our sanctification shows great prudence in a Christian and is a great art, particularly when God's cane strikes us intensely. But if evils, adversities, and calamities (especially the severest) by which God afflicts and drills His own are not accompanied by the divine grace necessary to sustain them well, instead of stirring a person up for his duties or promoting and perfecting in him a concern for holiness, these may cast down, confuse, and overwhelm a person's soul. These hardships may fill the soul with darkness and confusion, suffocate the flames of love toward God, or even provoke a person to revolt, as happened to Jonah (Jonah 4:3–4). None of the ancient pagan writers expounded more wisely the methods of divine providence than did Seneca. He prudently observed that "it is not the matter of *whether* or not you suffer, but *how* you suffer that matters."

To put it briefly, when we believers find ourselves suffering under the hand of God, (1) We should diligently seek out the cause or causes of the Lord's anger in sending these grievous afflictions (Lam. 3:40). (2) We should humble ourselves under the rod and whip of God and endure them patiently with proper submission of mind and reverence for His sovereign majesty. This has always been the response of the saints (note Hezekiah's attitude in 2 Chron. 32:26). (3) We must acknowledge and approve of the justice of God in the correction we are experiencing and praise Him for His grace in moderating the punishment, as did Daniel (Dan. 9), Ezra (Neh. 9:6), and Hosea (Hos. 14:1–4). (4) In short, we must sincerely repent, making a resolution to change and carrying it out consistently, chasing lukewarmness from our hearts, purifying ourselves from all clinging vices and blemishes, returning to our original course with the Lord, and continuing the race with greater eagerness and constancy (Heb. 12:12).

PART 5

The Goals of the
Spiritual Life

CHAPTER 16

# Spiritual Death

There is a kind of death opposed to the spiritual life that we have been describing thus far. Spiritual death is often referred to in the sacred Scriptures: "When we were in the flesh, the impulses of sins which were stirred up by the law in our members were bearing the fruit of death" (Rom. 7:5); "To be carnally minded is death" (Rom. 8:6); "Truly, truly I say to you that whoever hears My word and believes in Him who sent Me…has passed from death to life. Truly, truly I say to you that the time is coming and now is that the dead will hear the voice of the Son of God and those who hear will live" (John 5:24–25); "And you He has made alive, you who were dead in trespasses and sins" (Eph. 2:1); "Therefore He says, 'Wake up, you sleeper. Rise from the dead, and Christ will illumine you'" (Eph. 5:14); "Let the dead bury their dead" (Matt. 8:22). Saints under the old economy used the same terminology but made no distinction between spiritual and eternal death. Wisdom declares in Proverbs 8:36, "All who hate me love death." Similar statements occur throughout this book.

Everyone agrees that death is a certain kind of condition or state in a subject capable of life (whether animal or rational) and that the condition of death is directly opposed to the condition of life, whether considered literally or metaphorically. Death, in terms of one's spiritual state, can be considered from two points of view: privatively (as something that removes or nullifies) or positively. This distinction may seem a paradox or even an absurdity because when it comes to the *natural* condition of something, death is of a single kind—that is, privative, taking away life. Death can be called the overthrow of life. Death is the state in which a subject capable of living is deprived of its capacity for action or for feeling and sensation. Ecclesiastes speaks this way: "The dead understand nothing" (Eccl. 9:5). Sayings of this kind arise from common experience and are an argument from human sensation. The senses of the living are like a door by which the knowledge of things comes to their minds, and those in the state of death understand and know nothing by their senses. Death in the *spiritual* realm, however, can be considered both privatively, as when it denotes the lack of spiritual life, or positively, when it suggests the actions of a mind moved by sins and lusts. Such death seems to be a kind of living, but it is utterly dissimilar to the spiritual life. In this sense, death is a condition of slavery to sin and to lust.

Some of our pious theologians, whom I would generally call most learned, collapse this privative/positive distinction. They closely connect spiritual death to animal death, do so under the privative conception, and downplay any differences. They note that when an animal is deprived of life, there is not a complete cessation of all movement whatsoever. As the body decays it gives birth to various insects. In these worms that it feeds there is a new kind of movement that seems like life. The same thing takes place, so they say, with the man who lives in the state of spiritual death. In this state he is deprived of spiritual life; therefore, he is in the state of death. As long as he lives in this state, new movements of sin are bursting forth from his corrupt and putrid mind: lusts, base impulses, sensuality, and malice. These are like maggots that swarm about this spiritual cadaver; though utterly different from true life, they put forth the image of movement and life. If not authentic, at least it puts forth the appearance of the real thing.

Considered superficially, this concept has its attractions. But the comparison fails as soon as you consider it carefully. The life of maggots that feed on a cadaver is not the life of the animal (which is indeed dead) but of these insects. The life of sin and of lust in a spiritually dead person is, on the contrary, the life of the man's own soul and mind. It is the life of the man himself, even though he is said to be spiritually dead.

This first difference between spiritual and natural death gives birth to a second. The state of natural or animal death admits of no degree and has nothing to do with scale. No one can say that an animal is more dead or less dead. But the state of spiritual death admits of degrees. The person who lives in this state can be considered more or less dead, depending on the situation of his soul. I will explain this shortly under the positive concept of spiritual death (i.e., spiritual death as productive of something). But first I will deal with the idea of spiritual death considered privatively (i.e., as something that annuls or negates).

If you consider spiritual death according to its privative aspect, you will say that it is the state of a man alienated from the life of God. A person in this state lives and acts outside of communion with God, in ignorance of Him, destitute of His love, producing no fruit (that is, not bringing forward actions that are consistent with being in a spiritual state and that bring glory to God). He is like a cadaver bereft of life, deprived of any feeling for true pleasure that stems so much from communion with God and from a good conscience. He has no hope for a better and more perfect life. This is the simplest way to describe spiritual death: it is the state of lacking spiritual life. The apostle describes it as a state "alienated from the life of God" (Eph. 4:18). But within this state there is a wide degree of difference among people; it admits of degrees, unlike animal death.

The first and simplest of these degrees is when a person is devoid of the love of God and therefore has no share in His communion (which comes to a person only by a gracious revelation). This is the condition in which all people of whatever age or condition find themselves by nature. In the state of nature, apart from the life they have received from their parents, they have not received the principle of a nobler life, which only comes by grace from the Holy Spirit. For since the love of God (that is, a most intense desire for communion with Him and an ardent concern for His glory) is the source of the spiritual life, true love of God can only arise out of faith. And faith is founded on the revelation of grace, as we demonstrated above. Therefore, a lack of the love of God implies spiritual death. There is no exception to this rule.

In ancient times there were non-Christian men who were not only committed to the rules of social honesty but were learned in the principles of prudence, followers of wisdom, and teachers of moral philosophy. They gained all kinds of light either from the fountains of natural philosophy (i.e., from experience and observation) or from the scholarly traditions of which they were the heirs. Among these outstanding and commendable men can be listed Orpheus, Zoroaster, Theognis, Solon, Confucius, Pythagoras, Lycurgus, Socrates, Aristides, Theophrastus, Epictetus, Marcus Aurelius, and, if you will, Plato and Seneca. Examine their writings and opinions, however. What were they seeking? To what end did they bend their actions and their search for what they called virtue? If you ask what was their goal, they sought "to live in accordance with nature." In this way, through the use of reason they sought to find the tranquility of mind that they believed to be in their power. You scan their works in vain for anything about a zeal for the glory of God stemming from a pure love for Him founded on His grace. The essay entitled "What Is the Goal of Philosophy?" by Maximus of Tyre [late second century] is worthy of a philosopher— that is, a person zealous for wisdom and virtue. But notice what he would teach you. Nothing having to do with God enters into this philosopher's noblest exercise. What would this cultivated and brilliant man show you? What does he inculcate and advocate openly? That a man should not pray to God! I say nothing of Epictetus [55–135], who sought all things within himself. I will not deny that Marcus Aurelius [121–180] was one of the truly outstanding men of ancient times and that he mentions God more than anyone in his meditations and precepts. Nevertheless, because he was committed to the foundational presuppositions of Stoic philosophy, which are directly contrary to the doctrine of the gospel and the testimony of one's inner conscience, he sought for resources within himself rather than in God. He repeatedly returns to the foundational doctrine of pagan philosophy that all things must be sought within oneself in order to find the state of happiness in life. But those who seek nothing outside themselves are separated from the state of communion with God and have no real zeal for His glory. The state of living "in accordance with nature" is in the words of Scripture "to live according to the flesh." It is a state of death, not of life. What the apostle says is certain: "The purely natural man does not receive the things of the Spirit of God" (1 Cor. 2:14); "To be carnally minded is death" (Rom. 8:6).

It is also useful to carefully consider the way the Holy Spirit calls "dead" those who have come to the most extreme stage of the state of corruption. The ultimate degree of spiritual death consists in a heart hardened in vices and depraved affections joined to a profound ignorance of God and complete insensibility to Him. It is in this sense that the apostle says, "You…were dead in trespasses and sins" (Eph. 2:1). He goes on to interpret his own meaning graphically in Ephesians 4:17–19: "No longer walk as the rest of the Gentiles do in the vanity of their mind. They have their understanding blinded and darkened, alienated from the life of God due to the ignorance that is in them, and by the hardness of their own hearts they are past feeling [i.e., deprived of all sensation]. And they have given themselves over to lasciviousness and the devoted practice of every impurity." As long as the conscience is carrying out its proper work in a human being, it keeps him from the more serious sins and pushes him to seek truth, honesty, and virtue through its convictions, warnings, and instructions. Marcus Aurelius nicely calls these the "inspirations, suggestions and warnings of God." In scriptural language, these are "rebukes" or "warnings" from God when the conscience is doing its work in a person, and the person does not render himself completely deaf to its admonitions (cf. Ps. 94:10; Job 33:13–33). In this way a person is kept back from grievous vices. Although it is not able to lift up a man in the state of nature and bring him into the state of spiritual life, the light and life of reason seems to and actually does survive in fallen man. In many people who are in the state of death (if you consider their situation as a whole in terms of spirituality), there are still traces of conscience that maintain an obscure and imperfect image of the rational life in them.

But in this final stage of spiritual death, a man is enticed by lusts and thoroughly corrupted by vices. He neglects and refuses all the efforts and testimonies of his conscience, and he gives himself over to his faults and hardens himself against his crimes, despising the convictions of his conscience and public shame. He casts aside all feelings against sin and does wrong without any pain or remorse. This is the state of insensibility, stupor, disregard, and insensitivity that is properly called death since a characteristic of the dead is that they feel nothing. It is equally the case with a person in a state of confirmed unbelief and hardness of mind, weighed down by grievous prejudices, who utterly refuses to listen to the clearest possible demonstrations of saving truth. And the same can be said of atheism, a state that is the end result of all sins. This is the highest possible degree of the state of spiritual (or metaphorical) death. It is a tragic, horrible state—a condition in which a man's reason has been overthrown and he has been made similar to the beasts. It is the indication and prelude in this life of the coming judgment and eternal destruction that has been pronounced against such a person. And this fate is certain unless God in His infinite mercy rescues the man out of such a state. The Lord Jesus speaks of this state when He says, "If the light that is in you is darkness, how great is that darkness!" (Matt. 6:23).

Now let us deal with the notion of spiritual death from a positive rather than privative point of view (i.e., considering what it produces). Man has a mind that he has received as part of his nature. And this mind or spirit is the fountain and source of a constant variety of actions. Such is the case with everyone, even those devoid of the love of God, having no zeal for His glory and not moved by any desire for communion with Him. No one ceases to act, think, and work continually. Everyone is always in action, seeking his own desires. But the apostle calls this action and movement "death" in Romans 8:6: "For to be carnally minded [that is, to think, reason, propose, deliberate, and carry out actions in such a way] is death." He had already said in the previous chapter, "When we were in the flesh, the impulses of sins which were stirred up by the law in our members were bearing the fruit of death" (Rom. 7:5). This is similar to what he said to the Ephesians in 2:1–2, whom he called "dead in trespasses and sins in which you used to walk in accordance with the habits of this age." Here is a paradox! To say that there is a life within death. Or even stronger, that this life itself is death!

Spiritual death, then, considered in its positive aspect (i.e., what it gives birth to) is the state of a man alienated from communion with God and devoid of the love of God, and from this state the man lives in sins and vices out of a principle of lust in accordance with the movement of carnal affections. Having a bad conscience, he seeks to obtain those carnal goods to which he is drawn by his own vitiated and forbidden desire, which ultimately leads to his eternal destruction. All these qualities are similar to the description we gave of spiritual life, except they are the utter opposites! The motion or vitality of this state of death acts out of its own internal principle, freely and self-consciously as is the case with the state of spiritual life. But the principle or source of this life is not the love of God coming from faith; it is lust, which Scripture calls an inordinate and disordered desire for some sort of good thing or the love of any false or forbidden good that has taken root in the soul. I use this word *love* in the very broad sense of an attachment or habitual affection and inclination of the will away from the proper love of God and toward the love of a false good. These motions and actions take place in accordance with a law: not a divine but a carnal law—that is, the corrupt affections that a man obeys as his inclinations are conformed to the lusts of the flesh. He is a devotee not of a good conscience, as in the spiritual life, but of an evil conscience that disapproves and condemns the man's actions, convicting him of sin and making him afraid. He arrives at the proximate (i.e., near) goal of his actions: to acquire the things for which his soul had been consumed with lust. And eventually he comes to the remote goal of his doings: eternal destruction, which is the necessary outcome of this state of life in accordance with the just judgment of God. Unless, of course, the person averts it through swift and sincere repentance.

The content of this life of sin (i.e., the material through which this activity expresses itself) is wrongdoing, faults, and vices of all types. For the life of lust is lived out by sinning. The concept of sin is to be taken in the broadest sense used in Scripture (which is also its common meaning). Sin is any kind of activity that departs from the rectitude, the fairness, and the goodness (expressed in praiseworthy deeds) required by God's judgment and the judgment of conscience (which amounts to the same thing).

Every possible kind of error, crime, offense, and shortcoming should be considered part of this life of sin—anything committed against the light of reason and conscience or against the law of God known by revelation. Included with these are all omissions by which a person falls short of what this law requires. There are so many groups and categories of offenses, and the topic of transgression is such a wide one, that it is almost impossible to measure the depths of the gulf of human impurity. Should a person wish to understand this in greater detail, he can look at the classifications I set out above. These include acts of impiety, idolatry, superstition, malice, hatred, envy, injustice, cruelty, pride, inhumanity, revenge, greed, selfish ambition, lust, lasciviousness, self-indulgence, immodesty, salaciousness, dirty speech, and vanity. Not even the most diligent mind can categorize every category. Along with these come faults and vices of a negative or privative nature: sluggish laziness and inactivity; unconcernedness about salvation; unsociability; denying to one's neighbor the help, protection, and support to which he is due in accordance with the divine law; lack of reverence for religion; lack of respect for magistrates and parents; and many other similar transgressions. Peter says, "It is enough that we have lived in past time doing what the Gentiles delight in: living in sensuality, lusts, drunkenness, gluttony, wild reveling and the shameful worship of idols" (1 Peter 4:3). And in the next verse he calls this abandoning oneself to dissolution, over-indulgence, and unrestrained lusts. The apostle Paul says in Titus 3:3, "At that time we ourselves were foolish, disobedient, misled, serving a variety of lusts and pleasures, living in malice and envy, hateful, and hating others," and in Galatians 5:19–21, "But the words of the flesh are obvious, which are adultery, fornication, impurity, lust, idolatry, witchcraft, hatred, brawling, rivalries, murders, drunkenness, carousing, and such things." Despite all the diligence and the fertile genius of this man, a divine apostle, he still had to leave so much material out of his reckoning. The harvest of human wrongdoing is so vast, the breadth of corruption is so monumental, and the ability of sin to produce new shoots and propagate itself in a variety of forms is so fertile! This is what it means when a person gives himself over to live in sin: it is to "practice lawlessness" (1 John 3:4). He who conducts his life this way is giving rein to sin, being a worker of iniquity and a very slave to sin.

However, there are people who are not free from these vices but who do not give themselves over to them nor go through life like pigs. As I have shown above, some profess a concern for truth; frame their lives and mores in accordance with what is socially honorable; practice patience, self-control, and temperance as exemplary citizens; and yet still fall under the censure of the heavenly court. The apostle lays out the unerring rule by which the sanctuary above gives its verdict:

"Whatever does not come from faith is sin" (Rom. 14:23). Natural acts fall short, even those in terms of content and matter that are socially and commercially honorable and praiseworthy. Such acts are defective if they have nothing to do with God, if they do not proceed from the principle of knowing the true God, if they do not stem from faith in and love for God, or if they show no zeal for His glory or desire for communion with Him. If deeds are not directed toward God as the chief source of our happiness, if they manifest no searching for God or desire to be joined to Him—in short, if a person does not have as his goal pleasing God or devoting himself to have communion with God in this life in the hope of eternal life—then (as Scripture expresses it) in the judgment of the celestial court, these acts are adjudicated to have been committed in sin. We are not able to affirm that the acts done by even the most honest men, praiseworthy though they be, are completely free from fault and blame because of the reality of human weakness and fallibility. Even if a person's goal and purpose is good and honest, everyone knows by experience that it is extremely difficult to bring to the effort the requisite amount of diligence, care, vigilance, prudence, and precision. One may be as painstaking as he can and yet say to himself, "I was not careful enough." If such is the case with the regenerate, how much more is it the case that all those who are in the state of nature live in sin, cannot please God in accordance with the rule of His holy sanctuary, are alienated from communion with Him, do not seek or love God, and are destitute of His grace and without hope of eternal life? Such living is indeed a type of death.

Based on what has been said thus far, the better we understand the extremes of this state of death, the easier we will grasp what its middle state is (i.e., the common condition of most men, people who live in well-ordered societies and who do not completely neglect the demands of their consciences or of social customs and expectations). Those who have sunk to the extremity, the deepest point and final stage of this state, are utterly enslaved to sins and vices. They revel in every injustice and lust. There is no limit to their sinning as long as they think they can do so unpunished. This is the most deplorable and terrible condition for a person to be in. The laws of society are much laxer than those of conscience or of the precepts of Christ Jesus. But those who do not even respect society's laws or fear penalties do not walk but run along the broad path of sin into crimes and offenses. Isaiah says they are like the troubled sea, restless and surging (Isa. 57:20). The affections within such a person are like waves that crash on each other, storms that stir up billows clashing together, and torrents raging against one another. The sinner becomes the toy of his own disordered desires. His passions continually buffet him, first in one direction, then in another. Satisfying one lust, he seeks to fulfill the next with equal ardor. A frail vessel at the mercy of the waves, he never finds the rest he expects. The sinner's condition, to use Peter's image, is like a river that overflows its dikes, carries along anything that opposes it, and spreads widely across the fields (1 Peter 4:4). Once the limits of honor have been breached, nothing can stop him. Such a person thinks he can have whatever he wills. He repels and stifles the urging of his conscience toward better things. If he cannot completely eliminate the remorse it causes him, at least he can weaken its force through sinning habitually.

To use Hosea's image, the life of sin is like a blazing oven (Hos. 7:4). Like a baker, Satan is continually casting on new kindling to enflame it further. The sinner is ardent for transgression; he himself constantly stirs up new flames of impurity. As if he feared that they would die away, he is regularly stirring up his lusts to burst forth in new infractions. For Isaiah, this is to "draw on iniquity with cords of vanity and sin with cart ropes" (Isa. 5:18). This is when one adds sin to sin, fastening them like the links of a chain. The sinner is described in Job as a man "who drinks perversity like water" (Job 15:16). Such a one has become a reeking, putrid abomination. He has debased himself; he has cast off his rational nature and become a corrupt and rotting cadaver. What a lamentable state! How tragic that a man would set aside his reason (the glorious ornament of his nature that shows his superiority to the beasts) and strip off his own humanity in order to subject himself to bestial vices and savage deeds! One might have difficulty believing this if it were not confirmed by the examples not just of individuals but of entire nations. Consider the status of God's beloved people of old. If you remove from consideration the elect seed (i.e., true believers), at certain periods the people were entirely sunken in corruption and idolatry. This can be demonstrated from the exhortations of the Old

Testament prophets, the rebukes of the apostle Paul, and the writing of Roman and other historians.

But what I call living at the *first* stage or degree of sin is quite a different matter. Such people manifest an image or reflection of the rational life but are still described by the Scriptures as living in the state of sin and separated from communion with God. Good and upright citizens, prudent legislators, just judges, strict censors of their own actions, and useful to civil society, they provide others with a praiseworthy example of the moral virtues. They lack only one thing—not something from themselves, not something they merit by their own abilities, but something from God, something produced by divine grace. People in such a condition must abandon confidence in their own works. They need to learn to rest and rely not in themselves, but in God. They should learn to live in the hope of eternal life: acting not simply out of fear of offending their conscience but out of a grateful love for God and a desire for His glory. Those who fail in this essential condition may have the appearance of being alive but are actually dead while living.

I hope it is now clear why this life of sin, lust, and wanton longing may be called death. To summarize briefly, the reasons are, first, because it is a type of activity and movement [*actuositas*] that is completely contrary to that kind of activity which is properly called life. And because it is contrary and utterly opposed to life, it should be called death. Second, because the activity of the type I have described lacks an essential characteristic of what constitutes true life, which is a love for God stemming from the hope of eternal life. Without love for God springing from the hope of eternal life, neither the person nor his acts are really "alive" or capable of pleasing God. Such love is the fountain and bubbling spring of true life. The absence of this principle of life and motion is death. Third, because this activity and motion is connected to a bad conscience and therefore completely deprived of feeling for the true joy and pleasure that comes only from the persuasion that a person is the recipient of divine grace and in communion with God. A bad conscience convicts a man that he is guilty, worthy to be damned, cast away, and alienated from the God who is the source of eternal life and glory. It reproaches the man of his unseemly condition and ugly behavior. It places before his eyes the just judgment of God, the thought of which infuses him with fear and horror. This evil conscience and restlessness of soul accompanies all a man's acts. It stings and gnaws at the man's state of mind. And despite all his attempts to stifle it, it embitters the sweetness of every sin that he embraces. As the sage expressed it, "Even in laughter there is pain" (Prov. 14:13). There is no stage closer to eternal loss than when, after the desire for a particular sin has been fulfilled, a man is left empty, thirsty, and starving. Fourth and finally, because in every sin and every shameful act there is what Peter calls "corruption," a perverting influence (2 Peter 1:4). As a person continues in sin, he degrades himself and becomes more and more corrupt. The state of sin is a "bondage of corruption" (Rom. 8:21) because "the one who sows to his flesh will reap destruction" (Gal. 6:8). Therefore, one can say of this state of sin that "there is death in the pot" (2 Kings 4:40). To truly live means to thrive, to flourish and be happy, and this means to live in the joy of a good conscience, which comes from being in a state of communion with God and conforming our actions to that state. "There will be glory, honor, and peace to the one who does good, first to the Jew, then to the Greek" (Rom. 2:10).

One thing remains to be noted. Odd as it may seem, for believers, the life of sin is a death that is, in turn, the beginning of a new life: "How shall we who are dead to sin live in it further?" (Rom. 6:2); "Occupy yourself with the things above, not the things of earth, for you are dead [that is, to the life of sin]" (Col. 3:2–3). This is the destruction of the body of sin that the apostle refers to in Romans 6:6. This death and destruction of the life of sin is pictured and set forth for Christ's disciples in the symbolic rite of baptism. For even as immersion in and remaining under water extinguishes and suffocates the life of earthly creatures, this symbol is a reminder and warning to believers that the life of nature, sin, and lust that they had lived has been destroyed, extinguished, and abolished in them by the power of their communion with the death of Christ Jesus. And this took place so that they might rise up to a new, better, and spiritual life. This life has been obtained for the elect seed by the power of the death of Christ and by His Spirit, in both of which they share. What a paradox! The life of man in the state of nature is really death, and the death or destruction of this life is life indeed and the beginning of a better life!

CHAPTER 17

# Distinguishing Spiritual Life
# from Spiritual Death

There is the widest possible difference between life and death. It seems
at first glance that it would not be difficult to distinguish those who
are in the state of life from those who are in the state of death. And this
is indeed the case if you consider people in whom the vigor of life or
the power of death are clearly on display, whether spiritual or natural.
Though imperfect, there are analogies between natural and spiritual
life and death. Everyone knows that at times a person may be alive
with natural and animal life but fall into such weakness and fainting
that it seems life has been extinguished in him. It takes an expert doctor to distinguish whether such a person is dead or alive. On the other
hand, experience teaches that from time to time people who have just
given up the ghost may have an appearance of such vigor on their face
that they give the impression of life even though they are in the arms of
death. This shows that even in the state of nature, two utterly distinct
things may seem to have a certain resemblance.

What shall I say about the spiritual state? I have shown above (where
I dealt with the affections of the spiritual life) that true believers may
find themselves on the edge of life and death, in the throes and near
to the stage of death. If you considered the state of such people's souls,
you might reckon them as spiritually dead since the principle of true
life in them expresses itself so feebly. They deserve to be listed among
the dead more than among the spiritually alive. On the other hand,
in the world there are people who by their actions and habits make a
vivid impression of being spiritually alive. But whether this stems from
mistaken and twisted religious zeal, self-love, a desire for hollow glory,

or hypocrisy, death in fact reigns in their foul members. This is how the Lord described the Pharisees and scribes of His times: "You are similar to white-painted tombs that seem nice on the outside, but inside are full of dead men's bones and all uncleanness" (Matt. 23:27).

The first thing we should conclude from this, as anyone can clearly see, is just how difficult it is for men to give a definitive opinion or make a judgment that is certain regarding the internal state of people who live in the communion of the true church, frame their lives according to social expectations, participate in external worship, and do not undermine the confession that they have made with their mouths with their way of living. This is particularly the case if you do not know the intimate workings of their minds through familiar interactions with them over a long period of time or have not explored their inward dispositions through careful examination. In the case of those who neglect God and live in sins and vices, it is not difficult or doubtful for others to render an opinion on their spiritual state: they condemn themselves (1 John 3:20). But when it comes to those who make a profession of faith, unless a person has the gift of discerning spirits (which the apostles enjoyed), I think that even the ministers of Christ Jesus who best understand the spiritual life and its characteristics cannot make a confident and infallible judgment about a person's spiritual condition in every case. For "how deceitful is the heart of man!" (Jer. 17:9). The human heart is full of secret things that leave no outward trace and are known only to God and the person's conscience. There are so many covered secrets, so many subterfuges; hypocrisy brings out hidden things under false pretenses. What is closer to true zeal than false religious zeal? Many more people are deceitful, slanted, and crafty than are upright, candid, genuine, modest, and sincere.

Second, many people find it difficult to judge and make a determination about their own spiritual state and condition. You would think a person could simply set his mind to the task and come up with a clear conviction about his own spiritual status, even if the results were disagreeable. You would think that each person should be conscious about his own spiritual life, and that no matter how mistaken others might be, he could not deceive himself. But, paradoxically, nothing is more common than such self-deception! Even in natural life some people, whether through illness or a deep mental disturbance, do things of which they are unaware or things that they cannot remember having done. It is almost not necessary to discuss self-unconsciousness when it comes to the spiritual life—I take it as a given that is obvious to all. An excessive self-love afflicts most mortals (some more than others), blending itself into the way that they judge their own actions, merits, and spiritual state. Consequently, people weigh themselves on deceptive scales. What they have done well they value excessively. Furthermore, they devalue the significance of their own failings and minimize their habitual sins.

Consequently, among the many people called into the communion of the external church, there are very few who examine themselves carefully. Most consider themselves no worse than any others and, quickly absolving and acquitting themselves, they consider themselves to be in the state of grace (though they may actually be far from it). This happens because of the hypocrisy that is mixed up with their self-judgment. For this reason, certain saints fear to enter into an examination of themselves: they distrust their own judgment and discernment when it comes to their own case. Speaking for the church and not just for himself, Jeremiah says that "the human heart is deceitful above all things [that is, full of twistedness, deceits, and things that are covert and not straightforward] and deathly ill and corrupted. Who understands it?" (Jer. 17:9). So he calls out to God as the searcher of hearts, the explorer of man's inner workings, and the One who judges without hypocrisy or partiality. This clearly implies that it is extremely difficult for a person to make an honest judgment about his own spiritual state because pride and excessive self-love (the sources of hypocrisy) deceive him and (even against his will) worm their way into his self-assessment. This is why the wise and godly man distrusts himself and submits himself to the equitable and infallible judgment of God: "Search me, O God, and know my heart. Test me, know my thoughts, see if there is in me any harmful way" (Ps. 139:23–24).

But even if you assume that people genuinely want to undertake this examination of themselves with all possible openness and honesty, the matter is hardly straightforward. There are some true Christians in whom the principle of spiritual life is so weak and so hidden that the one who is able to make a diagnosis would say that they are "ready to die" (Ps. 88:15) or faintly burning wicks and nearly extinguished (Isa. 42:3). There are others who are so fearful, whose minds are so weighed down, who distrust themselves so much that even when they see in themselves very clear marks of grace that leave no room for doubt, they always fasten their eyes on the weaknesses that cling to them, and against all reason they continue to mistrust and waver. They do not dare to arouse their minds to glory in the Lord's salvation. Often this state of mind is encouraged by the person's emotional temperament. Finally, there are some people from whom God withholds the felt influence of His grace. They find themselves oppressed by troubles. And with minds filled with anxiety, they discover that they are in a state of darkness, spiritual gloom, fear, and even terror. They are bereft of any real sense of divine comfort. No one should encourage people who find themselves in any of the three states I have described to undertake a study of their own spiritual status until they experience a change in their condition. For in such plights, self-examination cannot be carried out equitably or fruitfully.

Nevertheless, believers are called to this work of self-examination, and it should not be evaded: "Let a man examine himself, and thus eat of that bread and drink of that cup" (1 Cor. 11:28); "Examine yourselves whether you are in the faith; test yourselves" (2 Cor. 13:5); "Let every person examine his own work" (Gal. 6:4). Compare these with Lamentations 3:40: "Let us test and examine our ways; let us explore, study, and return to the LORD." Also, this act of judging between the holy and the profane is not alien to the duties of the ministers of the word of the gospel as guardians of the house of God, pastors of the flock of Christ, and overseers of the sanctuary: "Into whatever city or town you enter, search as to who in it is worthy" (Matt. 10:11). As Lightfoot has properly noted, *worthy* is a term used often in Jewish discussions of worship and means "honest," "proper," or "capable." The meaning of what the Lord says here is this: when you enter into a town, village, or house, inquire into which people apply themselves with seriousness and a heartfelt mind to reverence God and to learn His ways, people who have the capacity of judgment for discerning the truth. This is what Lydia implied when she said to Paul and his companions, "If you have judged me to be faithful to the Lord, come into my house and stay there" (Acts 16:15). Need I say more? Are not ministers of Christ Jesus like spiritual fishermen described in the parable (Matt. 13:48), who sat down on the shore and, from all those drawn in by the net of the gospel, collected the good fish in containers but cast out the bad fish? This is, as He then explained, the act of "separating the wicked from among the righteous" (Matt. 13:49). Spiritually speaking, are not ministers, as overseers of the church, in effect the angels at the doors of the new Jerusalem who make distinctions among those seeking to enter the city of God (Rev. 21:12)? There are, however, certain principles that must be observed so that this holy and necessary work might be carried out in a balanced and proper way. For if not, it may prove damaging to the spiritual condition of souls.

In order that he can do so properly, I require of a person making an examination of his own spiritual state before God that he do so candidly, sincerely, and with absolute honesty. As reason and the very nature of the matter itself make this clear, he must seriously and very carefully consider the certain and indubitable criteria of a person being in a state of grace. And it is particularly important that the person's mind not be disturbed by any extraordinary mishap, adversity, or change. Great care must be taken against this. Souls that are afflicted, depressed, wrapped in darkness, shaken by unforeseen troubles and adversities, and suffering grief, melancholy, or anxiety are unprepared to undertake this examination. To be fruitful, a spiritual assessment should only be done when the mind is quiet, peaceable, and composed, and when none of the great setbacks of life have unsettled its condition and habitual course. Nothing clouds a person's judgment more than extraordinary emotions.

Very great and extraordinary prudence is required of ministers of Christ who explore persons' states of soul. They may do this when consulted by people who are afflicted in mind, distrust their own judgment, and present themselves for examination to their spiritual priests. Or they may conduct an interview as part of their duty of examining the condition of those who should be admitted to baptism or to communion in the Lord's Table—that is, whether the candidates are worthy or unworthy. Experience continually shows that the worst abuses are those committed in matters of the highest importance. Surely this is the case in what is called ecclesiastical discipline. When it is carried out by imprudent, ambitious, proud, ignorant, and inexperienced men, church discipline produces a flood of horrible scandals and disasters for Christianity. Is there anything less tolerable than when degenerate and impure men, who are unacquainted with spiritual things but have obtained a position of authority, boldly arrogate to themselves the right to judge the consciences of others who are better, more holy, and more knowledgeable than they are? They exercise this authority proudly and heartlessly and become conscience torturers by abusing something that is most holy. Therefore, if this work is to be carried out properly, great care must be taken to entrust such responsibility only to men who are upright, good, sincere, modest, and mature in age and experience—men who have been tested and are well known for having the characteristics of pastors—that is, shepherds of souls after the Lord's own heart who will lead His people with knowledge and prudence (Jer. 3:15). Since it is difficult to penetrate the depths of this topic, we will confine ourselves here to the following observations:

1. Great care must be taken that those who evaluate the internal state of souls do not do so proudly, with a high hand or magisterial tone, as if they themselves had been installed on the tribunal of God having supreme authority to adjudicate and give rulings on the consciences of others. We have known too many who engage in this serious sin and whom God has covered with shame (or will do so). This examination must be done not only with fairness and moderation but also with profound modesty and a complete absence of all pride and arrogance. The saying of the apostle should always be kept in mind: "Who are you to condemn the servant of another [i.e., definitively and without appeal]? To his own master he stands or falls" (Rom. 14:4).

2. An evaluation of the spiritual condition of those who are in the middle state can only be done in accordance with what seems probable, as we have already noted. Among people who consider themselves Christians, there are two states far from each other. On the one hand there are those who have lived and continue to live in a state of ignorance, of fleshly lust, and of injustice. These do not seek God and do not concern themselves about His grace or His favor. At the other

extreme are those who have lived for many years in the light of the knowledge of God's ways, who continue to follow the path of virtue, and who worship and serve God carefully. It is permissible to dare to pronounce a confident judgment in both these extreme cases. (However, on account of that profound hypocrisy that eludes the detection of the best judges, the evaluation of those who are outside the communion of God and continue to live in sins and vices is more certain than the assessment of the state of those who present the appearance of virtue and piety.) But it is the person in the middle state whose spiritual condition is most difficult to discern since many things known only to God may escape our notice.

Take, for example, a man who has some knowledge of the essential teachings of religion. He has made a beginning, but the depth of his knowledge is difficult to determine. He professes faith in Christ Jesus. He says that he feels his spiritual need and that he desires communion with God. His habits and way of life do not undermine the credibility of the confession of his mouth. You might wish he had a clearer understanding and experience of how the spiritual life works, but what prudence it takes not to go astray in dealing with such a person! What rashness and carelessness it would be to reject one whom the Lord may have elected! What audacity to discourage those who needed to be encouraged and comforted! Absolutely sure standards and criteria for determining whether a person is in a state of justification or condemnation are hidden from our minds and sometimes can be clearly discerned only by God and the man's own conscience. Let me add that the borders of divine grace are very wide. Who can see the boundaries of God's mercy? Unless a minister of Christ wishes to do damage in such cases, he must maintain a certain breadth and liberality.

Christ Jesus alone can make the definitive and infallible judgment. "These things says the Holy and True One, who has the key of David, who opens and no one shuts; who closes and no one opens" (Rev. 3:7). In time, "All the churches will acknowledge that I am the one who searches hearts and intentions" (Rev. 2:23). Brethren must judge their brethren fairly, modestly, and in many cases reservedly. And they must certainly only judge "in the Lord."

3. It would be safest and best for those who do not have the duty of examining the inner state of their brothers' souls to abstain from such decisions (unless necessity demands), to leave such determinations to Christ Jesus, and to judge themselves rather than others. Knowing his own weakness, every modest and right-thinking person will do this gladly. The Lord said, "Do not judge so that you might not be judged" (Matt. 7:1); James adds, "My brothers, not many of you should be teachers, since you know that we will incur a stricter judgment" (James 3:1) and "There is one lawgiver, who is able to save and to destroy. Who are you who judges [that is, to condemn when you judge] another?" (James 4:12); and Paul asks, "Why do you judge your brother?" (Rom. 14:10). Self-love is so strong that people who can discern and censure the faults of others are blind to their own. A character defect that they gladly put up with in themselves they utterly condemn in others. But disciplined and prudent people will restrain themselves from forming judgments rashly or maliciously. They will rarely judge the state of others, the goals and motives for what others do, or even their sayings and opinions if such can be received under any kind of favorable interpretation.

We are also not required to agree when others make judgments about our own spiritual state. For they may be misled by their feelings or lack of experience. Every person must consult his own conscience on this matter. If our conscience absolves us, we do not need to fear the judgments of others. If it condemns us, the supportive judgments of others, even of church overseers, are of no help.

It is impossible to come to any judgment about our own or others' spiritual state except on the basis of criteria. And these criteria must be taken from the nature of the spiritual life itself. It is only on the basis of these distinguishing features, norms, and points of comparison that we can possibly differentiate the state of grace from that of nature, the state of regeneration from the unregenerate state. Every type of life has characteristics that distinguish it from death. I will describe the principal features of the spiritual life under the economy of grace, first in general then in detail.

To use general terms first, what most characterizes true spiritual life is sound, genuine, and living faith in Christ Jesus based on a proper and sufficient understanding of the foundational teachings of religion:

"The one who believes in the Son has eternal life" (John 3:36); "The one who believes and is baptized will be saved" (Mark 16:16); "The just will live by his faith [i.e., the one who is righteous by his faith will live by that same faith]" (Hab. 2:4). I will refrain from citing any more of the many texts along these lines. True and living faith is the beginning and foundational source [*principium*] of the spiritual life. Every spiritual act is birthed by faith and connected to faith. Where there is faith, there is life. All good impulses and actions have their beginning in faith, and the springs of living water burst forth from faith as from a fountain.

But, since the word *faith* can have an ambiguous meaning, we should note that there is a genuine faith and a counterfeit faith, a complete and perfect faith as well as an incomplete and imperfect faith, a faith of the heart and a faith of the mouth, a faith accompanied by the affections (notably, charity) and a faith that does not touch the affections, a faith with trust [*fiducia*] and a faith without trust, a faith with works and a faith without works, a fruitful faith and a sterile faith, a faith that bears constant and lasting fruit and a faith whose fruit is only temporary. Therefore, in the examination of the interior state of a person's soul it is essential that everyone be clear about faith. Let no one imprudently take the name of faith for the substance. Let no one confuse faith with that insubstantial and vague assent that a person may give to the doctrine of the gospel but that does not pass into his affections or actions. (This is commonly called historical faith [*historica*]). Nor should anyone confuse the true faith of God's elect with an acquiescence to the truth that is based on prejudices and false foundations and does not affect the heart or impact one's actions in any durable way. (This is sometimes called temporary faith [*temporaria*].) Did not the apostle tell the Corinthian believers in Christ to examine themselves to see whether they were in the faith (2 Cor. 13:5)? It is possible, then, that a church member might not truly be "in the faith." Therefore, to determine the criteria of true faith is the same thing as to describe the characteristics of the spiritual life, which I will now summarize under six headings.

The first and most outstanding characteristic of the spiritual life, as I see it, is the serious, regular, and constant *seeking after God* both in private and (when possible) in public worship out of a sincere, overriding, and passionate desire for communion with Him in Christ Jesus: "This is the generation of those who seek Him, who seek [carefully look for and desire to find] the face of the God of Jacob" (Ps. 24:6); "May all who seek You diligently rejoice in You" (Ps. 40:16); "Blessed are those who seek Him with the whole heart" (Ps. 119:2); "My soul has desired You during the night; and the very spirit within me will seek You at the break of day" (Isa. 26:9); "O God, You are my God. I seek You; my soul thirsts for You; my flesh pines for You" (Ps. 63:1). This characteristic is never missing from the state of grace. The serious seeking after God—indeed, seeking Him in Christ Jesus out of a desire for communion with Him—is the first and truest act of the spiritual life. There is life wherever it exists and death wherever it is absent. Seeking God is a sign that a person loves Him and desires communion with Him since it emerges from the very nature of the spiritual life.

Please do not think I have in view here only public worship services. Certainly I include them here (e.g., Ps. 84:1), but hypocrites and true believers alike share these in common. When I speak of seeking God, I refer to the following: (a) To the confident and very free commerce, intercourse, and interaction that the Christian has with God in his private worship as he prays, makes supplication, and gives thanks. He approaches God familiarly day after day and engages in a communion with Him, not from some traditional ritual but out of a tender affection for God as His caring Father. (b) To the continual reference to God that he maintains in every act of his life. This means that the entire life of a man regenerated by grace becomes as it were a continual seeking of God. He does not live in doubt but is always exploring what is the good will of God (Rom. 12:2). He asks, "Does that delight or displease the Lord?" and "Is this more or less pleasing to God?" He always keeps in mind that God is the observer of his actions. This reference to and consideration for God is a seeking for God. It is never absent from the state of grace. It is a characteristic mark of saints that they walk with God and in the presence of God [*coram Deo*].

The second characteristic of the spiritual life is a serious, constant, and sustained resolution and diligent concern *to abstain from vices* that are damaging to one's spiritual condition and contrary to the law of God and Christ, and *to cultivate and practice* without discrimination every virtue prescribed by reason or the law of God and Christ. This commitment must lead to practice. This resolution must lead to an appropriate response that touches on all the activities of life and that is carried out with joy and a willing and content mind in communion with Christ for the glory of God in the hope of eternal life. This is a distinguishing feature and criterion of holy and elect people emphasized throughout the Word of God. And it arises from the very nature of the spiritual life. For life is only recognized when something is alive—that is, from the vital actions that life produces. The apostle John, our Lord Jesus, and many other biblical writers emphasize this: "We know that we have known Him in this way: if we keep His precepts. The one who says, 'I have known Him,' and yet does not keep His precepts is a liar, and the truth is not in him. But the one who keeps His word, truly in him the love of God has been fulfilled. By this we know that we are in Him. The one who says that he abides in Him ought to walk as even He Himself walked" (1 John 2:3–6); "Whoever is born of God does not practice sin because His seed abides in him; he cannot sin because he has been born from God" (1 John 3:9); "He who has My commandments and keeps them is the one who loves Me" (John 14:21); "If a person loves Me, he will keep My word" (John 14:15); "You will recognize them by their fruits. Do people gather grapes from thorn bushes or figs from cacti?" (Matt. 7:16); "Not everyone who says to Me, 'Lord, Lord,' will enter into the kingdom of heaven, but only the one who does the will of My Father who is in heaven" (Matt. 7:21); "What profit is there, my brothers, if someone says he has faith but has no works? Can that faith save him?" (James 2:14); "For as the body without the spirit is dead, even so, the faith that is bereft of works is also dead" (James 2:26); "He gave Himself for us to redeem us from every transgression of the law and to purify for Himself a particular people, on fire for good works" (Titus 2:14; cf. Eph. 2:10; Pss. 34; 119).

What more shall I add? Wherever there is life there is virtue, justice, piety, love. In other words, there is a concern to glorify God in the practice of good and praiseworthy actions, to perfect oneself in fellowship with God, and to edify one's neighbor (1 Cor. 13). Where there is life there is a genuine desire for holiness: "Whoever has this hope in himself keeps himself pure even as He is pure" (1 John 3:3).

And wherever there is holiness (i.e., the purity of the affections and of the way of life) there is an image and likeness of God. By the light of nature Plato described this as "being just and holy with wisdom," one of the most beautiful statements made by a pagan. I understand well the many weaknesses that surround the human condition, even for those living in the economy of grace. But such no longer live in sins and vices. Sin no longer reigns over them. If some offense gets the better of them, by faith they purify themselves; they repent, return to their course in the Lord, and press on toward better things.

The third characteristic of the spiritual life is the *exercise of charity*. Among everything called good works, actions of charity are particularly outstanding according to Holy Scripture. I mean by this that because of a believer's faith, which fosters liberality, he does good to those who are poor and needy, especially to fellow believers in accordance with the limitations of his abilities and circumstances. I hope no one will blame me for making this criterion so prominent. I realize that there are people whom God calls to His communion that have an illiberal and stingy temperament and how difficult it is for them to rise above this weakness. But everyone called into fellowship with God must imitate the example of divine goodness in works of charity: "Blessed are the merciful, for they shall obtain mercy" (Matt. 5:7); "But the one who has worldly provisions and sees his brother laboring under the lack of something and closes up his compassion for him, how can the love of God dwell in him? My little children, let us not love merely in word or tongue, but in truth and in action" (1 John 3:17–18); "If a brother or sister is naked or lacking daily sustenance, and if someone among you were to say to that person, 'Be warmed and filled,' but did not give them the things necessary for their bodily needs, what use would that be? In this way also, faith by itself, if it does not have works, is dead" (James 2:15–17); "Be therefore perfect [that is, perfectly good/kind], even as your Father which is in heaven is perfect" (Matt. 5:48); "There will be condemnation without mercy for the one who has showed no mercy" (James 2:13; cf. Matt. 25:35–36, 41–42; Ps. 12).

I cannot exclude anyone from this requirement except to say that each one should keep in mind the limitations imposed by his circumstances and abilities. All who want to be godly are good, generous, kind, and merciful, sharing what they have gladly with others. They do this moved by a sharp sense of the immense grace and charity that God has exercised toward them in Christ. And as a testimony of their grateful hearts and for the glory of God they are prepared to expend all their faculties to benefit Christ Jesus in the person of His members. As in Luke 7:47, the woman loved much because her sins, which were great, had been forgiven.

The fourth characteristic of the spiritual life is a *zeal for the glory of God*. No one who does not have a spiritual disposition has been placed in the state of grace. A spiritual disposition means an eagerness for the divine honor, a care to keep oneself in communion with God, a love for the truth of the gospel, and a concern about eternal salvation. This is a criterion that distinguishes flesh from spirit, life from death: "What is born of the flesh is flesh, and what is born of the Spirit is spirit" (John 3:6); "For those who are fleshly [i.e., according to the flesh] pay attention to the things that are fleshly; but those who are spiritual [i.e., according to the Spirit] pay attention to the things that are spiritual [i.e., of the Spirit]" (Rom. 8:5); "Having the eyes of your mind enlightened, that you may know what is the hope of His calling, and what are the riches of the glory of His inheritance in the saints" (Eph. 1:18); "If then you have been resurrected with Christ, seek the things which are above, where Christ is sitting at the right hand of God" (Col. 3:1); "Your law is my complete delight" (Ps. 119:77).

Of course, I acknowledge that true believers established in the state of grace are not exempt from carnal affections and prejudices. But no one shares in the divine communion except the person whose carnal affections have been subjected to spiritual affections, or to put it more clearly, one in whom a spiritual disposition and affection dominates and has the upper hand. I have already described these spiritual affections above. The pious soul rejoices and inwardly thrills if it can do something for the glory of God. It is afflicted with sadness if it has neglected its duty. It takes delight in the Word of God, in meditation on it, and in every holy exercise. It is ravished by communion with God and finds its deepest pleasure in fellowship with Him, which it prefers to every other good. It values the truth of the gospel as a most precious pearl above anything else. And it is moved more by a concern for eternal salvation than by all earthly advantages. It counts everything as loss and rubbish in comparison to the surpassing worth of knowing Christ (Phil. 3:8). Such affections are inseparable from the state of grace.

The fifth characteristic of the spiritual life is *brotherly love*. Among the indubitable marks of a person with truly spiritual affections is to love the image of God in one's brother. Brotherly love is a positive affection and disposition toward our brother that stems from this source: that we see in him the imprint of true Christianity—that is, reverence for God and genuine godliness. In the examination of a person's spiritual state, this evidence is particularly conclusive. It is unquestionable that a person who loves God will love and cherish the image of God wherever he recognizes it. How can a person who receives into himself the image of God by regeneration hate in a brother God's image that he loves in himself? Or if a man hates in a brother the image of God (by which I mean an eagerness for truth, righteousness, and piety and a zeal for God's glory and for religion), how can he love God, who is the source of these virtues? "If a person should say, 'I love God,' and yet hates his brother, he is a liar. For how is it that one who does not love his brother, whom he sees, can love God whom he does not see? This is the commandment we have from Him: that the one who loves God must also love his brother" (1 John 4:20–21); "All people will know from this that you are My disciples if you love one another mutually" (John 13:35). Love is an affection that springs from a variety of sources. There is a natural love and a social love, and considered in themselves these are harmless enough. But if someone loves another because he is persuaded that that person has communion with God and Christ and that the image of God and Christ shines forth from him, he can legitimately conclude from this fact that he himself is in the love and communion of God and Christ. To the extent that a person loves and worships God, the unregenerate man will hate him and the regenerate man will love him. As David says, "My eyes will be upon the faithful of the land, that they might dwell with Me; the one who walks in the way of integrity will minister to Me. The one who acts deceptively will not dwell in My house; the one who speaks lies will not stand before My eyes" (Ps. 101:6–7).

The sixth and final characteristic of the spiritual life that I will mention here is *the ability to discern between spiritual and fleshly things*.

Everyone in the state of grace can distinguish what is of the Spirit from what is of the flesh. He takes note of the operations of the Holy Spirit with his own spirit, and if questioned he is able to give an explanation of these workings. I freely admit that on this point there is a great difference between ability and practice. I understand, of course, that some people may not be in the state of grace and still may display a decent aptitude for making discriminating comments about spiritual things because they are accustomed to discussing divine things through interactions with godly people or contact with the Word. But a person's opinions and statements about spiritual things are either accompanied by an internal feeling and affection about them or detached from this inner sense and inclination. Admittedly, it is often difficult to distinguish between these two conditions. But I would assert and defend the principle that no one to whom God in grace has revealed Himself is unaware of or unable to distinguish the state of his own soul. Rather, such a person notices the workings and influences of the Spirit of grace, pays attention to the spiritual changes and vicissitudes that he faces, examines often his progress or backsliding, and if it is useful or necessity requires, he is able to give an account of the state of his soul. He possesses a spiritual light that enables him to test and exercise discernment about what he receives from the preaching of the ministers of the Word or the conferences and writings of learned people. For the workings of God (in which He comes to people's souls, reveals Himself in grace to their minds, and joins His divine Spirit itself to our spirit) are capable of being sensed. The feeling of these things does not escape the notice of our consciences. Where there is spiritual life, there is light and also eyes capable of discerning that light. Jesus said, "Why do you not understand My speech [the phrases that I am using to explain my spiritual doctrine]? Because you cannot hear My word" (John 8:43). That is, you are inexperienced and incapable of discerning the sense of My statements about spiritual things: "My sheep hear my voice, and I know them, and they follow me" (John 10:27); "But the natural man is not capable of grasping the things that are from the Spirit of God. They are foolishness to him, and he cannot understand them, because they are spiritually discerned. The spiritual person, however, is able to discern everything, though he himself is properly understood by no one"

(1 Cor. 2:14–15); "But you have an anointing from the Holy One, and you understand all things" (1 John 2:20); "There was no one who could learn that song except for the hundred and forty four thousand, that is, those who were redeemed from the earth" (Rev. 14:3); "As it is written, 'I believed, and I have accordingly spoken'; we also have believed, and so we too speak likewise" (2 Cor. 4:13; see also Ps. 116:10).

What shall I say further? All of the attributes of the spiritual life that I have discussed above can be sketched from and compared to the qualities that Jesus Christ requires in His disciples. You can find these characteristics expounded at length in Matthew 5:3–11, in the psalms of David, and scattered throughout the Holy Scriptures. Whoever wishes to know his own image will find there a mirror to look into. Most mortals find this work of examination burdensome since they refuse to acknowledge their faults. People who are truly godly, however, will not flee from this inspection of themselves. They will always do it with humility and modesty, hard on their own weaknesses and faults and unimpressed with their own virtues and good works. In fact, the better and more modest they are, the more strictly and concernedly they will judge themselves. They never find anything lacking on the part of Christ Jesus, whose grace toward the penitent is indeed enormously broad, but in themselves they see many defects.

I commend to you the example of that remarkable man, James Ussher [1581–1656], archbishop of Armagh in the Protestant Church of Ireland. The churches will always celebrate his memory not only as an amazing scholar who displayed evidence of a remarkable measure of grace starting in his youth but as a man of piety known for every kind of virtue. For seventy-five years he carried out a long and constant course of indefatigable labors for the glory of God and the benefit of the church. He accomplished this through his preaching, teaching, writing, pastoring the souls of the faithful in his charge, encouraging his clergy, comforting the afflicted, helping the poor, and not sparing himself right up to his death. Nevertheless, just before he died, when he heard a friend preach on Colossians 3:1, the pious man was much touched by the sermon and roused himself to speak to the minister. Opening to him his heart, he asked the intimate question, "I beg you to tell me what state you judge me to be in," to which his colleague responded that he was beyond doubt in a good spiritual condition. "Ah," he replied, "you indeed judge me by your charity, but God is the searcher of the heart." William Dillingham adds something similar in his *Life of Ussher*: "As he left London for the last time and was saying goodbye to his friend Bernard, he spoke of himself as being the least of all the saints with a frequent profusion of tears."

CHAPTER 18

# Eternal Life

Thus far we have been discussing the beginning stages of the spiritual life. Our life lived in communion with God now will have its fulfillment in the celestial life lived in imitation of the angels and in accordance with the example of Christ Jesus raised from the dead. As we have understood from the survey above, we live this divine life imperfectly while on earth. Nevertheless, we expect the fulfillment of these beginnings in the glorious and celestial life that is their consummation. In keeping with the order of grace, our present spiritual experience is so connected to our future life that they cannot be separated or torn apart. As Jesus said to the Samaritan woman, "Whoever drinks from the water that I will give him will never again be thirsty, but the water that I will give him will become in him a fountain of water bubbling up to eternal life" (John 4:14). Here we should understand the grace of Christ Jesus—this grace brings not only righteousness but also the eternal fruits of holiness and joy that are indivisibly tied to the glory that is the outcome and completion of grace: "For we understand in part, and we prophesy in part. But when the perfect comes, that which is partial will be done away with" (1 Cor. 13:9–10); "It is not as if I have already attained or were already made perfect, but I pursue so that I might attain, which is why Christ Jesus laid hold of me. Brothers, I do not consider that I have attained the goal. But I do this one thing: forgetting the things that are behind and striving for the things that remain in front of me, I make it my goal to win the palm of God's heavenly calling in Christ Jesus" (Phil. 3:12–14). The life of grace implies the life of glory. The latter follows infallibly from the former.

This is why believers are said to already possess eternal life (e.g., John 3:36). For the same Lord who gives grace also gives glory (Ps. 84:11).

The life of glory is that glorious and blessed state of life into which believers are transported who by faith have finished the course of this mortal life with perseverance. They will be freed from sin, misery, and all their consequences, such as all shame, sadness, grief, temptation, affliction, all reproaches, all vanities, and all the vicissitudes to which our status in this life is exposed. And they will delight in the happy and glorious life of heaven itself, enjoying in the house of their Father fellowship and the closest connection to God, Christ Jesus, the angels, the patriarchs, the apostles, and the saints. And being enlightened by the glory of God and of Christ, with perfect love and the highest pleasure, joy, and delight in a state that is absolutely secure and unchangeable, they will possess God and be possessed by Him unto all eternity. Believers will have a foretaste of this life when their souls have been separated from their bodies. And they will receive its culmination [*complementum*] when their bodies have been resurrected from death by the power of Christ Jesus and transformed into spiritual bodies, having been adjudicated by Him on that great and solemn day that will put an end to the vanity of this age. This is the confidence of the saints and their most secure hope. This is the end of the struggle, the crown of the games, the palm of the race, and the triumph of faith. All desires lead to this; such life is the incessant longing of all those who seek God.

This is a state that surpasses the highest thoughts of mortal minds: the day "on which God will be glorified in His saints and marveled at by all who have believed" (2 Thess. 1:10). Who can describe such things adequately? Not even the languages of angels are sufficient for such a task. Even if we knew its attributes, we can only stutteringly describe such a magnificent subject. Since our thoughts are accustomed to the economy of this present time, it is only with difficulty that we can possibly compare the grandeur and excellence of the things that make up the heavenly economy. After speaking with Nicodemus about regeneration, the Lord Jesus added, "If I have told you earthly things, and you have not believed, how will you believe if I tell you heavenly things?" (John 3:12). We must understand "earthly things" in this passage to refer to those things that pertain to the dispensation of divine grace in this life, or rather that relate to the present economy of the church, in distinction to the things that make up the celestial economy. Not all the attributes of this state of perfection are known to us, since they have not been revealed to us. And they have not been revealed, both because we are not capable of understanding them perfectly and because God's purpose in graciously revealing things to us is not to satisfy our curiosity but to nourish our faith and hope. As John said, "Beloved, now we are the children of God, but it has not yet been manifested what we will become" (1 John 3:2). But in fact enough has been revealed about the coming glory for the support and encouragement of our faith and hope—so much material that I could go on at great length about it if the restrictions of the present work did not forbid. So here I will note a few of the most necessary points on this subject and bring my book to a proper conclusion.

The state of eternal life is a *state of consummation* in which a person, being rescued from the miseries and griefs of this life, is perfected in every way, in all his parts and faculties. His status is ennobled. And the attributes of this excellent and perfected status are designated in the Word of God under various concepts and notions, such as glory, kingdom, salvation, eternal life, incorruptibility, perfect redemption, adoption as the children of God, and blessedness, which we will take up in turn. These conceptualizations provide us with such a sweeping and exalted picture of this state that they include the most excellent possible things that could ever be thought or said about the condition of mankind.

In both testaments, eternal life is frequently presented in Scripture under the idea of *glory*: "When Christ, who is our life, becomes manifest, then you also will be manifest with Him in glory" (Col. 3:4); "The God of all grace called us to His eternal glory in Christ Jesus" (1 Peter 5:10); "You will guide me with Your counsel, and afterward take me to glory" (Ps. 73:24). That is, you will make me to share in the coming glory. Peter calls this "the unfading crown of glory" (1 Peter 5:4), and Paul says it is "an inexpressibly excellent weight of glory" (2 Cor. 4:17). What a powerful expression! And this was written by a person who had heard ineffable words in heaven that cannot be expressed!

Glory conceptualizes for us a state of supreme excellence, splendor, and dignity. Those entering this state will be made completely happy and blessed. They will be furnished with every internal quality that does credit and adds distinction to an intelligent creature. Their knowledge and holiness will be perfected, and they will have the purest affections of love for God. Simultaneously they will be lavished with all the external circumstances possible to enhance their honor and enrich and perfect their status. They will be transported into the closest communion with God the Father, Son, and Spirit and placed with all the saints into a state of high dignity in keeping with the ordering of the celestial economy constituted by God. They will celebrate the victory over all the evils, miseries, and enemies that often troubled, tempted, and crushed them in this life. A man will look on his neighbor, and he on the next person, and they will all see the bright, shining image of God in one another. Each one will brilliantly radiate God's glory, and they will acknowledge, love, and honor that glory in one another.

*Kingdom* is close to the idea of glory. As Jesus said, "I appoint a kingdom for you, as My father appointed for me" (Luke 22:29). Or Paul, "But this I say, brothers, that flesh and blood cannot obtain that inheritance which is the kingdom of God" (1 Cor. 15:50; cf. 1 Thess. 2:12). The concept of kingdom or reign suggests complete majesty, grandeur, and stateliness. Kingdom implies a state of the utmost glory, abundance, wealth, honor, freedom, perfection, and joy. As nothing disturbs the glory there, so nothing can perturb the joy, which cannot be separated from it. Kingdom implies a state of supreme exaltation in which all enemies will be crushed, and we will have nothing to fear. This figure of a kingdom also shows that believers (having been glorified in a state of supreme dignity and liberty, vindicated from every charge and disgrace, and freed from every depraved affection) will be subject to God alone and joined so closely to Him that they will have a share in God's rule. In Him they will rule over all things, and all creatures will serve to enhance the dignity of their status.

A third related idea is that of *salvation*, a well-known term frequently used in Scripture: "The one who perseveres to the end will be saved" (Matt. 24:13); "The one who believes and is baptized will be saved" (Mark 16:16). Salvation has a wide range of meaning, but its deepest reference is not to the miseries, afflictions, and temptations of this life (though I do not exclude them) but to the eternal loss and destruction and the wrath of God that will be poured out in a terrifying way on the wicked and those who are insolent toward the gospel on the last day, the day of wrath that exposes the just judgment of God. "Since we are now justified by His blood, we will even more certainly be saved by Him from wrath" (Rom. 5:9). The term *salvation* alludes to how Noah was saved from the flood, Lot from Sodom, and the Israelites from Egypt, which was buffeted and ruined by the divine plagues. It also brings to mind those Jewish believers in Christ of the first century who were going to be saved from the "Jerusalem flood"—that is, its destruction by the Romans. We should regard all these judgments as symbols pointing to the great and terrible final judgment. Who then is the person who forms no proper notion of the greatness of salvation? Who is the person unaffected by any true sense of its importance? Only the person who has not set before his eyes (by faith and a vivid mental image) that weighty and dreadful judgment. On that day those who despise the long-suffering of God, reject His calling them to repentance, and disdain His grace offered to them in Christ will be punished, ruined, and (even though they will not pass out of existence) put to death.

A fourth term is *redemption*, or rather *perfect redemption* (for this is the force that the term often receives in Holy Scripture). It denotes how believers are delivered and brought into a state of complete liberation and wholeness (as texts such as Rom. 8:23; 1 Cor. 1:30; and Eph. 4:30 suggest). The concept is close to that of salvation except that it particularly underlines for us the cause of our liberation. Throughout Scripture, this cause is set forth as the blood of Christ Jesus as an atoning sacrifice offered to God the Father in order to redeem the elect from the power of Satan, the corruption of the world, the servitude to sin, and all sin's oppressive consequences that choke the state of man on earth and make it a veritable captivity and slavery. The blood of the Son of God—that is, the perfect obedience that He demonstrated toward His Father in pouring out His blood unto death—accentuates the idea of a ransom paid to satisfy the judgment of God so that the elect seed might obtain complete liberation and freedom. The powerful effect of redemption in this life is that the souls of believers are cleansed from their sins and set free from slavery to corruption. But this ransom will have its fullest effect in the life to come when not only our souls but our very bodies will be resurrected from death; set free from all shame, pain, and corruption; and have a share in the glory that the illustrious final day will bring about. This is why Paul speaks about the "redemption of our bodies" (Rom. 8:23). Surely at that time the redemption procured for us by Christ Jesus will have its full effect. Its consequences will not be limited, as is the experience of believers on earth, but its impact and repercussions will be absolute, all-encompassing, and perfect.

The expression "adoption as sons" has a similar meaning and denotes the privileges granted to justified believers in the economy of grace. Through adoption they have been brought into the family of God, they become sharers in the good things of the house of God, and they receive the right to conduct themselves as the heirs of eternal life (John 1:12). But when this notion is taken in its fullest sense (as is the case in Rom. 8:23), it refers to that benefit of grace by which those whom Christ Jesus has redeemed are brought into such a state of perfection that the image of God appears in them with all its force, all its beauty, and all its excellence shining forth in majestic resplendence. In that state they will experience all the power and strength implicit in the title "sons of God." For they will be made similar to God not only in holiness, in purity, and in having their intelligence perfected and purged from error, but they will share even in His glory, honor, and immortality. As the Lord said in Luke 20:36, "Neither will they ever be able to die anymore. They will be made equal in condition to angels; they will be sons of God since they will be sons of the resurrection."

The idea of *eternal life*, a term often used in the Word of God, is particularly important for us to consider. I would add to it the idea of incorruptibility and immortality from Romans 2:7: "To those who patiently through good works seek glory, honor, and immortality, He will give eternal life." A well-developed idea of everlasting life is presented in Daniel 12:2–3. It teaches us to think of a state of noblest and most perfect activity in which the blessed are energetically engaged for all eternity, enjoying the highest pleasure and delight. In both testaments of Scripture, this condition is often simply called life—that is, life par excellence. Many texts speak of life emphatically: "You made known to me the path of life" (Ps. 16:11); "The righteous by faith will live" (Hab. 2:4); "...the commandment that was intended [to lead to] life" (Rom. 7:10; cf. Lev. 18:5).

There are two outstanding characteristics of this perfect life. First, it is a state of the noblest activity, most appropriately called life. Second, it is a state joined to a supreme pleasure and delight from which all pain, care, and fear have been removed. This illustrious activity is lived out in a complete way involving the entire person. It is not only rational, involving the mind, but spiritual since it is animated by the Spirit of God. And it is celestial, following the example of the actions of the angels. What is this spiritual activity but things similar to these: being taken up in the contemplation of God with joy, freedom, and delight; viewing the excellence of His attributes, virtues, power, and works; having an ardent and pure love for Him; and glorifying Him with praise and celebration? This activity will include keeping one's place and carrying out one's responsibilities in the celestial economy and, since we will have been raised to the same state of glory, having close relations with the angels and the saints. Consider also that this is a state of activity that will endure unto eternity in accordance with the counsel and enactment of God. It will be subject to no harmful change, no decrease, and no damage. It will be constant and perfect, and no series of ages will ever bring it to an end. From this comes the concept that it is an incorruptible state in which there will be no imperfection or the possibility of any change for the worse.

All the benefits mentioned above join together to make up our *blessedness* [*beatitatem*—i.e., supreme happiness], though this new term draws its own unique characteristics to our attention. Such terminology is often used in the Word of God: "Blessed is the people whose God is the LORD" (Ps. 33:12); "Blessed is the man who reverences the LORD" (Ps. 112:1). This is certainly because such a person has the solid hope of happiness, which no person who fears God expects to have perfectly in this life. "Looking for that blessed hope, and the glorious appearing of our great God and Savior, Jesus Christ" (Titus 2:13). Blessedness, as all know, is the highest perfection of the state [*status*] of intelligent beings. It is a condition in which they all perfectly acquiesce. They are at rest. They lack nothing. They desire nothing but what they have and long to be nothing but what they are. This perfect contentment and satisfaction consists in the following: that a person, in keeping with his condition, possesses such a measure of all the good things of nature that his desires are perfectly fulfilled; that he can enjoy these things without any pain, sadness, or bitterness; that a person is completely convinced of the security and perpetuity of his status, which takes away all fear, concern, and anxiety; and that a person enjoys such a sharp and constant sense of his own happiness that it produces in him a joy, a pleasure, and a delight in his perfect state.

Therefore, the blessed person is not only the one who longs for nothing and desires nothing beyond what he is, but the one who also hopes for nothing, fears nothing, and is penetrated by such perfect joy that no care or anxiety can possibly trouble him. Blessedness means being satiated with consolation and happiness: "Before Your face there is the full abundance of joys [i.e., perfect joy and a satiety of happiness]; at Your right hand there are pleasures forever" (Ps. 16:11); "They will hunger no more, nor will they ever be thirsty. The sun will no longer beat upon them nor any heat, because the Lamb who is in the middle of the throne will pasture them. He will lead them to the fountains of living water, and God will wipe away every tear from their eyes" (Rev. 7:16–17). This is what the "joy of the Lord" means (see Matt. 25:23). But of all the good things that the blessed will possess, the greatest and highest is God Himself, who, at that time and in that condition, will be "all in all." He will communicate Himself intimately to His people and will give them such an enjoyment of Himself that it is impossible to express in this life. He will cover them with His shadow and penetrate them with His glorious presence in such a manner that they will be ravished with perfect joy. It is proper to think that this is the first and most outstanding part of their blessedness. The holy singer expresses this elegantly in Psalm 17:15: "I will see Your face in righteousness [i.e., truly]; I will be satisfied with seeing Your image when I awaken." Similarly, the apostles write: "We know that when He will be made manifest, we will be made similar to Him, because we will see Him as He is" (1 John 3:2); "And in this way we will always be with the Lord" (1 Thess. 4:17).

We have gained an overview of this glorious status and its attributes from these concepts by which it is set forth in the Word of God. Nothing they present for our thought and contemplation is merely ordinary. Everything we understand from them is excellent, magnificent, and glorious, and by comparison all human and earthly things seem worthless. Everything is remarkable; everything pleases. The more we meditate on these terms and ideas, the more we will gather from them just how glorious and celestial are the attributes of that state into which justified believers will soon be transferred. All or even a single one of these scriptural concepts are able to stimulate in our minds sweeping and majestic ideas of the state to come.

This is also the case with the types and figures [*emblemata*] that are used by the authors of Holy Scripture to depict this state. Examples of these include calling this state (a) *paradise*, or the rest of God, in reference to the land of Canaan, the inheritance of the people of God under the old economy, as a symbol of happy rest enjoyed after extensive and difficult labors, along with liberty and the abundance of necessary and delightful good things; (b) the *temple of God*, furnished and prepared as a fortress, in which the ministers of God are in close communion with Him, stand before His throne, are sanctified by His glory, have all their needs met by divine providence, and devote all their efforts and care to serve Him perpetually; (c) *Zion*, the seat of the reigning house of David, the fortified mountain whose temple stood atop the cliff; (d) the *New Jerusalem*, a city most splendid and broad described by the divine prophets Isaiah, Ezekiel, Zachariah, and John, the city par excellence, transformed into a paradise and a temple, for these three figures are brought together in the vision given to John so that he might set the excellency of the state of this city before our eyes and commend it to us more certainly; (e) the *harvest*, a time of joy and abundance; (f) *pasture*, a grassy land for flocks irrigated by fountains of living water; and (g) other symbols such as *the eternal Sabbath, the feast of tabernacles*, and similar figures for this time that I have passed over in this brief survey.

All of these force us to exclaim along with the sacred singer, "How great is Your good which You have treasured up for those who fear You! The things that You have prepared for those who live for You in the presence of the children of men!" (Ps. 31:19). Of course, I understand that the Holy Spirit used these same symbols to represent the flourishing condition of the New Testament church that would take place at certain periods. But even in using these figures to describe the state of the New Testament church, the Holy Spirit always had in mind the perfect ideal and consummation of the state of the church, and He depicted the church in all its perfection at the end of the ages. I cannot analyze, untangle, and tease out the implications of all these symbols here, however. It is sufficient for my purpose simply to point them out.

In addition to these general characteristics that the Holy Spirit has used to describe and illustrate the happiness and perfection of this state, He has also revealed particular characteristics. And these are too magnificent to pass over in silence. We can see that they fall into two categories: those that describe this state negatively and those that describe it positively.

In terms of the negative, the Word of God teaches that in the coming state, justified and resurrected believers will be freed from every evil that afflicts the human race on earth. They will also be delivered from all the imperfections that cling to the state of God's elect in this world. As we have said, this is the implication of the term *perfect redemption*. Accordingly, they will be released from all sin, spiritual struggle, temptation, affliction, and persecution along with all the calamities, adversities, and setbacks of this life that cause our souls such pain, bitterness, and sadness. We will be freed from the fear of hardships, from all anxiety about troubles, and from death itself, which comes at the end of all these things. We will be delivered from all the contempt, shame, scorn, lies, oppression, injustice, and every wrong to which we are often exposed on earth from our adversaries. And finally, we will be released from all the vanity of this life—that is, the feeling of meaninglessness that accompanies so much of what we do on earth. Often things that are not bad in themselves, even useful and beneficial things, become through repetition things that bore, displease, weary, and disgust us. But then we will enjoy perfect consolation in intimate communion with God: "And God will wipe away every tear from their eyes; and death will no longer exist, neither mourning, nor crying. Pain shall no longer exist, because the previous things will have passed away" (Rev. 21:4).

In terms of the positive, there is much we could say about the characteristics peculiar to the state of glory. We will spend the remainder of our discussion considering the following three areas: (1) the way that man will be perfected and brought into a state of consummation in all his parts and constitutive elements, (2) the transformation of all man's faculties, and (3) other characteristics of the new state and condition in which man finds himself.

1. By the consummation of all the parts of a man, I have in mind what will happen to him on the last day when, rising from death, the entire man will enter into this glorious, heavenly, and eternal life—not just his spirit but also his body. For the Word of God and the analogy of every aspect of the doctrine of grace teach us that at the coming of the Lord the bodies of believers will be resurrected from the dust of the earth. They will receive a new form that is suited for the blessed life of immortality in a way that our animal bodies of this life are not capable. Believers whom the Lord will find still living when He comes will experience the same transformation of their bodies. This is the teaching that the apostle lays down and explains in the clearest terms (1 Cor. 15:42–58), a doctrine that he must have received by revelation and from Christ Jesus Himself. Our bodies indeed do not cease to be corporal, but they will be changed—not with regard to their substance but with regard to their qualities and characteristics. They will be incorruptible, enduring, glorious, spiritual, and robust in comparison with the corruptible, imperfect, and animal bodies that are the homes of our spirits here on earth.

From this we understand that these bodies will no longer need nourishment fitted to this life: food and drink for building up the blood. Our bodies will no longer be driven by the natural desires and animal passions that are connected to animal bodies. We will have spiritual bodies, completely subject to the rule of our spirits. Spiritually sustained and invigorated, they will act according to the will and intention of our minds. They will be like the bodies of the angels, who take on some pure and ethereal substance given by God when He sends them to be the instruments of His working. The Lord Jesus speaks of this in Luke 20:35–36: "But those who will be considered worthy to gain that age with its resurrection from the dead will neither marry nor be given in marriage. They will no longer be able to die for they will be similar to the angels." This gives us a reliable view and proper idea of that state. The apostle says similarly in 1 Corinthians 6:13, "Foods are designed for the stomach and the stomach for foods, but God will abolish them both." Our body in that state will no longer be an instrument of temptation to every sort of lust, but it will be made completely subject to our sanctified minds and serve for holy and upright works appropriate to the state of glory.

Those bodies will be freed from all filthiness and anything that brings on shame. Here I do not have in mind simply those external and outward vices that cause disgrace. At that time even those aspects of our present bodies that are dishonorable (i.e., the parts of the body that serve for purposes of bodily excretions in this economy) will become honorable (cf. Rom. 9:21; 2 Tim. 2:21). As the apostle says in Philippians 3:21, "[Christ Jesus] will transfigure our humble body and bring it into conformity with His glorious body."

Those bodies will be strong and robust, not subject to any of the infirmities of our present animal bodies. No sickness, weariness, melancholy, or any other disorder will be able to hinder or trouble the free exercise of the faculties of the mind and spirit. In contrast with what we see in these earthly tents that conform to this earthly economy, our bodies then will not be subject to any corruption or harmful alteration, certainly not to death itself and the dissolution of our members.

It is certainly difficult to get a perfect image of the change that will take place in our bodies in that state and economy. But as we think about this change, reason leads us to believe along with the apostle that the transformation of the qualities of our bodies is clearly necessary to the coming state of glory that the Word of God reveals to us.

2. Regarding the perfection of man's faculties, which include the intellect, the will, and the affections, the Word of God clearly teaches us that there will be at least two differences. The first is that our intellect and knowledge in the state of our future life will be much more perfect than in the economy of grace in this life. The understanding of the blessed will be so perfected that all their desires to know will be perfectly satisfied as far as human capabilities and faculties allow. The apostle suggests this in 1 Corinthians 13:9–10: "For we understand in

part, and we prophesy in part. But when the perfect comes, that which is partial will be done away with." In this same text the apostle explains what will be the difference in our knowledge. First, it means that the object of our knowledge will always be present and contemporaneous, not something future or something from the past. For thus he says, "Love never fails. But if there are prophecies, they will vanish; if there are tongues, they will cease; if there is knowledge [that is, the knowledge necessary to understand prophecies and to examine carefully the ways of God], it will be done away with" (1 Cor. 13:8). There will be no reason for a knowledge of future things, because the state of celestial glory will be constant and unchanging. With regard to past things, the blessed will not have to trouble themselves, either because the greater part of human affairs are a series of crimes, miseries, and the vanities of the human race groaned out in service to corruption and under the rule of Satan, or—if God decides to give to His people the knowledge of the order and connectedness of the ways in which He administered the church during its different economies (which is not improbable)— then He will do it without any labor or wearying investigation on their part. He will so clearly illuminate their understanding at a single stroke that they will be able to contemplate as in a mirror the entire order of the ways of God until they are fully satisfied. But you may properly say that all things will be present to their minds as God leads them into the intimate contemplation of His glory and of His wondrous works. In the state of glory this contemplation may well cause them to admire the displays and effects of His power, goodness, and wisdom in such a way that the observation and vision of these things will fill them with the highest pleasure.

A second difference will be the way we will know. The blessed will know all things through an intuitive and sensory vision, through the clearest illumination of their minds, perhaps similar to the kind of enlightenment God gave to the prophets of old when they were carried off in ecstasy. The apostle says in 1 Corinthians 13:12, "For now we see in a mirror, darkly [*in aenigmate*]. But then we will see face to face. Now I know in part; but then I will know even as I have been known," and, "For we walk by faith, not by sight" (2 Cor. 5:7). Now between faith and sight there is the same difference as between a judgment

about something based on a rational demonstration and a direct vision
or sense experience of that same thing. I do indeed recognize that faith
involves a demonstration that can be rather certain, and if it is accompanied by the illumination of the Holy Spirit, it becomes indubitable
and invincible proof. However, there is a different and even clearer type
of perception when the truth is revealed immediately to our minds
and spirits. This is what the apostle calls seeing God "face to face," a
phrase he has taken from the sacred history of Moses (Ex. 33:11; Num.
12:8). It was the privilege of Moses, who was distinguished above all
the prophets, to enjoy an immediate commerce and communication
with God. He manifested Himself to Moses in the cloud, whether on
Mount Sinai or at the door of the tabernacle. Moses laid out the questionable matters and cases before God without being in any ecstasy or
having his mind affected in any extraordinary way. And he received
the responses through his senses: hearing the voice of God speaking
in a human form with nothing veiled, nothing expressed in riddles
or figures. In this connection with God where Moses had the free use
of his senses, he saw something of the glory of God and was himself
illumined by that glory. In that same passage this is called seeing the
image or the likeness of God. The holy singer refers to this experience
when he describes the state of glory in Psalm 17:15: "I will be satisfied
with seeing Your image when I awaken." Just earlier he had said, "I will
see Your face in righteousness." The Hebrew expression *in righteousness*
means "truly." It refers to knowledge that comes from sense experience
rather than through the reasoning and thinking we do in this life. In
the life to come our reasoning will be so purified and perfected, we will
be so enlightened and so able to see all the consequences of things, that
the rational and intellectual perception of our minds will be an intuitive vision similar to what we experience with our bodily eyes. We have
a picture of this in the four mystical animals described as "four beasts
full of eyes before and behind" (Rev. 4:6).

The second change that characterizes the new status of the rational
parts of our faculties will be perfect sanctification. Holiness will spread
its light through our entire mind and all its affections and actions. This
state of sanctity is a state of spiritual purity. Having been freed from
sin, from all temptation to sin and as firm as cherubim, believers in

that state will be unalterably confirmed in bearing the perfect image of God as far as possible for created beings. His glory will shine out from them, and they will bear the name of sons of God even as the angels do: "We know that when He appears, we also will be like Him" (1 John 3:2; cf. Luke 20:36). When the Holy Spirit in Scripture speaks about this sanctification, it does so in terms of the affections of love and of zeal for God's glory. Holiness of the affections implies that we will love God and desire to see Him glorified.

A third characteristic of this changed status regarding the rational part of our faculties flows from the second: a perfect love for God and for His saints that will consume every type of depraved affection. In the coming state of glory all wrath, hate, envy, and jealousy, which in this life so often slide in and trip up the best of us, will be done away with. A love for God accompanied by a burning zeal to see Him glorified will penetrate to the deepest parts of believers' souls and will set them entirely aflame as the apostle suggests in 1 Corinthians 13:8: "Charity never fails [i.e., love is never extinguished]." Faith will evaporate. Hope will be no longer necessary. But love and charity will remain. Since God's people will be equal and comparable to the angels, the purity of affections, the zeal, and the concern for the divine glory that we acknowledge in the angels will shine forth conspicuously in them. Certainly this is a characteristic of all God's outstanding ministers, whether in heaven or on earth (though in His earthly servants this quality will be only brought to perfection in the age to come). Ezekiel sets forth this characteristic symbolically in the figure of the cherubim, who are described as such: "The appearance of the living creatures was like burning coals of fire, like the appearance of flames" (Ezek. 1:13; cf. Isa. 6:2; Ps. 104:4).

A fourth characteristic of these changes will be the unspeakable joy and perfect satisfaction and acquiescence that we will take in our state and condition. I have described this above as a part of one's blessedness. I do understand that the joy of the blessed will come from an awareness of all the attributes of the state of blessing, and so it would be most natural to deal with this subject last. But since I am dealing with the characteristics of this state as they relate to the parts and faculties of man, it seemed proper for me to keep the train of thought and deal with this subject here. For joy has to do with the affections, and the affections lead to a person's inclinations and will. So the holy poet speaks in Psalm 16:11, "You will make known to me the path of life [a state of the most enjoyable activity]; before Your face there is the full abundance of joys; at Your right hand there are pleasures forever." Nothing could be said more powerfully. Isaiah expresses it in this way: "Everlasting joy will be upon their heads. Pain and sighing will flee away, and they will obtain happiness and joy" (Isa. 35:10; cf. the previously cited texts of Isa. 25:8; Rev. 7:17; 21:4). It is true that these passages of the prophet can be understood of the excellent state of the New Testament church on earth, which was a foretaste of heavenly joy. But the Holy Spirit never speaks emphatically about the joy of the church in this age (which is always laboring under its own imperfections) without suggesting that it will be completed in the state of heavenly blessedness.

Not only all public but all individual suffering and pain will be done away with in that state of eternal happiness. There will be no more tears, groaning, or sighing. There will be no more grief or sorrow. There will be no sad memories connected to bitter feelings, no regrets, no pangs of conscience over things poorly done, as is often the case in this life. No fear about the future will trouble the sweetness of that state nor any concern that bad things may happen to our condition. There will be no death nor any destruction. In contrast we will enjoy pure brightness, unmixed joy, perfect consolation, and solid pleasure, not carnal but spiritual. For all the affections of the blessed will conform to their spiritual state—they themselves will be truly spiritual people and, as it were, angelical: "They will be irrigated by the richness of Your house, and from the torrent of Your pleasures You will give them drink" (Ps. 36:8). He will lead them to the fountains of living water, and they will drink to their entire satisfaction [satietatem]. The shadow of God like a shelter will furnish them with security, protection, and refreshment against all the hot blasts that troubled them in this life. From our experience of spiritual joy, we can gain some idea of the bliss to come. But we are now surrounded by so many troubles, hindrances, and difficulties that it is difficult to grasp just how amazing that state will be. So we must keep in mind our imperfect present state as compared with our perfect future state. To simply list out all the symbols that point to it is difficult, but figures such as feasts, weddings, temple music, celebrations and jubilees, the Sabbath, and eating from the Tree of Life all point to the great joy to come.

3. The third way we can discuss the positive characteristics of the state of the blessed is by considering other attributes and characteristics that describe it. First among these is the fact that in glory we will have immediate commerce and direct fellowship with God and with Christ Jesus, the captain, prince, and firstborn of the brothers who will be glorified along with Him. We will also have fellowship and personal dealings with the holy angels, the patriarchs, the prophets, and the chosen people of God from every age. The following texts that I have already cited are relevant here: "I will see Your face in righteousness; I will be satisfied with seeing Your image when I awaken" (Ps. 17:15); "We will see Him as He is" (1 John 3:2); "Then [we will see] face to face" (1 Cor. 13:12); "We will always be with the Lord" (1 Thess. 4:17); "I desire to depart and be with Christ" (Phil. 1:23); "Many…will sit down with Abraham, Isaac, and Jacob in the kingdom of heaven" (Matt. 8:11; cf. Luke 16:22). It is indeed difficult to define how this immediate commerce with God will be experienced on our part, and it is not good to be too curious in wanting to penetrate this mystery in advance. But this I am absolutely sure of: that we will behold the glory of the Lord with unveiled faces (2 Cor. 3:18). We will have direct fellowship with Him, not simply as a mental communication but in a sensory way. We will see and we will hear amazing things in that place full of splendor, grandeur, and divine majesty.

A second characteristic of the status of the blessed is the beauty and external splendor that they will enjoy since they have a share not only in the communion but also in the glory of God. They will experience what happened with Moses, whose face shone after he had been in close communication with God, and the Israelites could not bear the rays of brightness (Ex. 34:29–30). The gospel history teaches that when God the Father wished to give Christ Jesus a taste of the future glory prepared for Him, He transformed Him in front of His disciples and "His face shone like the sun, and His clothing became as white as light" (Matt. 17:2). It is rather certain that Moses and Elijah appeared in this same form too. When angels appear among men, they take on this same appearance, according to Luke 24:4. I realize that I must take care not to reduce heavenly glory, something spiritual, into a mere external form or outward show that has little to do with its real nature. But what I say here is important to consider. The exterior form and appearance of those who have been resurrected will be entirely glorious. This is the teaching of the apostle (1 Cor. 15:41). He says in Philippians 3:21, "[Christ Jesus] will transfigure our humble body and bring it into conformity with his glorious body," and, "For those He foreknew He also predestined to become conformed to the image of His Son, so that He might be the firstborn among many brothers" (Rom. 8:29).

A third characteristic of this type is the holy activity and exercise (completely in keeping with their perfect and glorious state) that will occupy the blessed in glory. As I have explained above in the discussion of eternal life, they will exert themselves without intermission and with a sense of continuous delight and pleasure. We see a figure of this in those confessors of the truth who, during the times of the most violent persecutions of the church, "washed their robes white in the blood of the Lamb" (Rev. 7:14). The elder instructed the apostle John and gave this testimony about them: "Therefore they are [standing] before the throne of God. And they serve Him day and night in His temple" (Rev. 7:15). Believers in glory will actively contemplate the glory, majesty, powers, and wondrous works of God. God Himself will set out for their consideration and amazement the acts of His wisdom and the effects of His power and goodness. Every person in that glorious state and heavenly economy will serve God with extreme joy in His personal presence and, in close communion with God, will act like a priest. All of us will celebrate and glorify Him with a single voice in harmony and perfect concert both for His excellencies, virtues, powers, and works as well as for the immense benefits and many things more that we have received out of His infinite grace (cf. Rev. 4:8; 5:8–14; 15:3–4; Pss. 17:15; 65:8).

A fourth characteristic relevant here is that in this state the saints will see the enemies of God, of Christ, and of themselves thrown down at their feet. Those who despised believers in this life (derided, afflicted, and persecuted them, oppressed and tortured them)—these violent, evil, tyrannical, and wicked people—will be excluded from the fellowship of the saints and turned outside the gates of the heavenly

Jerusalem. They will go into a state of punishment as their conscience oppresses them, and they will lack all good things. The more they envy believers' happiness, the greater will be their despair (cf. Isa. 66:24). As the apostle says, "For He must reign until He has placed all enemies beneath His feet [that is, the feet of Christ and of those who are His]" (1 Cor. 15:25) and "The God of peace will soon grind Satan under your feet" (Rom. 16:20). Isaiah expressed this figuratively as he spoke about the state that the church would enjoy in a better time to come: "The sons of those who afflicted you will come and bow down at the soles of your feet" (Isa. 60:14). God forbid that we should take any delight in the miseries of others, but we should rest and be satisfied in God's most just economy and His most righteous management of all things.

A fourth way to approach the topic of this blessed state is by considering its accidents—that is, the circumstances that surround it. Among these, let me first note the place. The place destined for this glorious and happy state is called by Scripture the highest heaven, the third heaven (2 Cor. 12:2), the heaven of heavens (1 Kings 8:27), the paradise of God, the heavenly Jerusalem and celestial temple.

I piously and firmly believe that there is a place that is a part of this universe in the highest realms of the heavens, completely illuminated by the light of the divine glory, which has been prepared for when the salvation of God's chosen ones is brought to consummation. Christ Jesus, as the first one resurrected from the dead and having opened up the way there by His own blood, has entered and taken the throne of glory destined for Him by the Father. The Lord Himself speaks of this in John 14:2: "In the house of My Father there are many rooms, otherwise I would have said so. I am going to prepare a place for you." We read about Abraham, who was living in tents, that, "He looked for a city which has foundations [in contrast to tents], whose architect and builder is God" (Heb. 11:10). Another symbol of this place was the holy of holies in the ancient temple, which was simply called "the holy place" or the sanctuary of God (cf. Heb. 8:1–2; 9:12; 2 Cor. 5:1). The Lord had this in mind when He told us to pray, "Our Father which art in heaven." This sanctuary is the dwelling place of the good angels and the lodging of the righteous made perfect (Heb. 12:22–23). Here God makes known His presence, probably through external manifestations that are beyond human ability to explain. Here He has His throne, the seat of His majesty. Here He is adored, worshiped, and honored. Here He is attended by the angels. Most accurately and truly, this is God's place, as Ezekiel heard: "I heard behind me a voice of a great rushing wind, saying, 'Blessed be the glory of the LORD from His place'" (Ezek. 3:12). Amos spoke of the chambers or "dining rooms" of the Lord (Amos 9:6). We must believe that mortal human beings in the present state are not able to conceive anything equal to the magnificence of this celestial sanctuary, imagine anything equivalent to its grand and beautiful appearance, or envisage anything that can give the least glimpse of its construction and true form. But this we do know: it is a place filled with God and with His glorious and awe-inspiring presence. Who does not perceive and feel that this place will contribute much to the happiness, honor, and bliss of those who will enter there by grace?

A second attribute and circumstance surrounding the future state is its eternity. I have dealt with this more fully above in speaking of eternal life. It will be a state of immortality and incorruptibility (Rom. 2:7; 1 Peter 5:4). This is the circumstance that brings all the others to their full completion. For unless that state of blessing is eternal, and unless the blessed are conscious of its eternity, they could never have joy or any true bliss. Uncertainty about your status gives birth to concern and fear, which disturb your joy. The greater the good thing that you enjoy is, the dearer it is to you. The more you passionately love something, then the more urgently you desire to keep it and the more bitter would be the thought that your possession and enjoyment of it is only for a limited time. There is no true bliss and beatitude if it does not include the certainty that we will be able to enjoy it for an eternity.

Such is it to enter into the joys of the Lord Jesus (Matt. 25:23). Such is the "crown of glory prepared by the Lord for all who are desirous of His glorious appearing" (2 Tim. 4:8). Such is the celestial paradise—an eternal, perfect, and blissful life that is the consummation and fulfillment of the spiritual life. The hope and confident expectation of this happy life to come sustains believers throughout the difficult and painful race, throughout all the labors and afflictions of this life. The portrait I have given of it here is clumsily done, a mere sketch rather than a portrait.

If the reader of these few pages would understand more, let him use his own capacity to perceive the things to come that are imperfectly chalked out here, and he will be able to explain them better. For the present, however, it is sufficient to understand that an abundant recompense is coming, a "great reward" (Ps. 19:11). There are tremendous good things stored up for those who fear God (Ps. 31:19). The magnitude of these benefits cannot be grasped by the faculties of the human mind in this terrestrial economy. But it often happens that out of the great kindness He has toward those whom He so tenderly loves, God gives a foretaste of the delights of this future life. When they are involved in holy exercises, at times He may fill them with great clarity and light and give them an extremely vivid sense of His grace. With gentle comfort He may soothe and console them in the sorrows and adversities of this life. He may fill His people with unspeakable joy and lighten their way with serenity, contentment, all kinds of high thoughts, and a peace that passes understanding. He may stir them up to a most ardent love and desire for Himself. Seeming to have been loosed from their bodies and ravished in the contemplation of the wonders of His being and the marvels of His ways, God may saturate them with such a certain persuasion and overwhelming confidence in their future happiness, and the good things that they have by faith they seem to possess now as a present reality. These are delights that can only be learned in the school of the saints. Such pleasures are bread for God's elect, the white stone with a new name written on it that no one knows except the one who receives it, the supper of God where Christ feasts with those worthy to live in His house, the Spirit's testimony with our spirit (Rom. 8:16), the affirmation and strengthening of the faith and hope of those who are mature believers by the grace of God. And they in grateful response devote themselves completely to Him (cf. Ps. 63:3; John 14:23; Rom. 8:16; Phil. 4:7; 1 Peter 1:8; Rev. 2:17; 3:20).

Therefore, O man of God, you who are called in the hope of such good things, set forth toward the goal appointed for you! In this way you will find rest and you will rise to enjoy your portion on the last day (Dan. 12:13). Amen. Come, Lord Jesus!

Glory be to God through Jesus Christ. Amen.

# Bibliography

Baschera, Luca. "Ethics in Reformed Orthodoxy." In *A Companion to Reformed Orthodoxy*, edited by Herman Selderhuis, 519–52. Leiden: Brill, 2013.

Bauch, Hermann. *Die Lehre vom Wirken des Heiligen Geistes im Frühpietismus: Studien zur Pneumatologie und Eschatologie von Campegius Vitringa, Philipp Jakob Spener und Johann Albrecht Bengel.* Theologische Forschung: wissenschaftliche Beiträge zur kirchlich-evangelischen Lehre 55. Hamburg-Bergstedt: H. Reich, 1974.

Beeke, Joel R. "Gibertus Voetius: Toward a Reformed Marriage of Knowledge and Piety." In *Protestant Scholasticism: Essays in Reassessment*, edited by Carl R. Trueman and R. Scott Clark, 227–43. Carlisle, U.K.: Paternoster, 1999.

Bomble, Christianus Joannes. *Analysis nec non chronotaxis apocalypticae: (ad mentem...Campegii Vitringa...in suo commentario apocalyptico, editione altera).* Amsterdam: Henricus Strick, 1721.

Brine, John, and Campegius Vitringa. *The Moral Law the Rule of Moral Conduct to Believers, Considered and Enforced by Arguments: Extracted from the Works of the Late Rev. John Brine and Vitringa [Observationes Sacrae].* London, 1792.

Büsching, Anton Friederich. "Fortsetzung des Lebenslaufs des selige Herrn Vitringa: von seinem natürlichen und sitlichen Character." In *Auslegung der Weissagung Jesaiae*, 2:7–16. Halle, Ger.: Johann Gottlob Bierwirth, 1751.

———. "Lebenslauf des Verfassers dieser Auslegung." In *Auslegung der Weissagung Jesaiae*, 1:25–52. Halle, Ger.: Johann Gottlob Bierwirth, 1749.

Childs, Brevard S. "Hermeneutical Reflections on Campegius Vitringa, Eighteenth-Century Interpreter of Isaiah." In *In Search of True Wisdom: Essays in Old Testament Interpretation in Honour of Ronald E. Clements*, edited by Edward Ball, 89–98. Sheffield, U.K.: Sheffield Academic, 1999.

———. *The Struggle to Understand Isaiah as Christian Scripture*. Grand Rapids: Eerdmans, 2004.

Clark, R. Scott, and Carl R. Trueman, eds. *Protestant Scholasticism: Essays in Reassessment*. Carlisle, U.K.: Paternoster, 1999.

Diestel, Ludwig. *Geschichte des Alten Testamentes in der christlichen Kirche*. Jena, Ger.: Mauke, 1868.

Duff, Archibald. *History of Old Testament Criticism*. London: Watts, 1910.

Dunkel, Johann Gottlob Wilhelm. "Campegius Vitringa." In *Historisch-Kritische Nachrichten von verstorbenen Gelehrten und deren Schriften*, 2:748–50 (Teil 4), 1970. Hildesheim, Ger.: Georg Olms Verlagsbuchhandlung, 1756.

Glasius, Barend. "Campegius Vitringa, Zoon." In *Godgeleerd Nederland: biographisch Woordenboek van Nederlandsche Godgeleerden*, 3:36. Hertogenbosch, Neth.: Gebroeders Muller, 1856.

Halma, Francois. *Aan der eerwarden Heer, Campegius Vitringa, der H. Theologie en kerkelyke Historien Professor, als zyn Eerwaarde tot Rector Magnificus in Vrieslandts Atheensche Schoole plechtig wierdt ingewydt, den 2den van Wiedemaant, 1705* [Honorific Poem]. Franeker, Neth.: Franciscus Halma, 1705.

Hemsterhuis, Tiberius. *Oratio funebris in memoriam admodum venerandi ac celeberrimi viri Campegii Vitringa filii: SS. theologiae doctoris, & dum fuit, in illustri frisiorum academia professoris ordinarii, exequiis solenniter in templo academico habita die XXV. Januarii MDCCXXIII*. Franeker, Neth.: Henricus Halma, 1723.

Israel, Jonathan I. *The Dutch Republic: Its Rise, Greatness and Fall, 1477–1806*. London: Oxford University Press, 1995.

Kautzsch, Emil Friedrich. "Vitringa, Campegius." In *The New Schaff-Herzog Encyclopedia of Religious Knowledge*. Vol. 12. Edited by Samuel Macauley Jackson. New York: Funk and Wagnalls, 1912.

Kobus, Jan C. "Campegius Vitringa, Zoon." In *Beknopt Biographisch Woordenboek van Nederland*, 3:101. Zutphen: Royal Netherlands Academy of Arts and Sciences, 1861.

Kocsi, Stephanus Cs. *Epos lugubre in obitum viri dei longe celeberrimi, d. Campegii Vitringa, P. in inclyta academia Franequerana s.s. theologiae & historiarum professoris meritissimi. Fato functi XXXI. Martii MDC-CXXII.* Franeker, Neth.: Henricus Halma, 1722.

Lange, Joachim, and Campegius Vitringa. *Apocalyptisches Licht und Recht, das ist richtige und erbauliche Erklärung, des prophetischen Buchs der heiligen Offenbahrung Johannis: darinn, nach dem bisher auch bei der evangelischen Kirche sehr beliebt gewordenen Systemate Vitringiano, nach einem nöthigen Vorbericht, erstlich eine ausführliche Einleitung, und nach der exegetischen Abhandlung...eine genaue Ubereinstimmung gedachter Offenbahrung mit den Propheten des alten Testaments, sonderlich dem Jesaia, aus des niederländischen hochberühmten Theologi, Campegii Vitringae, grossen und vortrefflichen Commentario über den Jesaiam, dargeleget wird.* Halle, Ger.: Francke, 1730.

Muller, Richard A. *After Calvin: Studies in the Development of a Theological Tradition.* New York: Oxford University Press, 2003.

———. "Biblical Interpretation in the Sixteenth and Seventeenth Centuries." In *Dictionary of Major Biblical Interpreters,* edited by Donald K. McKim, 22–44. Downers Grove, Ill.: InterVarsity Press, 2007.

———. *Dictionary of Latin and Greek Theological Terms, Drawn Principally from Protestant Scholastic Theology.* Grand Rapids: Baker, 1985.

———. *Post-Reformation Reformed Dogmatics: The Rise and Development of Reformed Orthodoxy, ca. 1520–1725.* 2nd ed. 4 vols. Grand Rapids: Baker Academic, 2003.

Nicéron, Jean-Pierre. "Campege Vitringa." In *Mémoires pour servir à l'histoire des hommes illustres dans la république des lettres, avec un catalogue raisonné de leurs ouvrages,* 35:30–40. Paris: Briasson, 1727.

Postma, Ferenc, and Jacob van Sluis. *Auditorium Academiae Franekerensis: Bibliographie der Reden, Disputationen und Gelegenheitsdruckwerke der Universität und des Athenäums in Franeker, 1585–1843.* Minsken en Boeken: Rige bio- en bibliografyske skriften Fryske Akademy nr. 760. Leeuwarden, Neth.: Fryske Akademy, 1995.

Röell, Herman Alexander, and Campegius Vitringa. *Dissertatio theologica de generatione filii, et morte fidelium temporali:[Pars prima]: qua suas de iis theses plenius explicat, & contra clarissimi viri Campegii Vitringa objectiones defendit [Pars altera]: Opposita epilogo clarissimi viri Campegii Vitringa....* Franeker, Neth.: Johannes Gyselaar, 1689.

Sandys-Wunsch, John. "Early Old Testament Critics on the Continent." In *Hebrew Bible / Old Testament: The History of Its Interpretation: From the Renaissance to the Enlightenment*, 2:971–76. Göttingen, Ger.: Vandenhoeck and Ruprecht, 2008.

Schrenk, Gottlob. *Gottesreich und Bund im älteren Protestantismus: vornehmlich bei Johannes Coccejus; Zugleich ein Beitrag zur Geschichte des Pietismus und der heilsgeschichtlichen Theologie.* Gütersloh, Ger.: Bertelsmann, 1923.

Schultens, Albert. *Laudatio funebris in memoriam Campegii Vitringa, theol. prof.* Franeker, Neth.: Henricus Halma, 1722.

———. "Lykrede ter Uitvaart van den voornamen Godgeleerden Campegius Vitringa [Vader]." In *Uitvoerige Waarschuuwing, op verscheide stukken der Kategismus Verklaaringe van den Eerwaarden en Geleerden Heere Alexander Comrie, Predikant te Woubrugge, tot onerrrichting van dien Godvruchtigen Leeraar; tot vernedering van Niklaas Holtius, Predikant te Koudekerk; tot vernietiging der scheurgierige Aanslagen eener ongenoemde Societeit, die den Twist over de Leere van D. van der Os, naar het Voorbeeld van D. Holtius, betrekkelijk heeft gemaakt op eenige Stellingen, en op den Leertrant, der Heeren Vitringa en Lampe; tot Verdeediging van het Leids Advies over het Zwolfe geschil; en tot bewordering van Vreede en Rust in Land en Kerke; ontworpen en uitgevaardich door Jan Jakob Schultens...Voor af gat de Vertaalde Lijkrede van Alb. Schultens op Kampeg. Vitringa, den Vader,* 1–47. Leiden: Abraham Kallewier and Hendrik van der Deyster, 1755.

Singer, Isidore. "Campegius Vitringa, the Elder." *The Jewish Encyclopedia.* Vol. 12. New York: Funk and Wagnalls, 1906.

Spier, Johann Justus. *De sensu mystico vitringiano septem epistolarum ad septem asiae ecclesias.* Wittenberg, 1730.

Telfer, Charles K. "Campegius Vitringa (1659–1722): A Biblical Theologian at the Beginning of the Eighteenth Century." In *Biblical Theology: Past, Present and Future*, edited by Mark Elliot and Carey Walsh, 18–32. Eugene, Ore.: Wipf and Stock, 2016.

———. "Campegius Vitringa (1659–1722), Exemplary Exegete and Theologian of the Spiritual Life." *Hapshin Theological Review* 6 (2018): 69–90.

———. "Campegius Vitringa Sr.: 'Praefatio ad lectorem,' in: *Commentarius in librum prophetiarum Jesaiae*, 1716 and 'De interpretatione prophetiarum,' in: *Typus doctrinae propheticae, in quo de prophetis et prophetiis agitur, hujusque scientiae praecepta traduntur*, 1708." In *Handbuch der Bibelhermeneutiken*, edited by Oda Wischmeyer, 433–47. Berlin: De Gruyter, 2016.

————. "The Exegetical Methodology of Campegius Vitringa (1659–1722), Especially as Expressed in His *Commentarius in Librum Prophetiarum Jesaiae.*" PhD diss., Trinity Evangelical Divinity School, 2015.

————. *Wrestling with Isaiah: The Exegetical Methodology of Campegius Vitringa (1659–1722).* Reformed Historical Theology Series. Edited by Herman Selderhuis. Göttingen, Ger.: Vandenhoeck and Ruprecht, 2016.

van Asselt, Willem J. *Introduction to Reformed Scholasticism.* Translated by Albert Gootjes. Grand Rapids: Reformation Heritage Books, 2011.

van Asselt, Willem J., and Eef Dekker. *Reformation and Scholasticism: An Ecumenical Enterprise.* Texts and Studies in Reformation and Post-Reformation Thought. Grand Rapids: Baker Academic, 2001.

van den Berg, J. "Theology in Franeker and Leiden in the Eighteenth Century." In *Religious Currents and Cross-Currents: Essays on Early Modern Protestantism and the Protestant Enlightenment*, edited by Jan de Bruijn and Peter Holtrop, 253–67. Studies in the History of Christian Thought. Leiden: Brill, 1999.

van der Sleen, J. J. "Johannes Coccejus en Campegius Vitringa: een Vergelijking van hun Theologie op Hoofdpunten." MA thesis, Universiteit Utrecht, 2001.

van der Waeyen, Johannes, ed. *Kort Bericht opens het Geene so by de hooge Regeeringe en Heeren Curatoren, Mitsgaaders Rector en Senatus der Academie tot Franeker gedaan; als Elders voorgevallen is, in de Saake van Geschil over de Generatie des Soons Gods, tusschen de Heeren Vitringa En Röell [1653–1718], Doctoren En Professoren Theologiæ.* Franeker, Neth.: Hans Gyselaar, 1691.

van der Wall, Ernestine G. E. "Between Grotius and Coccejus: The 'Theologia Prophetica' of Campegius Vitringa (1659–1722)." In *Hugo Grotius, Theologian*, edited by G. H. M. Posthumus Meyjes, Henk J. M. Nellen, and Edwin Rabbie, 195–215. Leiden: Brill, 1994.

van Heel, Willem Frederik Caspar Johannes. "Campegius Vitringa Sr. als Godgeleerde Beschouwd." PhD diss. Gravengage: Utrecht, 1865.

Vitringa, Campegius. *Aanleiding tot het recht Verstant van den Tempel, die de prophet Ezechiel bezien en beschreeven heft.* 2 vols. Franeker, Neth., 1687.

———. *Aanmerkingen over de Leerwijse om kerkelijke Redenvoeringen wel op te stellen. Vermeerdert met einige betrachtende Overdenkingen, mitsgaders een Verhandelinge van 't H. Nachtmaal, alsmede van de geestelijke Blijdschap als gevolg van de staat eens christen Mensch.* Franeker, Neth.: Wibius Bleck, 1724.

———. *Anacrisis Apocalypseos Joannis Apostoli qua in veras interpretandae ejus hypotheses diligenter inquiritur & ex iisdem interpretatio facta, certis historiarum monumentis confirmamur atque illustratur; ea etiam quae Meldensis praesul Bossuetus in hujus vaticinii commentario supposuit, et exegetico protestantium systemati in visis de bestia ac babylone mystica objecit, sedulo examinantur.* Franeker, Neth.: Franciscus Halma, 1705.

———. *Animadversiones ad methodum homiliarum ecclesiasticarum, rite instituendarum.* Franeker, Neth.: Henricus Halma, 1721.

———. *Aphorismi, quibus fundamenta sanctæ theologiæ comprehenduntur: in usum scholarum privatarum.* Franeker, Neth.: Johannes Gyselaar, 1688.

———. *Archisynagogus: observationibus novis illustratus: quibus veteris synagogae constitutio tota traditur inde deducta episcoporum presbyteriorumque primae ecclesiae origine.* Franeker, Neth.: Leonardum Strick, 1685.

———. *Auslegung Der Weissagung Jesaiae, übersetzt und mit Anmerkungen Begleitet von M. Anton Friederich Büsching. Mit einer Vorrede von Hern J. L. von Mosheim. Mit Lebenslauf von Vitringa.* Translated by M. Anton Friederich Büsching. 2 vols. Halle, Ger.: Johann Gottlob Bierwirth, 1749.

———. *Commentarii ad librum prophetiarum Zachariae, quae supersunt cum prolegomenis, cura et studio Campegii Vitringa…opus posthumum.* Edited by Herman Venema. Leeuwarden, Neth.: Tobias van Dessel, 1734.

———. *Commentarius ad canticum Mosis: Deut XXXII cum prolegomenis, opus posthumum.* Edited by Herman Venema. Harlingen, Neth.: Folkert Jansz van der Plaats, 1734.

———. *Commentarius in librum prophetiarum Jesaiae.* 2 vols. Herbornae Nassaviorum: Johan Nicolai Andreae, 1722.

———. *De brief van den Apostel Paulus aan de gemeente der Galaten; als mede aan Titum: en uitgeleesene Keurstoffen van eenige voorname Texten des Nieuwen Testaments, voormaals opgegeven in de Latynsche tale aan de*

*Voedsterlingen van de Akademie te Franeker, en nu in 't Nederduits vertaalt.* 3 vols. Franeker, Neth.: Wibius Bleck, 1728.

———. *De decem viris otiosis: ad sacra necessaria veteris synagogae, curanda deputatis, liber singularis: in quo sententia Lightfooti de hoc argumento, non ita pridem a se acceptae, ratio redditur, quaeque illi nuper objectae sunt difficultates, e medio removentur: illustratis, ubi occasio est, cum locis S. Scripturae tum antiquis civitatis hebraeorum consuetidinibus.* Franeker, Neth.: Johannes Gyselaar, 1687.

———. *De synagoga vetere, libri tres: quibus tum de nominibus, structura, origine, præfectis, ministris, et sacris synagogarum, agitur; tum præcipue, formam regiminis et ministerii earum in ecclesiam christianam translatam esse, demonstratur.* 2 vols. Franeker, Neth.: Johannes Gyselaar, 1694.

———. *De theologia symbolica: liber posthumus. accedit index omnium locorum S. Scripturae quae in hoc opusculo explicantur.* Utrecht, Neth.: Guilielmus Croon, 1726.

———. *Doctrina christianae religionis, per aphorismos summatim descripta, cum Hypotyposis theologiae elencticae, graviores exhibens controversias quae super Cristianae religionis doctrina ecclesia reformatae cum diversis ejusdem sectis intercedunt.* Franeker, Neth.: Franciscus Halma, 1690.

———. *Epilogus disputationis, non ita pridem a se habitae, de generatione filii et morte fidelium temporali: in quo fidem ecclesiae de his articulis porro adstruit ex verbo dei, eandemque tuetur contra dissertationem, illi novissime oppositam.* Franeker, Neth.: Johannes Gyselaar, 1689.

———. *Essai de Theologie Pratique, ou traité de la vie spirituelle et de ses caractères, traduit du latin.* Translated by Henri Philippe de Limiers. Amsterdam: H. Strik, 1721.

——— *Geloove der Kercke Angaande de Geboorte des Sons ende de tydelicke Dood der Geloovige.* Franeker, Neth., 1695.

———. *Geographia sacra.* Edited by Daniel Gottfried Werner. Jena, Ger.: Johann Bernhard Hartung, 1723.

———. *Heilige und erbauliche Betrachtungen über die Wunderwercke Jesu Christi.* Frankfurt am Main: Andrëa, 1727.

———. *Hypotyposis historiae et chronologiae sacrae, à M[undo]. C[ondito]. usque ad finem Sæc[uli]. I. Æ[tatis].* Leeuwarden, Neth.: Franciscus Halma, 1698.

————. *Hypotyposis theologiae elencticae, graviores exhibens controversias, quae super christianae religionis doctrina ecclesiae reformatae cum diveresis ejusdem sectis intercederunt.* Franeker, Neth.: Franciscus Halma, 1706.

————. *Korte Schets van de christelyke Zeden-leere, ofte van het geestelyk Leven ende deselfs eigenschappen. Uit het Latyn vertaalt.* Translated by Johannes d' Outrein. Amsterdam: Hendrik Strik, 1718.

————. *Korte Verklaringe van het Gelove der algemeene Kercke aengaende de Geboorte des Soons, ende de tydelicke Dood der Gelovige.* Franeker, Neth.: Hans Gyselaar, 1691.

————. *Nauwkeurig Onderzoek van de goddelyke Openbaring des H. Apostels Johannes.* Translated by Mattheus Gargon. 2 vols. Amsterdam: Antoni Shoonenburg, 1728.

————. *Observationum sacrarum libri VI: in quo de rebus varii argumenti, & utilissimae investigationis, critice ac theologice, disseritur; sacrorum imprimis librorum loca multa obscuriora nova vel clariore luce perfunduntur.* Edited by Daniel Gottfried Werner. 6 vols. Franeker, Neth.: Johannes Gyselaar, 1683.

————. *Observationum sacrarum libri VII, in quo de rebus varii argumenti, et utilissimæ investigationis, critice ac theologice, disseritur.* Amsterdam: Horreum, 1683–1727.

————. "On the Interpretation of Prophecy." *The Interpreter* 4 (1835): 153–76.

————. *Oratio de synodes, earumque utilitate, necessitatem auctoritate; habita in templo academico ipsis kalendis Juniis CIC IC CCVI.* Franeker, Neth.: Franciscus Halma, 1706.

————. "Praefatio." In Heinrich Teelmann, *Commentarius criticus & theologicus…continens explicationum parabolarum evangelicorum de fermento, oeconomo, divite & Lazaro etc. in caput XVI Evangelii Lucae aliasque insignio res utriusque S. instrumenti partes…Praefationem adjecit Vir. & Cl. Campegius Vitringa,* 1–11. Amsterdam: Borstius, 1695.

————. *Rechte Verstant van den Tempel Ezechiels verdeedigt en bevestigt.* Haarlem, 1693.

————. *Redenvoering van Campegius Vitringa over de Synoden derzelver Nuttigheid, Noodzaakelijkheid en gezag, uit het Latijn overgezet door S. H. van Idsinga; Uitgespooken in de academie-kerk.* Translated by Saco Herman van Idsinga. Harlingen, Ger.: Jan E. Jongma, 1742.

————. *Schriftmäßige Erklärung der evangelischen Parabolen: vormals in lateinischer Sprache mitgetheilet, nachgehends in die niederländische übersetzt, und mit einigen Zusätzen und Anmerkungen erläutert von Johann d'Outrein, nun aber in die Hochdeutsche übergebracht.* Frankfurt and Leipzig: Johann Nicolaus Andreä, 1717.

————. *The Synagogue and the Church: Being an Attempt to Show That the Government, Ministries and Services of the Church Were Derived from Those of the Synagogue.* Translated and edited by Joshua L. Bernard. London: B. Fellowes, 1842.

————. *Typus doctrinae propheticae, in quo de prophetis et prophetiis agitur, huiusque scientiae praecepta traduntur.* Franeker, Neth.: Franciscus Halma, 1708.

————. *Typus theologiae praticae, sive de vita spirituali, ejusque affectionibus commentatio.* Bremen, Ger.: Saurmann, 1717.

————. *Uitlegging over het Boek der Profeetsyen Jezaias: In het Werk zyn ingevoegt de Kennisnemingen van het oude Moabitische Landt; uit het Latijn vertaald.* Translated by Boudewyn ter Braak. 6 vols. Leiden: Jan and Henrick van der Deyster en Abraham Kallewier, 1739.

————. *Verklaringe en heilige Bedenkingen over de verborgene Sin der Miraculen van Jesus Christus.* Edited by Herman Venema. Franeker, Neth.: Wibius Bleck, 1725.

————. *Verklaringe over de agt eerste Capittelen van de Brief Pauli aan de Romeinen, voormaals opgegeven in de Latijnsche tale aan de Voedsterlingen van de Academie tot Franeker… en nu in het Nederduitsch vertaalt.* Franeker, Neth.: Wibius Bleck, 1729.

————. *Verklaring van de evangelische Parabolen: voormaals opgegeven (in de Latynische Tale) aan de Voedsterlingen van de Academie te Franeker. Vertaalt en met eenige Byvoegselen en Aanteekeningen opgeheldert.* Translated by Johannes d' Outrein. Amsterdam: Hendrik Strik, 1715.

————. *Voorbeeld of Schets der wederleggende God-geleerdheid, vertoonende de swaarste Geschil-stukken welke over de leere van den christelyken Godsdienst tusschen de gereformeerde Kerk en verscheydene Secten van dien christen Godsdienst bezintwist worden; Uit het Latijn in 't Duytsch overgebragt.* Delft: Adriaan Beman, 1708.

Vitringa, Campegius, and Christianus Joannes Bomble. *Analysis nec non chronotaxis apocalypticae… in suo commentario apocalyptic (editione altera); adornante Christiano Joanne Bomble, eccles. Batavoduri.* Amsterdam: Henricus Strick, 1721.

"Vitringa, Campegius [Jr] (1693–1723)." In *Biografisch Lexicon voor de Geschiedenis van hed Nederlands Protestantisme*, edited by D. Nauta, C. Houtman, et al., 2:438. Kampen, Neth.: Kok, 1998.

"Vitringa, Campegius (Kempe) (1659–1722)." In *Biografisch Lexicon voor de Geschiedenis van hed Nederlands Protestantisme*, edited by D. Nauta, C. Houtman, et al., 3:379–82. Kampen, Neth.: Kok, 1998.

Witteveen, Klaas Marten. "Campegius Vitringa und die prophetische Theologie." *Zwingliana* 19, no. 2 (1993): 343–59.